Changing Religious Roles of Women in Pre-Modern Asia

Changing Religious Roles of Women in Pre-Modern Asia

Ramakant Tiwari

MD PUBLICATIONS PVT LTD
NEW DELHI
www.mdppl.com

Published by :

MD Publications Pvt Ltd
"MD House", 11, Darya Ganj,
New Delhi - 110 002
Phone : +91-11-45355555
E-mail : contact@mdppl.com
Website: www.mdppl.com

ISBN: 978-81-7533-254-6

Published and Printed by Mr. Pranav Gupta on behalf of **MD Publications Pvt Ltd** at Times Press, Delhi.

PREFACE

Religion and religious norms historically have played an important role in shaping public policies and public life in many countries around the world. Some countries may experience the impact of religion on their public life more than others. In many countries, this impact ebbed and flowed throughout the course of history. At the same time, it is important to acknowledge the role of tradition and cultural norms that may be formed separately from religious norms or affect religious ideology.

The 11 countries of Southeast Asia include over 550 million people. Despite great linguistic and cultural diversity, the region is characterized by the relatively favourable position of women in comparison with neighbouring East or South Asia. Over time, however, the rise of centralized states and the spread of imported philosophies and religions (Confucianism, Daoism, Buddhism, Islam, and Christianity) increasingly privileged males and stressed female subordination. Although such influences were most noticeable among the elite, the strength of local traditions was always a moderating force.

Asian Catholic women religious leaders find themselves entering an uncertain limbo, caught between their church's gospel teachings and lofty pro-women rhetoric, on the one hand; and limiting, social, cultural and ecclesial realities, on the other. It seems this is a place where countless educated Catholic women throughout the world find themselves, but it is a special reality in Asia where centuries of patriarchal religious customs resistant to change clash with Catholic women who are increasingly being exposed to contemporary spirituality and feminist theological thought.

Throughout this change, women in Asia have had greater access to education and with it have come more demands for gender equity. Moves in the direction of equity have gained foothold in politics, social and financial structures. A notable exception has been within the ranks of the Catholic Church. Educated Asian women religious, pious by nature and characteristically reluctant to challenge authority, nevertheless, feel pinched between the liberating mandates of the gospel, as they have begun to see them, and the more restrictive habits of local bishops. The pot has been simmering for four decades now. Asian women religious, meanwhile, have quietly found ways to take their missions increasingly into their own hands, breaking out of models of religious congregations that have worked to keep clerical institutions running.

I am very grateful to Mr. Pranav Gupta, Director of MD Publications Pvt Ltd, New Delhi, for his kind cooperation and support for this book.

Ramakant Tiwari

Contents

1

Introduction

WOMEN IN PRE-MODERN ASIA

The 11 countries of Southeast Asia include over 550 million people. Despite great linguistic and cultural diversity, the region is characterized by the relatively favorable position of women in comparison with neighboring East or South Asia. This has been explained by several factors: traditionally, kinship was traced though both maternal and paternal lines; a daughter was not a financial burden because of the widespread practice of bride price; a married couple often lived with or near the wife's parents; women had prominent roles in indigenous ritual; their labor was essential in agricultural, and they dominated local markets.

Over time, however, the rise of centralized states and the spread of imported philosophies and religions (Confucianism, Daoism, Buddhism, Islam, and Christianity) increasingly privileged males and stressed female subordination. Although such influences were most noticeable among the elite, the strength of local traditions was always a moderating force.

New Religious Movements (NRMs) present holistic social systems of beliefs and values, rituals for coping with crisis and uncertainty, daily routines, codes for dress, diet and relationships, ways of speaking, greeting, annual festivals and rituals for birth, marriage (where appropriate) and death, to converts across the globe. Joining such organisations radically changes a convert's cultural perspective on life. But even more important is the fact that many NRMs have made this impact across a global sweep of cultures with little perceivable variation in the way converts from different national origins accepts the new system.

This phenomenon is especially striking when the NRMs are from Asia and introduce radically different ritual and daily life practices from those found in the West. MNCs too have had the power to override traditional cultural values and practices through their globalised systems of production and consumption. For instance, young Muslim factory women in Malaysia leave their families and go unescorted into the night to work the third shift for multinational semiconductor corporations, transcending strict Islamic values about the supervision of unmarried women by their male relatives.

Working class Malaysian families take their children for a 'status' outing to a KFC outlet, even though the deep fried chicken drumsticks sold at roadside stalls may be tastier and cost one third of the price. But these are still piece-meal responses to global culture. It is only at the level of middle class affluence that the global values of consumer culture are imposed as a total lifestyle, as people cut traditional ties and consolidate their efforts to achieve prosperity for the nuclear family as the main unit of consumption.

The power of multinational economic organisations to transcend local traditional cultural values and material lifestyles is well documented, but wish to focus attention on the similar role of multinational or 'global' NRMs in having equal, if not more, power to transform the behaviour, values, material cultures and patterns of social relationships of people in both traditional and modern cultures with a uniformity and universality which is striking. Their effect is even more powerful than the piecemeal power of the MNCs because active membership frequently involves a total transformation of one's daily lifestyle and relationships.

In this way the NRMs present a comprehensive cultural package to their followers. What is even more striking is that this cultural package will be taken up equally by followers all over the world, and from every socio-economic stratum, often when it is quite different or even antithetical to their original cultural background. These global NRMs frequently originate from Asia, in which case their beliefs and rituals are grounded in the Asian culture of origin, often in its pre-modern form. This makes for quite an extreme form of cultural dissonance with followers from the West, Africa and Latin America.

Yet converts accept the total package of doctrine and lifestyle and modify their persona, personal values, daily routines, kin and voluntary relationships, not to mention diet, speech patterns and dress, in order to embrace their new spiritual path. And this happens to the same degree among all the members within one NRM, uniformly, across a global sweep of cultures both east and west. Because the NRMs are 'new', hybridity of practices and beliefs have not had time to develop, as is the case in the established religions.

NRMS AS MNCS

Organisationally, it is also significant that these NRMs can be compared to MNCs on many levels. Firstly, in terms of their global reach, many of them have branch centres in the capital cities and other major regional cities of countries in all continents. Moreover, some of them were constituted to have this global focus from the outset and their very name reflects this. For instance, a neo-Hindu movement based at Mt Abu, Ragasthan, India, is called the Brahma Kumaris World Spiritual University (BKWSU) and a Shintoistic NRM based in Japan, is called the Church of World Messianity (Sekai Kyusei Kyo).

The global focus is more than in name however. Many movements have pilgrimage places which attract members from all over the world, and it is a thought-provoking sight at a time when globalisation has become a cliché, to see members from widely disparate geographic and cultural regions mingling together, totally unified by their common adherence to the faith. In this sense, the 'corporate culture' of the spiritual organisation acts strongly to dominate national or ethnic cultures of origin.

The services are conducted with simultaneous translation in many languages. But the global mind-set of the organisation is not just a matter of making the doctrine available in foreign languages. It stems from a philosophy that all humanity is one, albeit with Japanese or Indian culture as the original culture. Often NRMs frame themselves as supra- religions, which, they assert, transcend the established religions and avoid their narrow and limiting conceptualisations. This philosophy is built into the name of another Japanese Shintoistic NRM, Sukyo Mahikari.

A striking example of a NRM with a global approach from the outset is Tenrikyo, with two million followers, 500,000 outside Japan, served by 200 overseas churches. Tenrikyo is Japan's earliest major new religion, founded before the Meiji Restoration by Miki Nakayama, a 41 year old woman from a peasant family, after she received divine revelations in 1838. It established its own library, university and ethnological museum in the 19th century, in order to aid the missionary activity of its early adherents.

The Tenri Museum displayed the daily artefacts of the countries where missionaries would be sent so that they would be familiar with the cultures they would have to interact with. The Tenri University was set up as an institution for teaching foreign languages to missionaries, and so strong is the movement's outward gaze that its religious texts were published in 16 foreign languages from the early days. All these institutions are located in Tenri City, established 1881, which is a pilgrimage place for members from all over the world.

As MNC style organisations, NRMs also have extensive property holdings. They usually have a headquarters complex which includes sacred spaces, often able to seat very large gatherings of tens of thousands of people, administrative offices and accommodation for pilgrims. Often the organisations include philanthropic institutions such as hospitals and environmental projects such as ecologically sensitive farms – Sukyo Mahikari's Yoko agriculture, or beautiful parks such as Sekai Kyusei Kyo's gardens in Japan.

In line with their extensive property, is the magnitude of the NRMs financial revenue, with the turnover of capital in the form of donations and events management – the BKWSU regularly feeds 10,000 pilgrims attending its ceremonies, for instance - demonstrating organisational expertise which rivals that of very large scale business enterprises. Like MNCs they have the challenge of recruiting, training and retaining good administrative staff, many of whom qualify primarily in terms of their spiritual stature and have to be trained thereafter to run an organisation or centre in a secular context.

However, the nature of the belief system makes staff posted to foreign centres more easily able to transcend the cross-cultural issues which bedevil corporate managers on overseas postings - as the NRMs 'corporate culture' which is shared by everyone, becomes the culture of interaction. Indeed the NRMs have policies to actively post their spiritual leaders and administrators to countries foreign to them. For instance in the BKWSU, which has 800,000 members worldwide, served by over 5,000 centres in 128 countries, the country coordinator in Greece is Australian, in Italy is British and in Japan is Indian

RMS AS AGENTS OF TRULY GLOBAL FORMS OF CULTURE

It is the ability of these global NRMs to provide a total cultural system to their members which distinguishes them from MNCs and gives them a higher level of global status. Conversion often involves members changing their daily lifestyles and even leaving long term relationships. Conversion to the religion is on an individual basis, taking the Individual away from established community patterns of worship and belief.

Often other family members may follow although this is not always the case and it can impose hardship if the dramatically altered lifestyles and values cannot be accepted or adopted by relatives or friends of the convert. Brahma Kumaris in the inner, committed circle, are vegetarian, celibate, and rise daily at 4am to practise raja yoga meditation. This lifestyle gives expression to the Indian spiritual traditions of brahmacarya (celibacy) and the satvic (pure) diet. Married converts have often had to forgo their marriage partnership.

Strict adherence requires that they only eat food cooked by themselves or other Brahma Kumaris in order to benefit from the pure vibrations of the person cooking the food. This has meant that some members do not eat food cooked by their mothers or other relatives who are not in the movement, thus challenging one of the most basic social activities which fosters social relationships, eating together. Brahma Kumaris attend their local centre for meditation, the reading of a revealed text and class discussion from 5.30 until 7.00 am.

In earlier times, Brahma Kumaris around the world dressed in white, a colour of spiritual practice in India and other Asian cultures, even during secular activities, but this has now been modified outside India. Yet the benefits of such a lifestyle include enhanced soul consciousness and a sense of peace which those from outside the movement notice and comment upon. At the same time, members are encouraged to participate fully in secular society and many hold full-time professional, clerical or manual jobs and remain incognito as far as possible.

Sukyo Mahikari does not impose dietary or marriage restrictions, but members are encouraged to come to the centre each day and engage in the practice of mahikari no waza, the transference of Pure Light or divine energy. The centres are very Japanese in style: members must wash their hands, as one does when visiting a Shinto shrine, and remove their shoes before entering, kneel on the floor and bow to the shrine and to each other, as in Japan, in many social and ritual contexts. Behaviour and attitude are very formal and emphasis is on thoughtfulness to others. The prayer which precedes the giving of Light, Amatsu Norigoto, is recited in archaic Japanese in a loud voice and all members have memorised it. I have observed centres in Japan, Australia, Singapore, Malaysia, Philippines, and everywhere, the atmosphere and practices are the same, despite the fact that some of these practices are very alien to the members' native cultures. It is also significant to observe, for instance, young women giving Light to elderly gentlemen, Indians to Chinese, in other words, not only ethnic boundaries but also gender and age differences are transcended to an unusual degree in an Asian cultural context.

Moreover, at home, members are encouraged to maintain an ancestral altar and offer food to the ancestors several times a day, a practice which has overtones of Japanese Buddhist observances in traditional households. In Sukyo Mahikari, these practices which focus on purification are associated with the occurrence of miracles in the healing of major illnesses, and other aspects of members' lives regularly turn for the better, but the relationships and social activities of the members gradually drift away from pre-conversion patterns and come to revolve around the centre and other members.

Speech patterns are also modified through membership of NRMs. Brahma Kumaris refer to other people as 'souls', and male and female members as 'brothers' and 'sisters'. Mahikari members speak with reference to their gratitude for everything that happens to them, both good and bad, and preface accounts of their own doings with "I was permitted to ...", thus showing respect for the divine plan of Su God.

In order to speak within the community of members, one must make a mental adjustment to the rules of discourse of the movement. This is of course easier if one is only interacting with other members but if one is moving in and out of secular society, it is a reminder of the layers of culture within which one exists. These outward speech patterns are a manifestation of an inner transformation which has taken place in terms of members' understanding of the divine underpinnings of human life.

Hence the Shinto emphasis on cleanliness, and the Hindu emphasis on purity in food, and brah- macariya, which are mainstream elements of these global NRMs, has been adopted without question by committed members of these religions, regardless of the degree of disparity between these ideas and practices and those of their original cultures or socio-economic and socio-political backgrounds.

WOMEN AND COLONIALISM

In the nineteenth century Southeast Asia's economic resources and strategic position between India and China led to increasing European involvement. By the 1890s the entire region except for Siam (Thailand) was under European control. In some areas women were recruited as cheap wage labor on plantations (tea, sugar, tobacco, rubber) and in processing factories. At the village level colonial regimes strengthened the male position as head of the household and "reformed" customary laws that had given women considerable autonomy. Similar trends can be found in Siam, the only non-colonized country, where legal codification strengthened patrilineality. These developments encouraged a preference for sons rather than daughters.

Nonetheless, women were still influential in community life, at times even leading anti-colonial rebellions. Increasing female literacy (especially in the Philippines) and exposure to Western feminism encouraged elite women to confront issues of gender inequality From the late nineteenth century nationalist movements developed across Southeast Asia. Male leaders focused on political independence, but educated women were equally concerned with polygamy, divorce, domestic abuse and the financial responsibilities of fathers.

For the most part, however, politicized women accepted the male argument that attention to "female" concerns should be delayed until after independence was attained. Yet despite active involvement in anti-colonial movements, sometimes as fighters, but more often as strike organizers, journalists, couriers and clandestine agents, women were viewed asauxiliaries rather than partners. Such attitudes were still evident inthe independence movements that exploded after the surrender of the Japanese, who occupied most of Southeast Asia between 1942 and 1945.

WOMEN IN CONTEMPORARY SOUTHEAST ASIA

The end of World War II signaled the demise of European colonialism in Southeast Asia. Theoretically, the independent states that emerged over the next 15 years were committed to gender equality, but this hasrarely been translated into reality. In recent years the number of women holding public office has increased, especially in local government, but only in the

Philippines has female representation in national government risen above 10 per cent. When women do manage to enter the political arena, they often find themselves marginalized in a male-dominated culture, with real power remaining in men's hands.

The few individuals who have attained the highest political offices (such as President in the Philippines and Indonesia) have done so because they are the daughter or wife of a famous man. They have not become advocates of women's issues, for this would risk alienating their male colleagues or the male electorate. Greater female involvement in politics is impeded by the way candidates are recruited as well as entrenched attitudes that see women's primary role as that of wife and mother. Gender stereotypes that favor males over females are often reinforced in school textbooks and are sometimes encouraged by religious teachings.

For example, Buddhists still believe that rebirth as a woman rather than a man indicates that less merit was accrued in past lives. Southeast Asian Islam has traditionally been very tolerant, but over the last 20 years there has been greater stress on "correct" dress (notably head covering) and public behavior. Although all Southeast Asian countries except Laos and Vietnam have signed the Convention on the Elimination of All Forms of Discrimination Against Women and have made advances promoting gender equality, it is difficult to change the preference for sons, especially in Vietnam with its strong Confucian heritage.

It is not easy to generalize about the economic position of Southeast Asian women because of the gap in development between Timor Lorosae, Cambodia and Laos (among the poorest countries in the world), and prosperous Singapore and Brunei Darussalam. Nonetheless, the continuing acceptance of the idea that a woman can generate and control her own income is still evident, although women receive less pay than men for the same work and the options for unskilled workers are limited. In poorer countries and impoverished regions this is apparent in the prevalence of prostitution and the disturbing trafficking of women. From the mid 1960s, however, as Southeast Asian countries gradually shifted to export-oriented economies, lower-paid women have become essential to factory work. In consequence, women have been more active in labor movements.

As overseas domestic workers, they have also been increasingly important to national economies, remitting large amounts of money to their families. Because of world-wide shortages, qualified women can find employment abroad in skilled occupations such as nursing. Obtaining vocational skills and academic qualifications is far more possible than hitherto as Southeast Asian women gain greater access to education. With the exception of Cambodia and Laos, the numbers of women progressing to post-secondary training is also rising, and in Brunei, Malaysia, Thailand and the Philippines there are more female graduates than males; the rates for Vietnam and Indonesia are almost equal.

The expansion in education has contributed to the blossoming of female-oriented Non-Governmental Organizations (NGOs) since the 1980s, which have given the knowledge and organization skills that equip them to argue for issues. Despite the region's economic, political and cultural diversity, Southeast Asian countries generally fare well in measures of human development. The heritage of relatively favorable gender relations and the resilience and pragmatism of local societies indicate that Southeast Asian women can look towards a promising future. It is perhaps instructive to begin by looking at Jonathan Israel's recent (2001) monograph, entitled Radical Enlightenment in which he argues that there was a radical underground European Enlightenment between 1650 and 1750 that has been generally regarded as marginal to the wider phenomenon but that he sees as central.

In his view 'the Enlightenment-European and global- not only attacked and severed the roots of traditional European culture in the sacred, magic, kinship, and hierarchy, secularising all institutions and ideas, but (intellectually and to a degree in practice) effectively demolished all legitimation of monarchy, aristocracy, woman's subordination to man, ecclesiastical authority, and slavery, replacing these with the principles of universality, equality, and democracy'. I do not cite Israel because I accept his grand view of modernity or enjoy his history of men and ideas approach or even because he places Spinoza and Holland in the center of world history, but because it is this wholesale, great transformation perspective, that we find also in many writings on Fundamentalism which is the catch phrase for writing about radical religion.

Radical in this case stands for a total rejection of secular global modernity (the product of Jonathan Israel's and Peter Gay's Enlightenment) by religious movements. When in the early 1990s I was invited to participate in the Fundamentalism Project of the American Academy of Arts and Sciences, I felt attracted to its comparative framework. I still think that due to the importance of the Middle East to U.S. global politics, there is too much emphasis on radical Islam and a neglect of the importance of global processes for a number of religious movements. To compare Muslim, Hindu, Buddhist, Christian, and Jewish movements therefore has an immediate appeal.

The problem, however, with comparison is that it is often not left at that, but that social scientists also want to come up with a general model to explain global phenomena. In the case of the Fundamentalism project this was basically the model of modernisation and secularisation. The argument is the following: fundamentalism is a social phenomenon that occurs during rapid social change, is marked by a profound experience of crisis, and tries to overcome that crisis by a revitalisation of religion and a search for authenticity. Fundamentalism is a global phenomenon in so far as it is a response to global processes of transformation.

Gabriel Almond, a political scientist, who had been a prominent modernisation theorist in the 1960s, was a leading influence behind the Fundamentalism Project and, indeed, the Project had a focus on secularisation or rather, the failure thereof, as a major structural factor. It was in outline accepted by Huntington for his theory of 'The Clash of Civilizations'. In a recent sequel to the multi-volume Fundamentalism Project

Gabriel Almond, Scott Appleby and Emmanuel Sivan have again proposed a general model of what they now call Strong Religion. They propose the following: 'strong religions are historical counterattacks from threatened religious traditions, seeking to hold ground against this spreading secular 'contamination' and even to regain ground by taking advantage of the weaknesses of modernisation.

The resistance to modern forms of secularisation is a defining common feature of religious fundamentalisms.' Secular Modernity is the Enemy against which radical religious movements rally, according to these authors. In their view secularisation is the main structural factor in the rise of these movements. It is clear that this is a view that belongs to the old orthodoxy of modernisation theory and that, after two decades of criticism of the secularisation thesis one might wonder whether this is a fruitful approach. In the case Hindu radical movements, it is not. These movements do not protest against secularisation, since they explicitly demand secularisation of India's legislation.

They object to what they call the 'pseudo-secularism' of India's Congress Party because they argue that this party thrives on 'pampering the religious minorities'. What is clear from the Indian case is that 'secularism' is a political ideology carried by political actors and opposed by other political actors in the name of religion. If liberalism is a secular ideology, radical Hindus accept most of it, such as liberalisation of the market, the free individual, democracy, but all in the name of a nationalist utopia in which the majority of Hindus dominate the nation-state. The Enemy is not secularisation but Islam that is seen as an obstacle to the secular ideal of progress that is shared by Hindus.

Of course, one could object that Hinduism and India are special cases that cannot be understood in general models. However, if the Muslim attackers of the World Trade Center can be considered followers of radical religion it is clear that they did not object to the secularisation of Saudi-Arabia, but to something far more specific, namely the close ties of the Saudi establishment with the American military-industrial complex and the presence of American soldiers on Saudi holy land. Therefore, do not think that a general model based on modernisation theory is what we should aim at, but that comparison between cases will bring out some general features of the movements we are interested in. The question whether they are religious or not may not be a crucial feature. In fact radical religious movements have much in common with a number of other movements- socialist, fascist, conservative, nationalist, that also want to use modern state power for total transformation of society.

Indeed, it is the focus on capturing state power that seems a defining feature of these movements and it is thus state formation as the framework of these movements that has to be understood. The modern state is directed to large-scale social transformation and, by and large, has the capacity to have such an impact (obviously with a large number of unintended consequences). No modern political movement (religious or otherwise) can ignore the state. While state formation in different societies has different trajectories there are also some general shared features. First of all, societies find themselves in a global order of nation-states, in which notions of borders, citizenship, elections, central state power and the enforcement of state law are operative. This implies that in many cases radical movements are nationalist.

South Asia has a number of examples: Muslim nationalism resulting in Pakistan, followed by Bengali nationalism resulting in Bangladesh, Hindu nationalism or Hindutva characterised by attacks on Muslims and Christians before elections, Sikh nationalism demanding a separate nation-state called Khalistan, Sri Lankan Buddhist Sinhala nationalism opposing Tamil Hindu nationalism, and so on and so forth. Borders, minority rights, electoral violence, centralisation and decentralisation, are all issues coming up here.

I would propose that it is not essential whether the focus of mobilisation is religion, language, regional identity or a mix of all these things and thus I would not claim a specific status for radical religion. Essential is the nationalist framework for political contestation. Secondly, all societies find themselves in a new phase of globalisation that complicates state formation but does not undo it.

Two major developments in this regard are connectivity through the internet and other forms of IT-enabled communication and the formation of transnational networks by migration. These developments may enhance the possibilities of radical movements to mobilise resources on a global scale and also to address the global political order. In the South Asian example the Sikh Khalistanis as well as the Tamil Tigers have been involved in transnational mobilisation of resources. But also the Hindu nationalists of the Vishwa Hindu Parishad have always seen their nationalist mission in global terms. This is not new or particularly religious, since much of this is already found in the Comintern, but the rise of the network society makes at least some movements less tied to specific spatial or social locales both in their operation and in their objectives.

Since the U.S. has become more and more the hegemon of the new world order it is clear that it is addressed both for specific regional problems, lobbying for Kashmir or Israel for instance, and for specific utopias like another Islamic world order. If religion is only a variable in all the movements that try to gain political power should we then pay specific attention to religious movements? I think that there is some need to do so for the simple reason that with the so-called 'End of History', the socialist utopia is not anymore carried by communist or socialist movements and religious utopias seem to be flourishing everywhere.

This is so also because mainstream social scientists continue to be inspired by secularist ideals and thus have difficulties to apply their perspective to religious movements. Therefore there is also a theoretical need to pay attention to religious movements. While I think that in their recruitment patterns, their resource mobilisation, and their creative response to opportunities religious movements can be studied like other social/political movements, their ideological core makes them religious movements. Striking in the ideological core is the reference to religious traditions. Often in South Asia and elsewhere we find a reference to a traditional, just, state.

This is the background to references to the Islamic state (dawla) or to Ram's Rule (Ramrajya). The first thing that has to be observed here is that references to earlier political forms show a deliberate misunderstanding of the radically different nature of the modern, developmental state. Those who call for the foundation of an Islamic state often use the Arabic term dawla that refers to 'dynasty' and indeed the pre-modern societies are governed by sultans, nawabs, rajas and the like. The modern state, on the contrary, is an instrument of the will of the people and penetrates deep into people's lives with a number of developmental projects, such as education and health care. It is, even when it is a weak state in Gunnar Myrdal's sense, still a beast of a completely different nature than the pre-modern state.

The second observation to be made is that the references to a religiously based 'just state' are relatively recent in modern Indian history and are actually quite marginal in Indian political thought and practice. The call for going back to the time of the Prophet Mohammad (pbuh) or the time of Ram and establish a so-called theocratic state is a very recent demand which has to be understood in the framework of modern political ideas of true Islamic democracy and so on. Contrary to what is often thought, there is no clear definition of the Islamic state in Pakistan. What is one to make of the tradition of dar-al-islam (the Abode of Islam) to which Muslims should migrate (hijrat) if they are in a minority position, or that of the jihad (holy war) against the dar-al-harb (an Abode of Unbelief or War)? None of this makes much sense in India where Muslims were always a minority and there were no Islamic states, but merely Muslim dynasties with Islamic legitimation.

It also ignores the fact of current large-scale migration to the dar-al-harb, or the West, rather than away from it. Similarly the reference to the rule of Rama, the virtuous king (dharmaraja) and the 'Lord of Propriety' (maryada purushottam), has very little specific content, even less than in the

Islamic context where the establishment of the Law (shariah) can at least be part of a political program, as it was in Pakistan under General Zia-ul-Haq and Nawaz Sharif. Certainly, in Hindu kingdoms the Ramayana may have given some guidance to the behaviour of rulers, but there is little in it that specifies the nature of the caste order and the rules of politics.

One should understand references to such traditions in the modern period primarily as a utopian rejection of current political formations rather than as a theological interpretation of the tradition. This is not to say that there are no theological interpretations of the tradition that have political implications. They certainly exist and are important, because they show that the tradition is alive. The violent political projects of activists like Osama Bin Laden, however, do not engage the tradition in such a fundamental manner. It is, in fact, striking how little theological training leaders of the major religious nationalist movements have had. They tend to be journalists, engineers, graduates of the humanities, educated in modern topics rather than in the tradition.

The same is true for leaders of Hindu and Muslim movements who want a just rule. Gandhi was absolutely not a theologian and when he came up with the notion of Ramrajya he used a cultural repertoire in which he had been socialised from his early youth, but not a political theology. In the case of Gandhi and many other great populist leaders one sees the function of a traditional religious repertoire for bridging the gap between elite politics and mass politics. However, it is also clear that this kind of reference to tradition for purposes of mass mobilisation needs to allow for a wide range of interpretations. Similarly, in contemporary Sri Lanka one finds major departures from Buddhist tradition and the invention of new traditions, such as the Sarvodaya movement that purports to give a Buddhist model of development.

Here we get to the heart of the matter: modern references to Ramrajya and Dar-al-Islam are inventions of tradition, but at the same time there are a number of living traditions, in which there are discourses and practices relating to state and violence. However, we are not speaking about separate universes (one of tradition, one of invented tradition) here, but about interaction, conflict, polemics. Some people are willing to use a lot of violence to establish their idea of traditional justice in the form of an Islamic state or of a Hindu state and others who think they are living in harmony with tradition are completely mystified by what the first are doing.

Often radical religious movements refer to traditions of gender as a way of signifying relations of power. An important transformation in these relationships in the nineteenth century is the rise of the gendered distinction between public and private. This distinction is crucial to the development of a modern ideology of the family, domesticity, and the moral order of the nation. A dominant line of interpretation in the study of nationalism is to argue that the nation is often imagined in terms of a brotherhood of men protecting their womenfolk.

Men are portrayed as strong and powerful; women as weak and powerless. Protection implies the exertion of male authority, to which women have to submit. The state represents male authority as if it were the father of the nation. While this pattern can be found everywhere, religious traditions shape this configuration in different ways in different cultures. While, for instance, Victorian ideas about 'domesticity', 'companiate marriage' and female education were influential all over the empire, in Hindu India, the ideal of the 'modern' educated housewife was almost always tied to that of Lakshmi. The problem we need to address, therefore, is how such traditions are transformed under the pressure of modernity.

2

Religious Change in Asian

In the nineteenth and twentieth centuries South Asian Muslims, along with Muslims elsewhere in the world, began to experience religious change of revolutionary significance. This change involved a shift in the focus of Muslim piety from the next world to this one. It meant the devaluing of a faith of contemplation on God's mysteries and of belief in His capacity to intercede for men on earth. It meant the valuing instead of a faith in which Muslims were increasingly aware that it was they, and only they, who could act to create a just society on earth. The balance which had long existed between the other-worldly and the this-worldly aspects of Islam was moved firmly in favour of the latter.

This process of change has had many expressions: the movements of the Mujahidin, the Faraizis, Deoband, the Ahl-i Hadiths and Aligarh in the nineteenth century; and those of the Nadwat ul Ulama, the Tablighi Jamaat, the Jamaat-i Islami and the Muslim modernists in the twentieth. It has also been expressed in many subtle shifts in behaviour at saints' shrines and in the pious practice of many Muslims. Associated with this process of change was a shift in traditional Islamic knowledge away from the rational towards the revealed sciences, and a more general shift in the sources of inspiration away from the Iranian lands towards the Arab lands.

There was also the adoption of print and the translations of authoritative texts into Indian languages with all their subsequent ramifications - among them the emergençe of a reflective reading of the scriptures and the development of an increasingly rich inner landscape. Operating at the heart of this process was the increasing assumption by individual Muslims of responsibility for creating Muslim society on earth - a great and heavy responsibility. Moreover, in the context of British India, where foreign power had colonised much public space, this was a burden of which Muslim women were asked to take a particularly heavy share. In the scholarship devoted to the Christian West the shift from other-worldly to this-worldly religion, which brought man to stand before the unfettered sovereignty of God, is regarded as a development of momentous importance?

Among its many outcomes was helping to shape the modern Western senses of the self, of identity. There is an assumption here, of course, which is that the 'self' is historically defined, that is that the late Roman self might be differently constituted as compared with the twentieth-century Western self. Let us consider some of the shaping processes at work. The new willed religion, which man entered into only of his choice, gave him a sense of his instrumentality in the world, of his capacity to shape it.

The new and heavy weight of this responsibility to an all-powerful God led to what has been termed the 'inward turn' - this started with the emergence of spiritual diaries in the Reformation and has continued with an ever deeper exploration of the psyche. Then, this new sense of human instrumentality, aligned to a deepening sense of self, helped to foster senses of individual personal autonomy. All this tended to affirm the worth of ordinary life, the value of ordinary human experience. There was value in productive work, in marriage, family life, love, sex; there was growing distress at human suffering and a growing sense that good consisted of human activities for the benefit of human welfare.

It is not suggested for one moment that we can look at the impact of the shift to this-worldly religion and somehow read off a series of developments or potential developments amongst South Asian Muslims. Nothing could be so crass. The particular circumstances of nineteenth- and twentieth-century India, not to mention the ideas and values inculcated by Islam, are different from those of Reformation Europe. Nevertheless, what is worth doing is noting the significance of the shift from other-worldly to this-worldly religion for shaping modern senses of the self in the West. And this should prompt us at least to consider the extent to which a similar change might have helped to shape Muslim senses of the self in South Asia.

Before embarking on this exercise, there are other factors contributing to the shaping of the self which need to be acknowledged. There is the growing influence of Western civilization with its ideas of individualism, personal fulfilment, and the rights of man - with its endorsement of earthly existence and earthly pleasures, and its celebration of individual lives, great and small. Such ideas and values were instinct in much Western literature and in many institutions; they were, of course, embodied by many of the colonial British.

There is also growing exposure to other forces which helped to fashion the more autonomous self: there is the spread of capitalist modes of production with their capacity to break down old communal loyalties and empower individuals; there is the emergence of the modern state with its concern to reach down through the thickets of the social order to make contact with each individual; there are the changes in the technology of communication - particularly of print and the shift it helped to bring from orality to literacy - which enabled individuals to command knowledge as never before and assisted them in the process of exploring their inner selves.

There are, of course, many forces at work in shaping the changing Muslim senses of the self. Our concern is to suggest that the shift from other-worldly to this-worldly religion is worthy of exploration. Before embarking on our exploration it is necessary to outline the nature and impact of the shift to this-worldly Islam. The nineteenth and twentieth centuries in South Asia saw a growing attack on intercessionary sufism, indeed, at times on all forms of sufism itself. The reformists were determined to rid the world of its enchanted places, that is of anything that might diminish the believers' sense of responsibility. They were determined to assert the principle of tawhid, that is of the oneness of God.

This theme ran through all the movements of the age from the Mujahidin of Saiyid Ahmad of Rai Bareli to the Jamaati Islami of Maulana Maududi. Not all movements gave quite the same emphasis to this theme. If the Ahl-i Hadiths and Ahl-i Quran were opposed to all forms of institutionalised sufism, the Deobandis on the other hand confined themselves to attacking practices at saints' shrines which presupposed the capacity of the saint to intercede for man with God. There were ironies, too. Maududi, while abhoring the tendency of sufism to compromise the oneness of God, nevertheless found an excellent organisational model in the sufi order which he used for his Jamaat. (His vision of the role of the Amir of the Jamaat was similar to that of the sufi master to whom all his disciples gave unquestioning submission).

This said, we should be aware that there was enormous sensitivity to behaviour at saints' shrines amongst almost all Muslims. It affected non-reformers as well as reformers. It was an important concern for the ulama of the Firangi Mahal family of Lucknow. The research of Claudia Liebeskind on three Awadhi shrines in this period, moreover, has illustrated how behaviour at them changed in order to accommodate some reformist preferences at least. What we need to be aware of is that in the nineteenth and twentieth centuries increasing numbers of India's Muslims from the upper and middle classes were finding the credibility of the friends of God, who had long provided them with comfort, undermined.

There could be no intercession for them. They were directly answerable to the Lord, and to Him alone. There can be no doubt that Reformist Muslims felt the weight of this new responsibility and were meant to feel it. They knew that it was their choice to will the good and forbid the evil. It was their choice as to whether a Muslim society which followed God's wishes existed on earth or not. Moreover, they knew that they were answerable to Him for their actions. Husain Ahmad Madani, principal of Deoband in the mid-twentieth century, often wept at the thought of his shortcomings. Rashid Ahmad Gangohi, one of the founders of the school, when reading the Quran alone at night, would weep and shake and appear terrified at those chapters dealing with God' wrath.

The Reformist God was certainly compassionate and merciful, as God always had been, but he was also to be feared. Indeed, 'Fear God' was the very first practice sentence that women in the reformist tradition, who were learning how to read, had to confront. There was a constant sense of guilt that the believer was not doing enough to meet the high standards of this most demanding God. "Oh God! What am I to do? I am good for nothing", Maulana Muhammad Ilyas, the founder of the Tablighi Jamaat, would exclain as he paced at night. And when his wife told him to come to bed, he said that if she knew what he knew she would be doing the same. 'I find no comparison between my anxiety, my effort and my voice,' he wrote, and the responsibility of Tabligh God has placed upon my shoulders. If He shows mercy, He is forgiving, merciful, and if He does justice, there is no escape for me from the consequences of my guilt.

Nothing brings home more the weight of responsibility with which Reformist Muslims were faced than their visions of Judgement. Consider the picture in Ashraf Ali Thanvi's Bihishti Zewar, which has been so ably translated and introduced for us by Barbara Metcalf. Thanvi draws on a vision initially generated by Shah Rafi al-Din, one of the four sons of Shah Wali Allah, and therefore at the heart of the Reformist tradition. Bihishti Zewar is one of the most influential books of twentieth century Muslim South Asia. The believer is first of all reminded of the Prophet's emotion at the thought of heaven and hell. 'He wept greatly until his blessed beard was wet with tears. Then he declared: "I swear by that Being in whose power is my life that if you know what I know about the afterlife, you would flee to the wilderness and place dust upon your head."'

Then the believer is told the signs of the coming of Judgement. The proper order of the shari'a will be reversed; people will think the wealth owed to God is their property: they will seek knowledge of religion not for its own sake but for worldly gain etc... The natural order will be reversed: stones will rain down from the sky; people will turn into pigs and dogs. The Imam Mahdi will appear to lead the Muslims into battle against the Nazarenes. The one-eyed Dajjal will appear claiming to be the Messiah. Hasrat Isa will descend from the sky with his hands on the shoulders of two angels to kill the Dajjal. The sun will rise in the West. A balmy breeze from the South will produce a fatal growth in the armpits of the believers. Then, on a Friday, the tenth Muharram, in the morning when all people are engaged in their respective work, a trumpet will suddenly be sounded.

At first, it will be very, very soft. Then it will grow so much louder that all will die from terror. The heaven and earth will be rent. The world will be extinguished. Then comes the Day of Judgement. After forty years God will order the trumpet to be blown again. Heaven and earth will again be established. The dead will emerge alive from their graves and will be gathered on the Plain of Judgement. The sun will be very close, and peoples' very brains will begin to cook in its heat. People will sweat in proportion to their sins. Only the Prophet Muhammad's intercession will persuade Almighty God to intervene. 'Angels in great number will descend from the heavens and surround everyone on every side.

The throne of Almighty God, on which will be the Illumination of Almighty God, will descend. The accounting will begin, and the Book of Deeds will be opened. Of their own accord, the believers will come on the right hand and the unbelievers on the left. The scales for weighing deeds will be set up, and from it everyone's good and bad deeds will be known. Thereupon everyone will be ordered to cross the Bridge of the Way. Anyone whose good deeds weigh more in the balance will cross the bridge and enter into paradise. Anyone, whose sins weigh more, unless forgiven by God, will fall into hell.... When all the inhabitants of heaven and hell are settled in their places, Almighty God will bring forth Death in the shape of a Ram, in between heaven and hell. He will display Death to everyone and have it slaughtered. He will declare: "Now death will come neither to the dwellers in heaven nor to the dwellers in hell. All must dwell for ever in their respective places."

There will be no end to the rejoicing of the inhabitants of heaven and no end to the anguish and grief of the inhabitants of hell.' The awfulness of this eschatological vision, the powerlessness of the believer to achieve salvation except through the preponderance of his good deeds on earth, gives real insight into how individual senses of responsibility were likely to be deepened. The penetration of this sense into the individual's inner self, its approach towards the quiddity of the human being, helps to explain the high levels of emotion it generated. It also helps to explain the growth of sectarianism - the many Muslim groups fashioned in nineteenth- and twentieth-century India that exist to this day - as Muslims in different social and intellectual locations strove with great sincerity to find the right way towards salvation.

It helps to explain the world of manazaras, fatwa wars and high combatitiveness that typifies these groups. This was the price to be paid for the huge release of religious energy generated by what could be called a process of personal religous empowerment. This sense of responsibility was not just felt amongst ulama of the reformist tradition, and those who followed them, it was felt no less by Muslim modernists, those who wished to build bridges between Western science and Islamic understandings. Listen to that very great man Saiyid Ahmad Khan: But since I have been the pioneer of Modern Education which, as I have said, is to some extent opposed to Islam, I regard it as my duty to do all I can, right or wrong, to defend my religion and show the people, the true, shining countenance of Islam. This is what my conscience dictates and, unless I do its bidding, I am a sinner before God. A similar spirit illuminated those other great modernists, Muhammad Iqbal and Fazlur Rahman, in their endeavours to show the people the shining countenance of Islam.

We should also note that this sense of responsibility has come to be spread more and more widely through the Muslim society of South Asia as the reforming movement has continued to develop, and as it has come to interact with a society where books were more widely available, and literacy slowly but surely growing. It is one of the ironies of this process that much of this activity was set going by ulama who, by translating key works of the Islamic tradition into Indian languages and by printing them largescale, aimed to give Muslim society strength to cope with colonial rule, but in the process they helped to destroy their own monopoly over religious knowledge.

If in the nineteenth century the effort was concentrated on a literate elite, the aristocracy which was attracted to the Ahl-i Hadiths and the Ahl- i Quran, the sharif classes which tended to go to Aligarh and the lesser bourgeois of the qasbas which tended to go to Deoband, in the twentieth century the effort was taken more widely into society, in part through the publications of the Jamaati Islami, which, though elitist itself, spoke to a whole new generation of Western-educated Muslims, but for the most part through the Tablighi Jamaat, or Preaching Society, which aimed, and aims, to involve ordinary Muslims in taking a basic understanding of reformist Islam to the masses.

The loss of the ulama's monopoly, this process implied, was a necessary sacrifice in striving to deepen the sense of personal responsibility in society as a whole. This democratisation of the possession of religious knowledge and its interpretation, which went hand in hand with the emergence of the concept of the caliphate or vice-regency of man in Muslim thought, is a development of enormous potential and importance for the future of Muslim societies. There is one final point which needs to be made about the shift towards this-worldly religion and the spread of a new sense of responsibility: it seems to have fallen rather more heavily on women than on men.

It is now a commonplace of the literature devoted to gender and identity in South Asia since 1800 that with non-Muslim occupancy of public space women move from their earlier position of being threats to the proper conduct of Muslim society to being the mistresses of private Islamic space, the central transmitters of Islamic values, the symbols of Muslim identity, the guardians of millions of domestic Islamic shrines. Women come, in fact, to bear an awesome responsibility. Thus they had a central role to play in the reformist project.

Their education, to the extent, as Ashraf Ali Thanvi declared, of acquiring the learning of a maulvi, was crucial to waging war on all those customs which threatened the unity of God and to maintaining fully in place the power of Muslim conscience in fashioning Islamic society. Thanvi also admitted that women would have to struggle harder than men to achieve this outcome. For Maududi and the Islamists women are expected to acquire knowledge of Islam, just as men do, and to examine the consciences in the same way.

On the other hand, they were biologically and psychologically different from men and their place was in purdah and in the home. They were to be the rulers of domestic space, sealed off from all those elements of kufr which polluted public space. 'The harim', he declared, `is the strongest fortress of Islamic civilization, which was built for the reasons that, if it [that civilization] ever suffered a reverse, it [that civilization] may then take refuge in it.' Muslim modernists sent out conflicting messages, on the one hand emphasising the spiritual and moral superiority of women, which might militate against their education, while on the other increasingly coming to see their education in Western learning and through the medium of English as the measure of the health and development of society.

Wherever women found themselves, a heavy weight of responsibility rested upon them. This weight is borne down to the present, although the extra burden of political pressures have come to join those of patriarchy and willed religion. Much of the discourse, both about Pakistani identity and about Muslim identity in India, has come to take place around the position and behaviour of women. If there is a correlation between burdens of responsibility and growing senses of the self, there is room for there to be increasingly stressful tension between women's expectations and those of the wider society in which they move. We now move from the shift towards this-worldly Islam and the new sense of responsibility it fosters to the impact of this responsibility on Muslim senses of the self.

There are four themes which should be noted. They are: self instrumentality, the idea of the individual human being as the active, creative agent on earth; self-affirmation, the autonomy of the individual; to which is connected the affirmation of the ordinary things of the self, the affirmation of ordinary life; and finally, the emphasis on self-consciousness, the reflective self, which in the Western experience is referred to as the 'inward turn'.

Self-Instrumentality

The first outcome of responsibility was that each individual Muslim had to take action to achieve salvation. The theme of individual instrumentality in this world runs through all the manifestations of this-worldly Islam. The life of Saiyid Ahmad Khan was a testament to his belief in self-help, and the need for the individual to take action for the good of his community and of Islam. Ashraf Ali Thanvi, in considering the process of character formation, insists that knowledge of what one should do is itself not enough: 'knowledge is not true knowledge unless it is acted upon', only thus is the inner self shaped.

For his contemporary, Muhammad Ilyas, Tabligh was the concrete manifestation of 'knowing meaning doing' in the light of the Quran's exhortation to Muslims both to acquire and to transmit knowledge. Maududi makes perfectly clear the duty of Muslims to act on their knowledge of God's commandments if they wish to be saved. This world is the ground on which men prepare for the next. But the clearest statement and vision of man's instrumentality comes in the thought of Iqbal who makes the role of the human self, or ego, in the creative activity of shaping and reshaping the world the focus of much of his work.

For him the reality of the individual is demonstrated not just in thought but in action in this world - not 'cogito ergo sum but 'ago ergo sum'. 'The final act', he declares in his Reconstruction of Religous Thought in Islam, 'is not an intellectual act, but a vital act which deepens the whole being of the ego and sharpens his will with the creative assurance that the world is not just something to be seen and known through concepts, but to be made and remade by continuous action.' Man must not only act but he was the prime mover in God's creation. The new Muslim self is a doing self. Hence the bursts of creative energy released by Indian Muslims during the past two centuries.

Self Affirmation

Individuals who will their religion on the basis of their own knowledge have the capacity to be increasingly autonomous and self-affirmative. They make their own choices. Ashraf Ali Thanvi, for instance, aims to give this capacity to women by giving them the learning of a maulvi and much practical knowledge as well. Iqbal's moral and religious ideal is of the man who achieves self affirmation by being more and more individual and more and more unique. In both cases unrestrained individualism is constrained by the godly purposes these authors have in mind for their subjects. There is, however, an essential tension between this-wordly Islam's desire to empower humankind on earth and on the other hand to continue to focus their attention on godly ends. Once the genie of individualism has been let out of the bottle, there is no guarantee that it will continue to submit to Islam.

Affirmation of ordinary life

With the affirmation of self there also comes the affirmation of the ordinary things of the self, the ordinary things of daily life, which the philosopher, Charles Taylor, terms 'one of the most powerful ideas in modern civilization'. We can see this process at work in the new trends which emerge in the sirat literature that is in the biographies of the Prophet whose number increase greatly in the twentieth century. Increasingly Muhammad is depicted not as the 'Perfect Man' of the sufi tradition but as the perfect person. He is said to have been 'beloved, charitable, frugal, generous, gentle, honest, lenient, a lover of children, modest, pure, steadfast and successful'.

Less attention, as Cantwell Smith has pointed out, is given to his intelligence, political sagacity and capacity to harness the new social forces in his society and more to his qualities as a good middle class family man - his sense of duty and his loving nature - and his qualities as a good citizen - his consideration for others and in particular those who are less fortunate. This transition is also mirrored in changes which take place in biographical writing more generally; the concern is less with what the individual might have contributed to Islamic civilisation and the transmission of knowledge and more on his life in his time and his human qualities. Even in the writings of the ulama it is possible to see them responding to the humanistic preferences of their times and depicting much more rounded lives to support their didactic purpose.

Another dimension of this process is the growing discussion of family and domestic issues, and particularly women, in public space. This discourse is begun by men such as Nazir Ahmad, Hali and Mumtaz Ali in the nineteenth century but in the twentieth century it is increasingly taken up by women and not least by the tens of women who aired their views in the pages of those remakarble journals Ismat and Tehzib un Niswan. All matters are discussed in public from education, diet and dress to love marriages, divorce and the sources of women's inferiority. The writing is often assertive in style, demanding that women and their lives be given respect.

Finally, the rise of the short story and the novel is, of course, an indication of the new value given to understanding human character and the many ways of being human. The themes, often shocking in their day, which were taken up by leading practitioners such as Manto and Ismat Chughtai - family life, relationships, feelings, sex - indicate the new arenas of life in which Muslims are finding meaning. Such is the new importance of these profoundly human matters that religous thinkers cannot afford to ignore them. 'The Islamic pattern of inner life,' declares the religious philosopher Syed Vahiduddin, `finds expression in religious and moral acts, in prayer, in love, in forgiveness, in seemingly mundane activities such as sex and domestic life, which should be radiated by the glow of the world beyond...'.

The Inward Turn; the Growth of Self-Consciousness and Reflection

The final theme is the growth of self-consciousness and reflective habit. A major element of this-worldly Islam in almost all its forms is the requirement for self-examination - a willed Islam had to be a self-conscious one, Muslims had to ask themselves regularly whether they had done all in their power to submit to God and carry out His will in the world. In book Seven of Bihishti Zewar Ashraf Ali Thanvi has a rather charming way of illustrating the process of regular self-examination to ensure purity of intentions and avoidance of wrongdoing. He suggests to the believer that she set aside a little time in the morning and in the evening to speak to her lower self [nafs] as follows: O Self, you must recognize that in this world you are like a trader, Your stock-in-trade is your life. Its profit is to acquire well-being forever, that is, salvation in the afterlife.

This is indeed a profit! If you waste your life and do not gain your salvation, you suffer losses that reach to your stock-in-trade. That stock-in-trade is so precious that each hour - indeed, each breath - is valuable beyond limit. O Self, recognize God's kindness that Death has not yet come. O Self, do not fall into the deception that Almighty God will surely forgive you. [Don't bank on his mercy] Say to yourself, "O Self, you are like a sick person.

A sick person must follow good regimen. Sinning is a bad regimen... Say to the Self, "O Self, the world is a place of journeying, and on a journey complete comfort is never available. You must endure all kinds of trouble. Travelers put up with these troubles because they know that when they reach home they will have all comfort. In the same way, you must endure hard work and distress as long as you dwell in this world. There is work in acts of worship; there is distress in giving up sin; there are all kinds of other troubles. The afterlife is our home. When we arrive there, all trouble will be ended.

This theme of self-consciousness and self-examination is to be found in many religious thinkers of the late nineteenth and twentieth centuries, whether we look at Muhammad Ilyas, Maududi and Vahiduddin or Saiyid Ahmad Khan and Iqbal. In seventeenth- century Europe, as we have noted, this process was accompanied by the emergence of the spiritual diary. Some similar, although not directly comparable materials exist for twentieth-century Muslim India. There is, for instance, Maulana Mahomed Ali's semi- spiritual My Life: A Fragment, which was written while he was interned in World War One. There is also Dr. Syed Mahmud's record of his spiritual reflections while in jail after the non-co- operation movement.

Beyond such works there is a great deal of correspondence with sufis which often does contain processes of self-examination. With such evidence for the reflective habit, alongside the widespread exhortation to examine the self, it is arguable that the development of this-worldly religion helped to open up an interior landscape. Whereas in the past the reflective believer, the mystic, might have meditated upon the signs of God, the new type of reflective believer meditated increasingly on the self and the shortcomings of the self. Now the inner landscape became a crucial site where the battle of the pious for the good took place. Doubtless, there had been Muslims in the past - in particular times and in particular contexts - for whom this had been so.

The importance of the shift towards this-worldly Islam, however, was that self-consciousness and self-examination were encouraged to become widespread. The role of reformism in helping to throw open a window on the inner landscape does not end with the end of belief. Once the original purpose has been lost the window may still remain open for purely secular purposes. The exploration of the inner territory may equally be the quest of one who is purely Muslim by culture. How far the exploration may be a consequence of early religious upbringing, or of values in society widely shared, or of exposure to Western culture will always be hard to judge, even on a case by case basis. That the process of exploration was taking place is evident in books as varied as Ismat Chughtai's remarkable novel of psychological insight Terhi Lakir (The Crooked Line) published in 1944 through to K.A. Abbas's I am not an Island: an Experiment in Autobiography published in 1977.

Arguably the shift towards this-worldly Islam has emphasised new strands in Muslim selves. There is the sense of empowerment that comes with the knowledge that it is humanity that fashions the world. There is the sense of personal autonomy and individual possibility that comes with the knowledge that the individual makes choices. There is the transfer of the symbols and centres of meaning in life from the signs of God and the friends of God to the mundane things of ordinary life. And there is the development of that extra dimension to the self, the interior space. Arguably the individual has become more complex and the possibilities for human fulfilment have become greater. We have noted the central role of the human self for the thinkers of this-worldly Islam.

The fashioning of a new human self was the central activity of the reformist project. The unlimited capacity of man to create and shape the external world is a central feature of Iqbal's thought exemplified in this challenge he makes man hurl at God: You created the night - I lit the lamp. You created the clay - I moulded the cup. You made the wilderness, mountains and forests I cultivated the flowerbeds, parks and gardens. We should note, too, that these manifestations of this-worldly Islam empower man but do not give him unlimited freedom. His power is in the service of God's word (Thanvi). His power is to be within the limits set by Him (Maududi). His power, his human potential, can only be fully realised within the framework of the community created by Him (Iqbal). There remain a few reflections.

First, there is an essential tension between the forces of individualism, potential and actual, set loose by this-worldly religion, and the continuity of the Muslim community as the community of all Muslims. We have noted that a central feature of this-worldly Islam is the empowerment of individuals, indeed the requirement placed on individuals to act on earth. What makes sure, for most Muslim thinkers, that these actions are designed to promote Islamic ends is fear of Judgement and faith, or just faith.

But, willed Islam would appear to be a two-edged sword. It can release great religious energy and creativity, as it has done in South Asia and elsewhere. But, on the other hand, it opens the door to unbelief. Muslims, who can choose to believe, can also choose not to believe, and become Muslims merely by culture. Once belief goes those mundane areas of life which reformist Muslims cherish in the name of God - work, home, family, relationships, sex - now could become prime theatres of meaning in themselves.

With the shift towards this-worldly Islam, and the increasing disenchantment of the world, I wonder, has Islam turned onto a track that, as in the West, leads down a secularising path? Certainly, here is a package of ideas ready to be powered forward in society by the growth of capitalism and the individual freedoms the modern state can fashion. Secondly, we have noted how the responsibilities for this-worldly Islam came to bear with especial weight on women. Nevertheless, there is no doubting the tension which exists between ideas of family and community on the one hand and individualism on the other.

"There was a sense of a collective in the lifestyle of this house', declares Gaythi, the heroine of Altaf Fatima's Dastak Na Do [The One who did not ask], `the selfish god of individualism had not yet crossed its threshold.' And wonder if the strident tone of many of the contributions to Ismat and Tehzib un Niswan in the 1940s was a reflection of the pressure that women were expected to endure. And too, if this might not explain the desire of some to test the boundaries of what was acceptable. Thirdly, willed Islam, self-conscious Islam, leads to a powerful concern to assert and to police the boundaries of difference; it surely also leads to a deepening of community affiliation in the psyche. By the same token, it may also form part of the groundwork for the development of a Muslim political identity and responsiveness to Islamic symbols in politics.

This said, we should note that leaders of this-worldly Islam have gone in very different directions in the political sphere from Muhammad Ilyas and Abul Hasan Nadvi, who have insisted that Islam is all about fashioning individuals and has nothing to do with the political sphere, to Maulana Maududi, who insisted that mastery of the political sphere is essential to achieve right guidance for society. More thought needs to be given to the implications of the deep cultural transformation brought about by the shift in Muslim piety firmly towards this-worldly religion. It is important to get a stronger grasp on its role in shaping modern Muslim selves.

Among other things it would be useful to have a sense of its contribution, as compared with global processes, to fashioning the greater individualism of some twentieth-century Muslim selves. But we also need a sense of how it may be leading to abrasive interactions between the search for individual fulfillment and the obligations of community, an abrasiveness often felt most particularly by women. Doubtless, as the different paths trodden by Nadvi and Maududi suggest, those travelling down the high road of this-worldly Islam can branch off in different directions. Among them may be that of a well-developed ethical self and a largely private faith.

Definition of political parties has changed for some from the time of Edmund Burke as "an organized assembly of men, united for working together for national interest" to one that may not accept members from the minority community and is insistent on establishing Islamic rule or Khilafat. Indeed the head of the Hizb ul Tehrir (Bangladesh) as did few other Islamist parties publicly announced that "we always want to oust all governments in all Muslim countries in the world to establish Khilafat states".

The world is already mired in the militant activities of al-Qaeda operatives, their latest victims being the carnage at Mumbai and the Marriot Hotel in Islamabad. The ongoing conflict for recapture of Swat displacing hundreds of thousands of people is a grim reminder that wars of religion did not end with the Treaty of Westphalia in 1648, as historian Webster had claimed, but continues till today. The form of the conflict has changed from identifiable foes to non-state actors. The conflict is not only inter-religious or intra-religious, the hydra headed Medusa has taken advantage of under development, poverty, tribal and cultural differences among people to unleash its fangs of poison.

Islam is the official religion of the Islamic Republic of Pakistan. In the 1998 census, it found 96% of the total population were Muslims, and in 2007 at 96% and out of Muslim population (Sunni 70%, Shi'a 30%). The estimated population of Muslims of Pakistan in 2008 is 169,800,000. Pakistan has the second largest Muslim population in the world after Indonesia. The majority of Muslims in Pakistan are Sunnis, and the Shi'a Muslim population is the second largest in the world after Iran, more than 50 million.

The Badshahi Masjid, literally the 'Royal Mosque', was built in 1674 by Aurangzeb. It is one of Lahore's best known landmarks, and epitomizes the beauty and grandeur of the Mughal era. Islam arrived in the area now known as Pakistan in 711 CE, when the Umayyad dynasty sent a Muslim Arab army led by Muhammad bin Qasim against the ruler of Sindh, Raja Dahir, whose pirates attacked Arab ships. The army conquered the northwestern part of Indus Valley from Kashmir to the Arabian Sea.

The arrival of the Arab Muslims to the provinces of Sindh and Punjab, along with subsequent Muslim dynasties, set the stage for the religious boundaries of South Asia that would lead to the development of the modern state of Pakistan as well as forming the foundation for Islamic rule which quickly spread across much of South Asia. Following the rule of various Islamic empires, including the Ghaznavid Empire, the Ghorid kingdom, and the Delhi Sultanate, the Mughals controlled the region from 1526 until 1739. The The Muslim technocrats, bureaucrats, soldiers, traders, scientists, architects, teachers, theologians and Sufis flocked from the rest of the Muslim world to Islamic Sultanate and Mughal Empire in South Asia and in the land that became Pakistan.

Sufism has a strong tradition in Pakistan. The Muslim Sufi missionaries played a pivotal role in converting the millions of native people to Islam. As in other areas where Sufis introduced it, Islam to some extent syncretized with pre-Islamic influences, resulting in a religion with some traditions distinct from those of the Arab world. The Naqshbandiya, Qadiriya, Chishtiya and Suhrawardiyya silsas havea a large following in Pakistan. Sufis whose shrines receive much national attention are Data Ganj Baksh (Ali Hajweri) in Lahore (ca. eleventh century), Baha-ud-din Zakariya in Multan and Shahbaz Qalander in Sehwan(ca. twelfth century). and Shah Abdul Latif Bhitai in Bhit, Sindh and Rehman Baba in NWFP.

The Muslim poet-philosopher Sir Allama Muhammad Iqbal first proposed the idea of a Muslim state in northwestern South Asia in his address to the Muslim League at Allahabad in 1930. His proposal referred to the four provinces of Punjab, Sindh, Balochistan, and the NorthWest Frontier-essentially what would became Pakistan. Iqbal's idea gave concrete form to two distinct nations in the South Asia based on religion (Islam and Hinduism) and with different historical backgrounds, social customs, cultures, and social mores.

Islam was thus the basis for the creation and the unification of a separate state, but it was not expected to serve as the model of government. Mohammad Ali Jinnah made his commitment to secularism in Pakistan clear in his inaugural address when he said, You will find that in the course of time Hindus would cease to be Hindus and Muslims would cease to be Muslims, not in the religious sense, because that is the personal faith of each individual, but in the political sense as citizens of the State. This vision of a Muslim majority state in which religious minorities would share equally in its development was questioned shortly after independence.

Salafi Islam was introduced to Pakistan from the early conquerers of Islam. It is represented by the Ahle Hadith movement in India, Pakistan and Bangladesh. A historically strong presence of the movement in Pakistan can be found in the cities Faisalabad, Gujranwala and the region Azad Kashmir, where most of the populations follow the movement, but also in Karachi, Sialkot, Islamabad and Jhelum. Today, more and more, mainly young people are affiliated to the movement, due to a growing number of mosques and many madrassas which teach the Salafi views of Islam. The largest islamic party, the Jamiat Islami, is strongly influenced by the movement. Today, approximately 20% of the Pakistani population feel theirself appropriate to the Ahle Hadith. This makes Pakistan the country with the highest number of Salafi muslims with more than 30 million followers, even more than Saudi-Arabia.

POLITICIZED ISLAM

From the outset, politics and religion have been intertwined both conceptually and practically in Islam. Because Prophet Muhammad established a government in Madina, precedents of governance and taxation exist. Through the history of Islam, from the Ummayyad (661-750) and Abbasid empires (750-1258) to the Mughals (1526- 1858), Safavis (1501-1722) and the Ottomans (1300-1923), religion and statehood have been treated as one. Indeed, one of the beliefs of Islam is that the purpose of the state is to provide an environment where Muslims can properly practice their religion. If a leader fails in this, the people have a right to depose him.

In 1977, the government of Zulfiqar Ali Bhutto outlawed alcohol and changed the weekend from Sunday to Friday, but no substantive Islamic reform program was implemented prior to General Zia-ul-Haq's Islamization program. Starting in February 1979, new penal measures based on Islamic principles of justice went into effect. These carried considerably greater implications for women than for men. A welfare and taxation system based on Zakat and a profit-and-loss banking system were also established in accordance with Islamic prohibitions against usury but were inadequate.

Census data indicates that over 96% of the population is Muslim. The Muslims belong to different schools which are called Madhahib (singular: Madhhab) i.e, schools of jurisprudence (also 'Maktab-e-Fikr' (School of Thought) in Urdu). Around 70% of Pakistani Muslims are Sunni Muslims and there is sizeable minority 30% Shi'a Muslims. Nearly all Pakistani Sunni Muslims belong to the Hanafi school with a small Hanbali school represented by Wahabis and Ahle Hadith. The Hanafi school includes the Barelvis and Deobandis schools.

Although the majority of Pakistani Shia Muslims belong to Ithna 'ashariyah school, there are significant minorities: Nizari Ismailis (Aga Khanis) and the smaller Mustaali Dawoodi Bohra and Sulaimani Bohra branches. Many people on the Makran coast of Balochistan follow the Zikri sect of Islam. The difference among Sunni schools (Hanafi, Maliki, Shafi, and Hanbali) are small in practice, and they may pray together in any Sunni Masjid. In Pakistan, adherents of the Barelvi and Deobandi schools also pray together in same Masjids.

The Shia Ithna 'ashariyah school has its own Masjids and Hussainias. Mustaali Dawoodi Bohra and Sulaimani Bohra also have their own Masjids. While the Nizari Khoja Ismailis (Aga Khanis) pray in Jama'at Khanas. There are small non-Muslim religious groups: Christians (1.6%), Hindus (1.85%), Ahmadis, Sikhs, Parsis, Bahá'ís, Zoroastrians (Parsis) and others making up 4% of the population.

MORALITY IN GOVERNANCE

The question of morality is justifiably now being raised in judging both the national and international behavior of states and the evaluation of the code of conduct, more or less uniform in character, prescribed to be followed by the civilized states, to retain one's position as a responsible member of the global community. Yet there is, no denying the fact that the world divided as it is into First, Second and the Third(or even Fourth) worlds does testify to the great existential divide among the people living in these well defined worlds where division is more vertical than horizontal.

A few individuals through diligence and/or accident may move residentially from the Third to the First world thus forming a part of the Diaspora who after the tragic events of 9/11 impelling the West to legislate various forms of anti-terrorist acts are facing "spiraling progressive alienation" and forced to continually negotiate the parameters of minority citizenship. As it is from the beginning of history social stratification or societal division based on wealth, power and status has been a defining characteristic of civilizations. Social stratification took global shape with the advent of colonization and poverty began to be distributed among the people living in the periphery and the wealth of the periphery was shipped to the metropolis.

During and after the process of decolonization the newly and aspirant independent countries began to question the hypothesis inherent in the modernization theory which explained underdevelopment in terms of lack of certain qualities in the "underdeveloped" societies such as drive, entrepreneurial skill, creativity and problem solving ability.

The decolonized people rebelling against intellectual dystrophy and sanitized academic orthodoxy by and large put their faith in the dependency theory which explained that the continued impoverishment of the Third World was not internally generated but was the result of a structural condition of global domination in which the dominant forced the dominated to be producers of raw materials and food stuff for the industrialized metropolitan center. However the entire colonial discourse should not be seen through the prism of Manichaeism expressed in binary structure between good and evil because the colonizers were not totally exploitive in nature but were also donors of liberal values so much in demand in the world today.

On the other hand even if the sub-alterns were to be magnanimous and forgiving for the politico-socio-economic exploitation in the by-gone days by the advanced countries it is not certain, despite occasional camaraderie shown by the West through aid to tsunami victims and the expected financial pledge following publication of the report by the Africa Commissionand the London Conference of G-20 in the aftermath of global recession that the West would sincerely like the developing countries to move forward at a sprinter's speed.

ODA is yet to be given at 0.7% of the GDP pledged by the developed world decades ago. The US and EU are yet to get rid of farm subsidies which is many times more than the assistance given to the Third world. Tariff and Para-tariff barriers imposed by the developed countries on the exports of the developing nations are yet to be removed. Debts owed by the poorest countries are yet to be entirely written off.

WESTERN PERCEPTION OF MUSLIMS

Though some Muslim scholars consider the essentialist construction of the people and the religion of Islam dominant in the western academic orthodoxy as grossly distorted, yet one must also acknowledge that the deviants of Islamic religion immersed in their own grotesque interpretation of pristine Islam do pose serious threat not only to the West but also to Muslims who they consider to have deviated from the "true" path. Time is past for the Muslim world to hold on to tortured nationalism by blaming the West for failing to seize the moment when western technology was on its way to irreversibly change the contours of global civilization. It is past time for the Islamic world to clean up the Augean Stable, get its act together and unite with the West and others to fight the common enemy-terrorism.

Islamic renaissance is unlikely to emerge from the destructive acts of Osama bin Laden. Efforts should be directed towards achieving "global civic ethics" as recommended by the Commission on Global Governance echoing Immanuel Kant's theory of "universal moral community" that derives from the principle that all people are bound together morally regardless of their distinctive culture and identity. If it is recognized that human security is central to global peace then a government's right to rule must be weighed against its people's right to security.

In cases if it is found that people's security is being threatened under the cloak of religious activism then the state should assume its responsibility to put ban on such religious activism which incipiently tries to crawl towards staging a so-called Islamic Free Election Trap to stage a coup to establish a theocratic state. Devoutly Muslim Bangladeshis are unlikely to countenance any Machiavellian machination by religious extremists because Bangladesh has a tradition of secular culture which is neither atheistic nor agnostic. The government in power regardless of political expediency is duty bound to arrest any movement towards religious extremism and ensure freedom of choice to the people.

Though the just concluded Indian elections have announced the victory of secularism over communalism perhaps also for stability in current uncertain global economic environment, global discomfort is evident these days over overt preeminence of religion in politics in some countries. The question that arises in the minds of the many is whether religion-conservatism has become the order of the day or the current religious doctrinaire is to be regarded as a quirk of history in an otherwise sequential historical progress of the world towards Francis Fukuyama's liberal democracy constituting the "end point of mankind's ideological evolution" and the "final form of government" and as such signaling the "end of history".

But Fukuyama himself has conceded that "one is inclined to say that the revival of religion in some way attests to a broad unhappiness with the impersonality and spiritual vacuity of liberal consumerists' societies". After Afghanistan, Islamic fundamentalism went global with its appeal to a section of Muslim society based on moral, cultural and political grounds. The Islamists argue that western culture particularly the one practiced by western women is essentially degenerative and incompatible with Quranic literalism. They argue that the values propagated by the West threaten Islamic "purity" and hence their advance is to be thwarted at any cost.

Political argument is by far the easiest to sell to the wayward Muslim population who despite declaration of piety could have nursed in the darkest corner of their heart a desire to commit the original sin. The Islamists argue that the reasons for economic backwardness, political repression and societal dysfunction were caused by western, particularly American assistance given to the repressive regimes in the Muslim world. So Osama bin Laden's deputy Egyptian Ayman al-Zawahiri faced little problem in becoming an ideologue of hatred to some marginalized Muslims living at the fringe of an often affluent society. In his Knights under the Prophet's Banner, a manifesto on jihad, al-Zawahiri explains that it is legitimate to strike western population, not just their governments and institutions, because they "only know the language of self-interest, backed by brute military force".

The problems faced by the Islamic secular movements have been compounded by the iconic presence of Samuel Huntington and Bernard Lewis in literatures trying to explain the democratic deficit generally suffered by the Muslim world. To Huntington in Islam God is Caesar, in Confucianism Caesar is God, and in European Orthodox Christianity God is Caesar's junior partner. Unhesitatingly Huntington declares: "The underlying problem for the West is not Islamic fundamentalism. It is Islam". Historian Bernard Lewis perceived Muslim world's "downward spiral of hate and spite, rage and self-pity, poverty and oppression" being caused by the Islamic world's defeat at the hands of Judeo-Christian civilizations.

But in this sweeping critique of Islam Lewis and others have forgotten that refusal of western hegemony does not necessarily mean wholesale abandonment of western values. Professor Robert Hefner correctly asserts that there is no clash of civilizations between Islamic and Christian world and the really decisive battle is being waged within the Muslim civilization where ultra-conservatives are competing with the moderates and democrats for the soul of Islam. In understanding the intensity of the battle it is necessary to distinguish between neo-fundamentalists with transnational reach and secular Islam which believes in the subordination of religion to the state. In this debate one may have to make the difficult choice of whether or not to ban religion based political parties.

DEMOCRACY AND ISLAM

An inconclusive debate remains about the incompatibility of democracy with monotheistic religions. Robert Dahl in his classic book Polyarchy had set eight essential requirements for democracy: - right to form and join organizations; freedom of expression; right to vote; eligibility for public office; right of political leaders to compete for support for vote; and institutions for making government policies dependant on vote and other expressions of preference. Other political scientists have added that democracy must also have a constitution that by itself is democratic in that it respects fundamental liberties and offers protection to minorities.

Additionally democratically elected governments must rule within the confines of their constitutions, be bound by law and be accountable. From historical observations it has been found that religions place inherent obstacles in the way of democracy.

Philosopher John Rawls found it particularly difficult in a pluralistic society in which citizens hold a variety of socially embedded, reasonable yet deeply opposed comprehensive doctrines to arrive at an overlapping consensus. In the case of Islam some western scholars have found that because of Prophet Mohammed(sm)'s fusion of military and spiritual authority and because Quranic laws are deemed to be final the space for democratic debate for the formation of secular laws does not exist in Muslim societies.

Some other scholars however have found that appropriation of political Islam by Islamic fundamentalists is untenable and millions of Muslims living outside the Arab world live in intermittent democracies and they may not become victims of so-called Islamic Free Election Trap in which fundamentalists use democratic means to get to power only to abolish democratic practices through legislation.

Democracy is a dynamic process and "a state's raison d'etre does not lie in the protection of equal individual rights but in the guarantee of an inclusive process of opinion and will formation in which free and equal citizens reach an under standing on which goals and norms lie in the equal interest of all".

Clearly then an ethical question would arise as perceived by Italian political scientist Luigi Bonante while discussing the difference between the individual and the state. He argues that while the state has sufficient tools to defend its rights and reject its duties; for the individual as recipient it is much harder to elude his duties than to achieve his freedom.

This kind of asymmetry of power during the BNP-Jamaat rule in Bangladesh provides strong argument for the protection of human rights. The Orwellian tyranny of the majority was further compounded by increasing activism of Islamists who wish to recreate a truly Islamic society not simply by imposing the sharia but by establishing an Islamic state where religious edicts will be integrated into all aspects of society.

Washington based Center for Strategic and International Studies in its Transnational Threat Update before the 1/11 change over stated: "The current security climate in Bangladesh may allow terrorist groups to organize attacks using a radiological dispersal device. Concerns over this possibility are plausible given that radio substance have proven accessible to terror groups within the country".

If we accept David Held's (of London School of Economics) assertion that we no longer live in a world of discrete national communities but in a world, in David Held's words, " overlapping communities of fate"; then the Muslims in Bangladesh do not constitute the majority community as they are surrounded by Hindu majority India and Buddhist majority Myanmar and in the vicinity by non-Muslim South East and Far East Asian countries.

Pakistani Intelligence Services (ISI) has been trying to destabilize North Eastern India from Bangladesh. Last year India had clearly warned that she would not ignore her neighbors' conduct "to allowing the use of their territories for cross border terrorism and hostile activities against India".

Predictably then Bangladesh authorities continued to dismiss these allegations.

The number of madrashas in Bangladesh is estimated to be 64000 (sixty four thousand) divided into two broad categories Aliya madrashas run with governmental support and control, and Dars-e-Nizami or Deoband style madrashas who are totally independent. Jamat-e-Islami, founded by Maulana Abu ala Maududi, had grown out of Deoband madrasha system.

Jamat from the very beginning was inspired by Ikhwan ul Muslemin or Muslim Brotherhood of Egypt with the aim of bringing about an Islamic revolution and creating an Islamic state. Initially in undivided India Jamat was opposed to the concept of Pakistan. Later, however, when Jamat came to support Pakistan as the Islamic state for the Indian Muslims, Bengali nationalism was totally unacceptable to them. Unsurprisingly therefore Jamat sided with the Pakistani occupation forces in East Pakistan and fought against the war of liberation.

MADRASA-EXTREMISM NEXUS

Most madrasa are used to educate male students while a few also impart education to girls. Since madrasa education does not carry much financial benefits in a labor market demanding non-ecclesiastical skills the students graduating from madrasas are forced to become madrasa teachers or priests in mosques. Coming from impoverished families they are forced back into poverty in a world racing for material advancement. This vicious cycle of poverty and deprivation may find expression in anti-western feeling particularly in the aftermath of the decimation of Afghanistan and the illegal invasion of Iraq.

Many madrasa students may find it difficult to understand the venality of the Taliban regime and of their participation in the 9/11 carnage necessitating regime change in Afghanistan. To many of them Osama bin Laden is a hero. Understandably the US Congress keeps itself informed of the madrasa education in South Asia. A report by the Congressional Research Service (International Terrorism in South Asia) states that among the approximately ten thousand madrasas in Pakistan some that have been implicated in teaching militant anti-western, anti-American and anti-Hindu values. Many of these madrasas are financed and operated by Pakistani Islamist political parties and foreign entities.

Foremost US analyst on South Asia Stephen Cohen states that the largest Islamic sects with the greatest control over religious schools are the Deobandis (as opposed to the Barlevis) who are among the most militant in their demand for Pakistan to become truly Islamic. Incidentally Deobandi groups were in the forefront of declaring Ahmadiyyas as non-Muslim in Pakistan. Cohen believes that the reaction of Parvez Musharraf's generation of army officers against Zia ul Huq's Islamic zealotry in no way represents a rejection of the limited strategy of using radical Islamic groups as instruments of Pakistani foreign policy, especially against India. This tour d'horizon of Pakistani religious extremism was necessary because terrorism, particularly religious terrorism, is almost always transnational.

During his latest visit to South Asia Ambassador Cofer Black, State Department coordinator for counter terrorism spoke of Indian allegations relating to terrorist camps in Bangladesh (denied by Bangladesh authorities) and of the "need to determine exactly the threat not only to Bangladesh but also the potential utilization of Bangladesh as a platform to project terrorism internationally". Noted Indian journalist Prem Shankar Jha felt that the 8/21 assassination attempt on Sheikh Hasina was possible due to a combination of political expediency and ambivalence over whether to ride the tiger of religious intolerance or to confront it". He warned against the propagation of "an intolerant arabicised brand of Islam that was alien to Bangladesh's secular culture".

Despite Bangladesh government's claim that militancy is under control frequent reports on the arrest of militants and discovery of their arms factories cause alarm among the people. This emergence of religious intolerance in Bangladesh, despite the present government's efforts to secularize the political environment, documented by Amnesty International, Human Rights Watch, and US State Department among others, should be seen in global context.

If the Muslims are to prove historian Bernard Lewis wrong that "Islam was never prepared, either in theory or in practice, to accord full equality to those who held other forms of worship, and that the centuries old rivalry between Christianity and Islam is no less than a clash of civilizationst perhaps irrational but surely historic reaction of an ancient rival against our Judeo-Christian heritage, our secular present, and the world wide expansion of both", then the Islamic world would have to adorn itself with all the traits of modernity.

Globalization is no longer a choice; it is a reality that all countries have to deal with. In this game the West has a decided advantage over the Muslim world, particularly the least developed among them. Countries like Bangladesh will remain dependent on the developed economies and international financial institutions if they are to transform their societies into more advanced ones.

This quest is fraught with difficulties that should not be further compounded by inviting religious extremism, however politically expedient such a move may be. If the worry of the international community is to safeguard its values and its way of life against the onslaught by Islamic fundamentalists' inflexible and nihilistic war of attrition then care should be taken of Jamaat's politics in Bangladesh.

Fusion of military and spiritual authority and Quranic literalism as opposed to the concept of the separation of the Church and the State is intrinsic to Jamaat's political philosophy. Problem with Islamic political parties like Jamaat in Bangladesh is "the persistence of ambiguity" suffered by Islamists almost everywhere.

Marina Ottaway and others define this ambiguity as "tensions remaining between the old goals of creating Islamic states and enacting uncompromising versions of the Sharia and the new goal of becoming influential players in a pluralistic, democratic system". Jamaat's spiritual Guru Maulana Maududi described the movement's purpose "to initiate the deen in the form of a movement so that religiosity does not become static in our personal lives, but we struggle to implement this deen and also try to crush those forces that are against its implementation".

On another occasion Maulana Maududi declared "we take a person in Jamaat when he understands the meaning of Kalima-e-Tayyiba and makes it mandatory that he fulfills the minimum criteria of Islam". Evidently Jamaat's philosophy does not allow inclusiveness of other religions or democratic norms. This partly explains Jamaat's initial opposition to the Muslim League's demand for a separate homeland for the Muslims in British India, and its opposition to Bangladesh liberation movement can be seen from Jamaat's perspective as dismemberment of a Muslim state caused by the machination of a Hindu India.

That the occupying Pakistani army was brutalizing Bengali Muslims (along with Hindus) was seen as "collateral damage" that must be borne if the Bengali Muslims were to be freed from the contagion of Hindu influence. Jamaat's current acceptance of democratic pluralism and female leadership in the stewardship of the country is tactical and was undertaken when Jamaat was convinced of the irreversibility of the existence of Bangladesh as a sovereign and independent state. Character of Jamaat-e-Islami is not only apocalyptic, it is nihilistic.

The confessional statements made by the terrorists relating to terrorism committed on 17th August have proved unambiguously their connection with Jamaat or its students' wing at some point during their political career. Little doubts remain that religion based politics generates fear among minority communities the protection of whom has been pledged by all civilized countries both in their domestic law and international commitment. In Bangladesh for example the recent events involving terrorist activities allegedly perpetrated by Islamic extremists have strengthened the demands of the secularists to put a ban on religion based political activities.

The 1972 Bangladesh Constitution did provide for such a ban. The post-1975 conservative establishments amended the Constitution once in 1977 and again in 1988 by passing the 8th amendment making Islam the state religion. Additionally the Vested (Enemy) Property Act enacted during Pakistani rule through which 2.1 million acres of Hindu owned land were confiscated remains in our statute book even today. Every year US State Department's Religious and Human Rights reports, reports by Amnesty International and Human Rights Watch chronicle abuses perpetrated on minority communities in Bangladesh.

3

Nineteenth-century Indian Islam and Women

'Islamization' of India did not occur as a result of mass conversions. The process took several centuries. Though the province of Sindh was conquered in early 8th century it was not until the incursions of Mahmud of Ghazni and Muhammad of Ghor that serious settlement of the subcontinent with Muslims took place. Even then contrary to belief it was not the forced conversions that increased the number of Muslims in India. Of course, the unfair taxes called jizya of all non-Muslims had an effect. Many Hindus were forced to convert to Islam to escape from the punishing taxes. The invading sultans like Qutb ud-din Aibak and Ala-ud-din Khilji often offered clemency to the enemy after their defeat if they converted to Islam.

Many of these local rulers switched back to Hinduism as soon as the sultans turned their backs and returned to Delhi. The major reason for mass settlement of India by Muslims was the invasion of Mongols into central Asia. Genghis Khan, his grandsons and later Timurlane wreaked havoc in the Central Asian countries causing migration of countless number of people seeking refuge in the relative safety of India. Just how disastrous Muslim conquest was for India and how much resistance had been offered to preserve its heritage by Hindu rulers are controversial subjects. Much of the history was written by Muslim historians and could be biased. The little history documented by

Indians was also written with an eye towards glorifying their kings. These as well could be simply exaggerations.

Hindu writers write about countless accounts of heroism by their warrior, some of them mere boys in their teens. Some of the fiercest resistance probably came from lesser tribes and simply went undocumented. However, it is clear that the Muslim conquest of India took several centuries. Idolatry was condemned but many sultans simply ignored the practice by the Hindus and did not impose Islam on them forcibly. Better results were obtained by imposing taxes on non-Muslims, although the Brahmins and some Buddhists were exempt form it until the rule of Feroz Shah Tughlaq in the latter half of 14th century.

When the Mughals established their empire, the whole of India was almost completely under the Muslim rule, especially during the rule of Aurangazeb. Religious fanaticism of Aurangazeb, unlike his ancestor Mughals finally led to the cessation of Muslim control of India. As a consequence of his intolerance, the Mughal Empire weakened precipitously after his death and steadily shrank in size over the next century and a half, to finally be taken over by another foreign force in the nineteenth century, the British. What Akbar had achieved with tolerance and reconciliation was reversed by Aurangzeb's zeal to force Islam on Hindus.

The religion of Islam stormed into India in a similar manner as it did in the Arabian countries. Powerful regimes succumbed to the religion at a remarkably fast pace as evidenced by the fact that within a century after its inception, it had spread to the entire Middle East and Northern Africa. But in India, Islam had a more difficult time to insinuate into the Hindu and Buddhist societies. Even then, 'Islamization' of India took several centuries and was never complete. The barbaric nature of the sultanates rule and the invasion of Mongols may have had a negative effect on the Hindu practitioners. The earlier Mughals had breeched the division somewhat, but Aurangzeb in his zeal to turn India into an Islamic nation alienated all other religions. From then onward 'moderate Muslim rule' was an oxymoron. It is also apparent that the Hindus revered their idols much more than the Muslim conquerors estimated. A sweep of India never occurred and India remained predominantly Hindu, with only about twenty percent of its population as Muslims, at any given time in its history.

Greater India once included Pakistan and Afghanistan. Gandhara (Kandahar) is mentioned in Mahabharata epic (Gandhari, wife of Drtarashtra hailed from Gandhara). Ashoka and Kanishka ruled Afghanistan and it was an integral part of India until it was lost to Islam. Afghanistan had been lost to India for many centuries until Babur, the founder of the Mughal Empire, united it with India. Lost to Shah of Persia by Humayun, Akbar had re established the sovereignty in Afghanistan by conquering both Kabul valley and Kandahar. Then Jahangir and Shah Jahan lost Kandahar forever to the Shah of Iran, never to be regained though Kabul remained in Mughal hands until the reign of Aurangzeb. Even the British in the nineteenth century were unable to re-conquer it. India lost further territory when Pakistan and Bangladesh were lost to India in the modern era, in the middle of twentieth century.

The myth that the Mughals were more detrimental to Hindu dominance of India than any other dynasty. If destruction of Hindu temples is any measure the Sultans of Delhi did far worse damage than the Mughals (except Aurangzeb). The marauders like the Mahmud of Ghazni, Muhammad of Ghor, Timurlane, Nadir Shah and Ahmad Shah Abdali did loot and destroy idols in the temples all over the North, but the rulers like Aibak, Iltumish, Khilji and Feroz Shah Tughlaq, continued to do the desecration of temples in the name of cleansing the religion of Hindus and Buddhists over a long period of time in a sustained way. A large library of Buddhist literature was set ablaze by Khilji in Odantapuri, even before knowing what they contained.

Their stories are forgotten because Indians never developed the habit of writing down history. They relied on their memory to remember events (just as the Vedas had been memorized for generations). But this was regretful, as history shows that the Hindus eventually forgot their history and made the mistake of repeating it, often committing the same mistakes over and over again. This folly was exploited fully by the invading Muslims as well the British at a later date.

Muslim influx and influence in India started almost at the inception of the religion. The traders from Arabia were frequent visitors to the Indian subcontinent even before Prophet Muhammad revealed the Koran. They brought the word of Muhammad to India in the 7th century and this resulted in some peaceful conversions of Hindus to Islam. Following this, Mohammad-ibn-Quasim in the year 712 A.D conquered the Province of Sindh. However, this event in history does not seem to have influenced India as much as expected. Beginning with the invasion of Mohammad of Ghazni in the 10th century, followed by a barrage of invaders from Persia, Turkey and Afghanistan in the 11th and 12th centuries, a full force of Islam was thrust upon India. Forcible conversions of people of other faiths with inducements as well as unfair taxation resulted in spread of the Islam in Hindustan. The British conquest in India that started insidiously with the establishment of the East India Company, eventually usurped the Muslim stronghold of India, in the 18th century.

Today there are more than a quarter of a billion Muslims living in the Indian subcontinent (India, Pakistan and Bangla Desh). This amounts to more than a quarter of the total Muslim population of the world. Muslims form about fifteen percent of the Indian population. It is unique that the Muslim population of India has been influenced by the Hindu religion throughout history. Sufism, for example is an adaptation of Vedanta. Over many centuries, Islam in India has undergone several attempts at reforms, some towards modernization and some leaning more towards fundamentalism.

The Muslims in India are categorized into two distinct classes based on their origins. This is similar to the caste system of Hinduism (so called Varnashrama). Muslims are broadly divided into two groups, namely, Ashraf and Ajlaf. Ashraf are again grouped as Sayyeds, Sheikhs, Mugahls and Pathans. The

Sayyeds are said to be descendents of the Prophet and regarded in high esteem. The Sheikhs are of Arab descent and are next in line in prestige. The Mughals are descendents of the greatest Muslim rulers of India, the Mughals and occupy third place. Pathans including Sepahis hail from the northwestern regions including Afghanistan and form the last group of Ashraf. The Ajlaf on the other hand are the Indian converts and are considered to be of common ancestry. They are considered to be of inferior class when compared to the Ashraf.

Nineteenth century India saw great socio-religious reform in Hinduism. The reform movements of Rajaram Mohan Roy in 1827 first started the abolishing of Sati and recognition of widow marriage as well as education of women by founding of his Brahmo Samaj in Bengal. Many reform movements followed this, significantly the Prarthana Samaj started by Keshab Chandra Sen in 1867 (later popularized by G.M.Ranade and Bhandarkar), Arya Samaj established in 1875 by Dayananda Saraswati and Ramakrishna Mission of Vivekananda.

The Theosophical Society of Colonel Cleott popularized by Annie Besant in 1886 in Madras, the Rehnumai Mazdayasan Sabha of the Parsees established by Dadabhai Navaroji in 1851 in Bombay and the Sri Narayan Dharma Paripalan Yogam started by Sri Narayana Guru in 1903 in Travancore were some other reform movements of late 19th century. All these reforms were attempts at steering the Hindu religion towards Vedanta, which is the backbone of its philosophy. Unlike Hinduism, which is flexible and amenable to reform, Islam is rigid and difficult to change. Criticism of old archaic practices is shunned and viewed as anti- Muslim rhetoric. Modernization is seen as a threat to the way of life of a Muslim. In the face of such persistent orthodoxy all the reforms of the 19th century generally have been reverting to more fundamentalism rather than modernization. Two such reforms were the Wahabis and Tabligis.

THE WAHABIS

The Wahabi movement started in Saudi Arabia in the 18th century by Muhammad ibn-Abd-al-Wahab (1703–1792) regards all other religions as heretical and thus intolerant towards them. The Indian Wahabi movement was founded by Syed Ahmed Brelavi (1789-1831) belonging to Rai Baraili. When he saw Islam drifting towards superstitions and exaggerated veneration of saints and prophets, he steered Islam to its more fundamental roots similar to the Arabian Wahabi movement. However, the Brelavi Wahabis had no direct contact with their counterparts in Arabia. Its aim was to establish Muslim sovereignty in India or a Dar-ul-Islam. Though the Wahabis took part in fighting the British, the basic tenet of the movement did not change, that is to establish Muslim supremacy over all of India.

Influenced by the Wahabi movement, two other fundamentalist movements came into existence. Shariatullah started Fairazi movement in attempt to aid the poor peasants in Bengal against the oppressive zamindars. Soon this became an anti-Hindu movement as well. More significant was the second movement called the Deoband. They established the Muslim schools for education, the model of which is still followed in the madrassahs around the Muslim world. These Deoband faction attracted students from all over the Muslim world. Financed by the rich Muslim Arab nations, fundamentalism was institutionalized in these schools. In India there is an undercurrent of discord between the Deoband faction and the Brelavi Wahabis, mainly due to the financial disparity. In course of time the movements started as reform of Muslims shifted course and has been preoccupied with power and control of the populous.

THE TABLIGIS

Dayananda Saraswati's Arya Samaj targeted Muslim converts and attempted a purification drive (shuddhikaran). As a response Maulana Iliyas of Mewat in Rajastan started the Tabligi movement in 1927. The Hindu converts were practicing a mixed form of Islam as they were culturally more Hindu than Muslim. Maulana Iliyas started his movement to transform these converts into 'complete Muslims' and put forward the slogan, 'Aye Musalmano! Musalman bano' (O Muslims! Be Muslims). True Islamic teachings and practices were taught in an uncompromising way. Initially localized to Mewat, the movement caught on and spread rapidly after the death of the Maulana.

The Tabligis follow strict codes of the Islamic law. They are bound by the religious dogma, dressing patterns, detailed methods of religious practices. Meetings of thousands of Muslim gatherings (Jama'at) are held where minute details of the religious practices are taught for Muslims to follow. Half the populations of Muslims in the subcontinent are now adherents of this movement. Though apolitical in its organization, they have a capacity of mobilizing a large number of Muslims at short notice to gather. More moderate reforms of the Islamic religion also occurred simultaneously. The adherents of such reforms are much less in number today. The Aligarh and the Ahmedia movements are the two main moderate attempts at reform.

THE ALIGARH MOVEMENT

Sir Syed Ahmed Khan (1817-1891) attempted a social upsurge amongst the Indian Muslims with his so-called Aligarh movement. His main contribution was to enhance education with starting of many schools and colleges. Much importance was given to Urdu language. He undertook reconciliation between Islam and Christianity and he pointedly showed the similarities between the two religions.

He even published a sympathetic study of the Bible. Urdu translation of books on western arts and sciences were done by a translation society founded by him. Despite all the successful launching of social reforms, Sir Syed failed to bring about much needed moderation of the religion such as women's education and the purdah system for oppressed women. Only the education of upper and middle class and has been criticized for not going far enough with his reforms of the entire Muslim society.

THE AHMEDIAS

Founded in 1889 by Mirza Ghulam Ahmed, the movement was based on universal religion of all communities. It spread western liberal education among Muslims by starting a number of schools and colleges. It was opposed to Jihad but at the same time infused vigorous religious spirit among Muslims. It is the most closely knit and organized group of Muslims in the country. Its perceived mysticism was its downfall.

THE AGA KHAN'S FLOCK

Apart from the Sunnis (the followers of Omar, the Caliph) and Shiites, (followers of Ali, Prophet's son in law) there is another sect in Indian subcontinent called the Aga Khanis. It is the Nizari Ismaili community with Aga Khan as their Imam. It originated as a splinter group of Shi'ite sect, when they accepted Ismail as the seventh Imam instead of his brother. They trace an unbroken line of Imams up to the current day Aga Khan (Prince Karim), who is 49th in succession. Many Shiite sects refused to accept any Imams after the elevnth Imam died without an heir. In this way the Nizari Ismailis are different.

Thirteen generation after Ali, the Shiite sect further divided between followers of Nizar and his brother (later came to be known as Bohra community). Nizari Ismailis follow Aga Khan as their leader and celebrate his birthday as a holy day rather than the Muharram, which most of the Shiites celebrate as a holy day because of the death anniversary of Hussein, son of Ali. Followers of Aga Khan are more westernized than any other Muslim community. Most of the recent Aga Khans have been educated in England. Thousand years ago they were rivals of the caliphate of Baghdad and ruled as the Fatimid caliphate of Cairo. After the decline of their influence in Egypt and Asia, they remained in Persia until 1840, when the 46th Imam was forced to leave Persia.

They then moved to India and Pakistan where they formed an amicable relationship with the British. They were not accepted into Mecca and did not undertake pilgrimage.

In 1866 their interpretation of the Koran resulted in dissension among its followers and many left the faith and reverted to some other form of Shiite sect. The Aga Khans were also accused of mishandling the Nizari finances in 1905 though they won a court battle in this regard. However, the modernization of the religion by the Aga Khans did not sit well in the Muslim world. The Nizari Ismailis of Gujarat are called Khojas.

During the 16th and 17th centuries, for example, Indian Nizaris often deemed it necessary to consult Hindu texts as well as The Holy Koran; in fact even today a fair number of Aga-Khanis enjoy and derive some inspiration from the Bhagavad-Gita. Unlike other Muslims, they sometimes sing hymns during their services, usually in an Indian language such as Gujarati. In addition, many Nizaris believe that reincarnation of souls is possible under certain circumstances. Mostly these are Muslims who embrace Sufism. An attempt was once made to categorize Hazrat Ali as the tenth avatar of Vishnu by Aga Khan though they no longer believe this.

As a result of the rift between the reformers and the orthodox sections of the religion, many deserted and joined other Shiite sect, thus becoming indistinguishable from them. It was thought that only about four million Muslims remained faithful to Aga Khan. However, after the breakup of the Soviet Union and birth of independent countries like Uzbekistan, Turkmenistan and Tajikistan where many Aga Khanis were found to be followers of the faith. Now it is believed that there are about 20 million followers.

OTHER ATTEMPTS

Other attempts have been made to modernize the religious practices with varying effects. Shibli Numani attempted Muslims to adopt a more flexible attitude towards Hindus and accept new ideas, but failed. Barruddin Tyebji (1844-1906) attempted to do away with the Purdah in Bombay. Moves toward re-interpretation of scriptures, history and behavior have been attempted by Hali and more recently by Maulana Vahiddudin Khan. Traditional Muslim forces are too strong to allow any radical changes in the socio-religious front.

Unlike Hindu reforms, real radical reforms of Islam have remained a dream of certain individuals over the course of history. Phadke wrote in 1989 that " So tight has been the hold of orthodoxy on the Muslim mind that nowhere in India has Muslim society been so far able to support a vocal group of liberal Muslims committed to modern values. There has been no serious attempt of a thorough critical appraisal of their heritage". After Indian Independence the reform of the Islam has become even more difficult as any attempt is viewed with suspicion because of the minority status of the Muslims. Another moderate Muslim movement attempting to reform is the Bohra Reformist Group. Bohras are mainly business people mostly in the hardware and gun smithy. This is a modern movement attempting to soften the authority of the religious leaders on the religion.

Started by Engineer, Contractor and Poonawala they have even attempted to interpret Koran in the perspective of a Christian liberal theology. In the 1970's a reformist named Hamid Dalwai made a serious attempt at modernizing Islam in India. He proposed abandonment of purdah and more freedom to women among the Maharashtra Sunni Muslim community. For this effort he was branded as heretic and his movement did not survive after his death. Dalwai's movement was called Muslim Satayshodhak Mandal (MSM). Many more similar attempts have so far failed to produce significant results in reforming the socio-religious aspect of Islam in India. The fundamentalism is readily accepted whereas the moderate reforms are shunned.

THE FUTURE

Any attempt to bring the religion in par with the modern scientific world is perceived as a threat to Islamic identity. Religion is law in Islam and any change is thought to be breech of faith and belief. Sir Syed (Aligarh Movement) was called a kafir or infidel for his attempts and Dalwai (MSM) was branded as munafique or a heretic. Religion forms an integral part of the day-to-day practice of Islam that any reform devoid of religion is bound to fail. At the same time the injudicious reliance on religion can result in extreme fundamentalism like the Wahabi or directionless organization of the Tablig Jama'at. Being a minority status in India has resulted in any attempt at modernization to be called as an attempt at 'Hindu-isation' of Islam.

Even the purdah system is defended as a religious identity, discarding the humanitarian aspect and discrimination. Somehow a middle ground has to be sought both by the minority Muslims and the majority Hindus in India. There has to be an exchange of moderate ideas in a non-religious context that does not cross the line of infuriating the religious faction. From a distance this looks like an impossible feat as both sides have vowed not to give an inch. This rigidity has made the clash of two of the great religions all the more difficult to avoid. The divergent paths followed by both in their philosophy and theosophy seems to be drifting apart at a rapid pace.

The advent of Islam in the Ganges basin at the end of the 12th century resulted in the withdrawal of royal patronage from Hinduism in much of the area. The attitude of the Muslim rulers toward Hinduism varied. Some, like Fîrûz Tughluq (ruled 1351–88) and Aurangzeb (ruled 1658–1707), were strongly anti-Hindu and enforced payment of jizya, a poll tax on unbelievers. Others, like the Bengali sultan $usayn Shâh Alâ al-Dîn (reigned 1493–1519) and the great Akbar (reigned 1556–1605), were well-disposed toward their Hindu subjects. Many temples, however, were destroyed by the more fanatical rulers. Conversion to Islam was more common in areas where Buddhism had once been strongest-Pakistan, Bangladesh, and Kashmir.

On the eve of the Muslim occupation, Hinduism was by no means sterile in northern India, but its vitality was centred in the southern, Dravidian-speaking areas. Throughout the centuries, the system of class and caste had become more rigid; in each region there was a complex hierarchy of castes strictly forbidden to intermarry or dine together, controlled and regulated by secular powers who acted on the advice of the court Brahmans. The large-scale Vedic sacrifices had practically vanished, but simple domestic Vedic sacrifices continued, and new forms of animal, and sometimes vegetable, sacrifice had appeared, especially connected with the cult of the mother goddess.

By that time, the main divinities of later Hinduism were worshipped. Rama, the hero of the epic poem, had become the eighth avatar of Vishnu, and his cult was growing, though it was not yet as prominent as it later became. Similarly, Rama's monkey helper, Hanuman, now one of the most popular divinities of India and the most ready helper in time of need, was rising in importance. Krishna was worshipped with his adulterous consort, Radha. Strange syncretic gods had appeared, such as Harihara, a combination of Vishnu and Shiva, and Ardhanarishvara, a synthesis of Shiva and his consort Shakti.

TEMPLE COMPLEXES

From the Gupta period onward, Hindu temples became larger and more prominent, and their architecture developed in distinctive regional styles. In northern India the best remaining Hindu temples are found in the Orissa region and in the town of Khajuraho in northern Madhya Pradesh. The best example of Orissan temple architecture is the Lingaraja temple of Bhubaneswar, built about 1000. The largest temple of the region, however, is the famous Black Pagoda, the Sun Temple (Surya Deula) of Konarak, built in the mid-13th century. Its tower has long since collapsed, and only the assembly hall remains.

The most important Khajuraho temples were built during the 11th century. Individual architectural styles also arose in Gujarat and Rajasthan, but their surviving products are less impressive than those of Orissa and Khajuraho. By the end of the 1st millennium ce the South Indian style had reached its apogee in the great Rajarajeshvara temple of Thanjavur (Tanjore). In the temple the god was worshipped by the rites of puja (reverencing a sacred being or object) as though the worshipers were serving a great king. In the important temples a large staff of trained officiants waited on the god.

He was awakened in the morning along with his goddess; washed, clothed, and fed; placed in his shrine to give audience to his subjects; praised and entertained throughout the day;

and ceremoniously fed, undressed, and put to bed at night. Worshipers sang, burned lamps, waved lights before the divine image, and performed other acts of homage. The god's handmaidens (devadasis) performed before him at regular intervals, watched by the officiants and lay worshipers, who were his courtiers.

These women, either the daughters of devadasis or girls dedicated in childhood, may have also served as prostitutes. The association of dedicated prostitutes with certain Hindu shrines can be traced back to before the Christian era. It became more widespread in post-Gupta times, especially in South India, and aroused the reprobation of 19th-century Europeans. Through the efforts of Hindu reformers, the office of the devadasis was discontinued. The role of devadasis is best understood in the context of the analogy between the temple and the royal court, for the Hindu king also had his dancing girls, who bestowed their favours on his courtiers.

Parallels between the temple and the royal palace also were in evidence in the Rathayatras (Chariot Festivals). On festival days, when the king issued from his palace and paraded around his city, escorted by courtiers, troops, and musicians, the god also was paraded in a splendid procession, together with the lesser gods of the minor shrines. The god rode on a tremendous and ornate moving shrine (ratha), which was often pulled by large bands of devotees. Rathayatras still take place in many cities of India. The best-known is the annual procession of Jagannatha ("Juggernaut"), a form of Vishnu, at Puri, Orissa.

The great temples were (and still are) wealthy institutions. They were supported by the transfer of the taxes levied by kings on specific areas of the nearby countryside, by donations of the pious, and by the fees of worshipers. Their immense wealth was one of the factors that encouraged the Ghaznavid and Ghûrid Turks to invade India after the 11th century. The temples were controlled by self-perpetuating committees-whose membership was usually a hereditary privilege-and by a large staff of priests and temple servants under a high priest who wielded tremendous power and influence.

In keeping with their wealth, the great walled temple complexes of South India were (and still are) small cities, containing the central and numerous lesser shrines, bathing tanks, administrative offices, homes of the temple employees, workshops, bazaars, and public buildings of many kinds. As some of the largest employers and greatest landowners in their areas, the temples played an important part in the economy. They also performed valuable social functions, serving as schools, dispensaries, poorhouses, banks, and concert halls.

The temple complexes suffered during the Muslim occupation. In the sacred cities of Varanasi (Benares) and Mathura, no large temple from any period before the 17th century has survived. The same is true of most of the main religious centres of northern India but not of the regions where the Muslim hold was less firm, such as Orissa, Rajasthan, and South India. Despite the widespread destruction of the temples, Hinduism endured, in part because of the absence of a centralized authority; rituals and sacrifices were performed in places other than temples. The purohitas, or family priests who performed the domestic rituals and personal sacraments for the laypeople, continued to function, as did the thousands of ascetics.

HINDUISM UNDER ISLAM (11TH–19TH CENTURY)

Before the Muslim invasion of the subcontinent, the new forms of South Indian bhakti had spread beyond the bounds of the Dravidian south. Certain Vaishnava theologians of the Pancharatra and Bhagavata schools gave the growing Vaishnava bhakti cults a philosophical framework that also influenced some Shaivite schools. Several Vaishnava teachers deserve mention, including Ramanuja, a Tamil Brahman of the 11th century who was for a time chief priest of the Vaishnava temple of Srirangam, near Tiruchchirappalli (Trichinopoly), and Nimbarka, a Telugu Brahman of the 12th or 13th century who spread the cult of the divine cowherd and of Radha, his favourite gopi (cowherdess, especially associated with the legends of Krishna's youth). His sect survives near Mathura but has made little impact elsewhere.

More important was Vallabha (Vallabhacarya; 1479–1531), who emphasized the erotic imagery of the Vaishnava doctrine of grace and established a sect that stressed absolute obedience to the guru (teacher). Early in its existence the sect was organized with a hierarchy of senior monks (gosvami), many of whom became very rich. The Vallabhacarya sect, once very influential in the western half of North India, declined in the 19th century, in part because of a number of lawsuits against the chief guru, the descendant of Vallabha. The Shaiva sects also developed from the 10th century onward. In South India there emerged the school of Shaiva-siddhanta, still one of the most significant religious forces in that region and one that, unlike the school of Sankara, does not accept the full identity of the soul and God.

A completely monistic school of Shaivism appeared in Kashmir in the early 9th century. Its doctrines differ from those of Shankara chiefly because it attributes personality to the absolute spirit, who is the god Shiva and not the impersonal brahman. An important sect, founded in the 12th century in the Kannada-speaking area of the Deccan, was that of the Lingayats, or Virashaivas ("Heroes of the Shaiva Religion"). Its traditional founder, Basava, taught doctrines and practices of surprising unorthodoxy: he opposed all forms of image worship and accepted only the lingam of Shiva as a sacred symbol. Virashaivism rejected the Vedas, the Brahman priesthood, and all caste distinctions. It also consciously rejected several religious and social conventions, such as the ban against the remarriage of widows, and practiced burial rather than cremation of the dead.

Shaivism underwent significant growth in northern India. In the 13th century Gorakhnath (also known as Gorakshanatha), who became leader of a sect of Shaivite ascetics known as Nathas ("Lords") from the title of their chief teachers, introduced new ideas and practices to Shaivism. The Gorakhnathis were particularly important as propagators of Hatha Yoga, a form of Yoga that requires complex and difficult physical exercises and that has become popular in the West. These yogis, who are still numerous, influenced the teachings of several of the bhakti poets.

The poets and saints (highly respected ascetics who were at times believed to be incarnations of a deity) of medieval bhakti appeared throughout India. Although all had their individual genius, the bhakti lyricists shared a number of common features. Unlike Sanskrit authors, mainly well-educated members of the Brahman class whose learning and status shaped their outlook, bhakti poets were not restricted to a single language or class. They brought to their poetry a familiarity with folk religion unknown or ignored in the Sanskrit texts.

The use of the spoken language, even though it was formalized, made possible the expression of an unmediated vision that needed no further context; thus, the lyrics are short, intensely personal, and precise. These works illustrate the localistic and reformist tendency evidenced throughout India in the vernacular literatures, especially in Tamil, Bengali, and Hindi. Some of the new forms of Hinduism have been attributed to the influence of Islam, including popular emotional bhakti, since the practice of singing ecstatic hymns in the current local language began in South India at a time when the sea trade brought many Arab Muslims there.

Moreover, the presence of rulers of alien faith and the withdrawal of royal patronage from the temples and Brahmanic colleges may have encouraged the spread of new, more popular forms of Hinduism. The psychological effect of the Muslim conquest may also have predisposed the people to accept the powerful teachings of the poets. Much has been said about the synthesis of Hinduism and Islam in the period of Muslim dominance. Numerous Muslim social customs were adopted, and Persian and Arabic words entered the vocabularies of Indian languages.

The teachings of such men as Basava and Kabir may have been influenced by Muslim observances and social customs. A still greater synthesis took place among the Muslims, most of whom were Indian by blood. In Hindi, Bengali, Gujarati, Punjabi, and Marathi there is much poetry, written by Muslims and commencing with the Islamic invocation of Allah, which nevertheless betrays strong Hindu influence. Thus, there are texts that proclaim Krishna as being in the line of the prophets of Islam and as the teacher of the unity of God. Much mystical poetry, though written by authors with Muslim names, uses Hindu imagery and Hindu terminology.

This literature originated in the accommodating character of early Indian Sufism, which, well before Kabir, proclaimed that Muslim, Christian, Jew, Zoroastrian, and Hindu were all striving toward the same goal and that the outward observances that kept them apart were false. Some Indian Sufis were greatly influenced by Hindu customs. For example, a school of Kashmiri Sufis-whose members call themselves rishis, after the legendary Hindu sages of the same name-respect and repeat the verses of Lal Ded, a 14th-century poet and holy woman from Kashmir, and are strict vegetarians.

Tolerant Muslim rulers encouraged syncretic tendencies, which reached their zenith in the reign of Akbar (1556–1605). Taking a great interest in the religion of his Hindu subjects, Akbar tried to establish a single, all-embracing religion for his empire. Although his efforts failed, they influenced India for more than 50 years after his death. Orthodox Muslim theologians complained about the growth of heresy, however, and the emperor Aurangzeb (reigned 1658-1707) did all in his power to discourage it. Popular Muslim preachers throughout the 18th and 19th centuries worked to restore orthodoxy. Thus, syncretic tendencies were somewhat reduced before the imposition of British power in the mid-18th century.

Furthermore, British rule emphasized the distinctions between Hindu and Muslim and did not encourage efforts to harmonize the two religions. It is generally assumed that Islam is opposed to change and rejects modernity. Those who think like this are found both among Muslims as well as non-Muslims. In fact this debate has been raging among Muslims since nineteenth century i.e. since colonial experience began. However, there is tendency to stereotype Islam and simplistic assumptions are made. Those who know would agree that the matter is much more complex than generally realised.

The debate goes on generally on theological grounds ignoring sociological aspects of the phenomenon. For some it is only theological that is important and for others theological phenomenon has to be placed in sociological perspective for better comprehension. Thus it would be more appropriate to say that there are Islams, not Islam, as different societies develop different Islamic traditions. The modernity too is generally stereotyped. Modernity also has to be understood in sociological, rather than rational perspective. Thus there are modernities rather than modernity. Also, those who work for change and for modernisation, are often selective, emphasising certain aspects and rejecting certain others, depending on chances of acceptability or rejection in their own society. It would be relevant to give some examples.

Sir Syed, a great reformer of nineteenth century India, was a great modernist in his own right and worked tirelessly for modernising the Muslim society of nineteenth century India. He emphasised the importance of science and interpreted the Qur'an in a way to show that it was not against promotion of science. He even coined an interesting slogan and popularised it that the word of God (the Qur'an) cannot contradict the work of God (nature which science studies). He also emphasised the importance of modern education and even established an institution to promote it. However, he rejected social reforms in favour of women. When his admirer and colleague Maulvi Mumtaz Ali Khan wrote a book Huquq al-Niswan (Rights of Women), he not only advised him not to publish it but also opposed his views.

Sir Syed also advised Muslims to keep away from politics, an important aspect of realising modern democratic rights. Thus Sir Syed's whole emphasis was on modern education and proper understanding of the Qur'an. Sir Syed's modernity had no place for promoting women's rights (whether he was opposed to women's rights or not, is debatable). Maulvi Mumtaz Ali, on the other hand, though Sir Syed's contemporary, and a co-worker, was great advocate of women's rights. For him, the concept of modernity or for that matter, that of Islam could not be complete without empowering women. He worked for women's rights as tirelessly as Sir Syed worked for modern education.

Though both were champions of modernity, their visions of modernity differed, considerably. For Sir Syed, women's rights were hardly of any significance for ushering in modernity in the Muslim society whereas education was. For the Maulvi, on the other hand, empowering of women was quite a significant aspect of modernity. Many Muslim theologians until today not only reject modernity but also reject any idea about the plurality of Islam. For them Islam is a monolithic phenomenon and anyone talking of plurality is on the path of error. Anyone accepting plurality may even be denounced as kafir. These theologians consider society as of no consequence. For them only theology is central, every thing else being peripheral. Society, for them, must conform to theological vision and society should not have any impact on theological vision. Thus sociological plurality must be rejected outright.

For them Islam is Islam, monolithic in structure. Thus one cannot talk of Indian Islam or Malaysian or Persian or Indonesian Islam. All local traditions are impurities and have no place in Islam. However, there are theologians who would concede the importance of local traditions and would acknowledge the significance of local customs called aadats. Shah Waliyullah, for example, maintains that if the Islamic injunctions based on Arab social customs bring hardships to non Arab nations and cultures they can be modified in the light of the universal principles and be adapted to the customs of a particular nation. Shah Waliyullah formulates very progressive principle in this regard.

He says in his magnum opus Hujjat-ul-lahil Balighah, "There is no method of legislation regarding injunctions and penalties better and easier than that taking into consideration the customs of the peoples in which the Prophet (PBUH) has been sent. It must also be taken into consideration that these laws are not so rigid as to create hardships for future generations." Shah Waliyullah, a great theological thinker of eighteenth century India thus concedes the possibility of Islamic pluralism depending on the local social realities and societal desideratum. One will find many different traditions in different societies which, over a period of time, get assimilated with religion practised by the people of that area and it is in that sense that one talks about Indian or Persian or Indonesian Islam.

Strictly speaking it is anthropological and not theological term. Also, in post-modern societies the significance of pluralism is being universally realised and ideological monolith is being rejected. Thus one should not talk of Islam but Islams and modernity but modernities. There is one significant aspect of modernity, besides plurality, which is quite significant. The modernity uses the idiom of rights whereas theological discourse is entirely built around the idiom of duties. Thus the traditional Islam imposes duties and rejects the idea of rights.

The Ulama, as well as some traditional political leaders in the Islamic world reject the discourse of rights. Mohammad Mahathir, Prime Minister of Malaysia, for example, said in a statement that the concept of human rights is a Western concept and is alien to eastern societies. Many Ulama would readily support him in this regard. This was also pointed out by a noted writer of Iran, Abdul Karim Suroush, in a seminar in Amsterdam on "Islam and the Modern World". Dr. Suroush maintained that the clergy in Iran talks only of duties and is not prepared to concede rights to the people.

They want all rights for themselves including the right to interpret Islam. The concept of Wilayat-e-Faqih (the authority of the jurist) which Ayatullah Khomeini claimed for himself and now his successor Ayatullah Khamenei claims for himself places entire authority in the hands of the Faqih (the jurist). People will have no right whatsoever at all. And if the elected representatives of the people make any law it will also be subject to the approval of the Jurist who is not even elected by the people.

Some other modernist Muslim thinkers, on the other hand, give right to the elected representatives of people to legislate and usher in necessary changes. The noted poet and thinker Dr. Muhammad Iqbal wrote in early twenties of twentieth century an essay on ijtihad (creative interpretation) in Islam and maintained that ijtihad is a principle of dynamism, it means independent opinion and decision and means complete authority in law making. According to him, an elected assembly of representatives of people constitute ijma' (consensus) of the people and thus any law made by such an elected assembly will be a valid exercise.

It is important to note that Iqbal wrote this chapter taking all caution and after consultation with many prominent Ulama of his time. It took more than 4 years for him to complete this chapter which is included in his well known work Reconstruction of Religious Thought in Islam. In this book he makes an interesting observation which is worth quoting here. Iqbal says, "It (society) must possess eternal principles to regulate its collective life, for the eternal gives us a foothold in the world of perpetual change. But eternal principles, when they are understood to exclude all possibilities of change, which, according to the Qur'an, is one of the greatest 'signs' of God, tend to immobilize what is essentially mobile in its nature. The failure of Europe in political and social sciences illustrate the former principle, the immobility of Islam during the last five hundred years illustrates the latter. What then is the principle of movement in the structure of Islam? This is known as ijtihad".

Iqbal has put the whole problem of change and modernity quite succinctly in the above passage. What some theologians do not realise is that though the principles are eternal and immutable there application is not. What constitutes justice in a feudal society (justice being an eternal principle) may not be just at all in a democratic society. The feudal society is essentially an authoritarian society and only discourse of duties would be an acceptable discourse in such an authoritarian society.

A democratic society, on the other hand, is an open society and people, not a central authority, are at the centre of political power, and hence the discourse of 'rights' is the most acceptable discourse. To demand duties and deny rights will constitute injustice in a democratic society. Thus while accepting the eternity of principles one should not deny the possibility of change in application of the principles. There are several advocates of change in the Islamic world today. It would be grievous error to think that the Islamic world is totally static and immobile. The processes of change may be slower or faster depending on the objective conditions in a particular country, but its signs are unmistakable. No society can be immobile in the modern world.

The process of change is of course a complex process and related to the prevailing conditions in a society. The principle of gender justice is very emphatic in Islam but it could not be realised in feudal societies in which Islam subsequently spread. And in the Islam world the transformation from feudal to democratic society is far from complete and hence empowerment of people, particularly women remain incomplete.

Gender justice again is a highly sensitive issue and while other changes may be more easily acceptable, the one related to women's empowerment will be very difficult to realise. Dr. Iqbal had enthusiastically welcomed the changes in the gender laws in Turkey during the Kemalist revolution and been a great admirer of Zia Gokulp, the poet and socioloist who was enthusiastic advocate of gender justice; he, however, cautioned that such changes may not be acceptable by the Indian Muslims as prevailing conditions are very different. Iqbal has proved to be prophetic in this matter.

4

Confucianism and Women

In Han dynasty, Confucianism was adopted and other schools suppressed by the Han rulers to consolidate their reign. Then Confucianism flourished and became dominant in Chinese history and culture for almost 2 millenniums. Later it even spread to Korea and Japan and has been influential in the two cultures. Confucius and his Confucianism had so great an impact on Chinese civilization that you can't imagine how Chinese culture and history would be otherwise. In the whole 2,000 years, Confucianism has influenced the Chinese attitude toward life, set the patterns of living and standards of social value, established standards for training government officials, and provided the background for Chinese political theories and institutions.

Confucius (551 B.C. - 479 B.C.), founder of Confucianism, was born in today's Qufu, Shandong province. He was named Kong Qiu and styled Zhongni and respected by Chinese as Kong Fuzi or Kong Zi. He was an outstanding thinker and educationist in the late Spring and Autumn period. He was born poor, however he managed to get good education. It was said that at the age of fifty Confucius finally ascended to Prime Minister of State Lu. However, his political foes conspired to force him to retire at the age of fifty-five. Then he led his disciples to trek around those competing states to advocate his teachings and to advise rulers how to govern. However he was frustrated.

In his late years, he engaged in education, with 3,000 disciples and 72 famous ones according to legend. Politically, he insisted strict social stratification to maintain public order and contended moral cultivation and opposed tyranny. Main ethic feature he advocated was benevolence, called Ren in Chinese. On the educational theory, he stressed individual aptitude education and combination of learning and thinking, proposing "learning without thinking leads to bewilderment; thinking without learning results in idleness."

Confucianism is a system of philosophy and humanism instead of a religion though it features a few religious characteristics. Confucius and Mencius never intended to set up a religion although they were enshrined in almost everywhere in the nation. Confucius lived in a time of social and moral chaos, when common values were generally rejected or simply disregarded. In the ethos of uncertainty and fear created by warlords, Confucianism flourished and eventually transformed Chinese society with its values and dominated it for centuries.

Since Confucius saw a sharp difference between the disunity and lack of harmony that existed in this chaotic society as opposed to the harmony and orderliness of nature, his philosophy sought to consciously restore primary set values and norms. In the Qin dynasty (221B.C. - 206B.C.), Emperor Qin Shi Huang slaughtered Confucian intellectuals and burnt Confucian canons, in order to unite chaotic thoughts to facilitate ruling. It was soon over thrown. In the Han dynasty under the reign of Emperor Wu (140B.C. - 87 B.C.), Confucianism was accepted as state ideology and orthodoxy since Confucianism claimed regality was god-given, and other ideologies were banned to maintain law, social stratification and social order with Confucian values. From then on, other ideologies never got a chance to attempt a comeback.

The reason why Confucianism was dominant was it conformed to needs of the ruling classing. It presented a utopian world for both the ruling class and the common people. Confucianism thinks that ruler be a father to his people and look after their basic needs. It encouraged officials to be loyal to their rulers and refuse to serve the corrupt; advocated absolute authority of a king over his subject, a husband over his wife, and a father over his son; and stressed five constant virtues, namely benevolence (Ren), righteousness (Yi), propriety (Li), wisdom (Zhi) and fidelity (Xin) as basic ethical code. Confucianism was an androcentrism in which women has no dignity and human rights.

According to Confucianism, women had to obey absolutely their fathers when they were not married, and obey their husbands absolutely after in the wedlock and to obey absolutely their sons in their widowhood. Morality, proper speech, modest manner and diligent work were basic virtues they ought have. In case women were barren, unfilial, talkative, jealous, heavily sick, or in adultery and theft, they would be divorced no matter what the reasons were. Although Confucian is condemned for some of its views, it has branded Chinese and their life.

Underlying the beliefs of many cultures is an assumption that, beyond biology, women and men possess essentially different capacities and functions. Understanding this assumption helps make sense of the perpetuation and even institutionalization of male/female difference with regard to behavior expectations, position within the family, legal rights, public status, education, and types of work. While this most often results in the subordination of women's position in society vis-a-vis men, it sometimes can be a source of women's special strength.

In China, the concept of gender difference appears visually in the male/female aspects of the yin/yang Taoist symbol. The dark swirl within the symbol's circle is the passive, yielding, feminine yin; the light swirl the active, aggressive, male yang. Neither principle is considered subordinate to the other; each complements the other and is capable of expressing both female and male characteristics. Within Taoism, then, women were able to seek spiritual fulfillment beyond their family duties. Some joined convents, others gathered with men to discuss philosophy and religion, a few became Taoist adepts.

Ancient China's highest goddess, Hsi Huang Mu (Queen Mother of the West), found in the classic tale Journey to the West, also expresses aspects of yin/yang beliefs. As yin, this goddess is compassionate, promising immortality; as yang, she is a force who had the power to disrupt the cosmic yin/yang harmony. This pervasive fear that women could bring chaos by upsetting the cosmic harmony was an obstacle for women who aspired to male political leadership. Those who succeeded were accused of breaking one of nature's laws, of becoming "like a hen crowing." Years after her reign, this derogatory term was applied to China's only female emperor, Wu Zetian (Tang dynasty, 625-705 C.E.).

Buddhism as practiced in Japan and China also granted women some areas of empowerment. Women went on pilgrimages to Buddhist temples, retreated to nunneries, sometimes gave public lectures, and led temple groups. Chinese Buddhism was at its height during the reign of Wu Zetian who promoted the religion and even justified her rule by claiming she was a reincarnation of a previous female Buddhist saint. During Wu's reign, and throughout the early to mid Tang period, women enjoyed relatively high status and freedom. Lovely Tang era paintings and statues depict women on horseback, and as administrators, dancers and musicians. Stories and poems, like those from the pen of the infamous female poet Yu Xuanji, also attest to the almost modern openness of the period.

In contrast, Confucianism became the most pervasive doctrine to promote the belief in women's "natural place." Confucius himself did not inherently denigrate women, although he placed them at the lower end of the patriarchal family structure. Yet, through the ages the assumption that men's and women's social places and expected behaviors were quite distinct was based on Confucian hierarchical precepts, and were reinforced by prescriptive advice manuals like Lessons for Girls. Written by the female historian Ban Zhoa (Han dynasty, ca. 45-120 C.E.), Lessons became one of China's most durable sources of advice about female behavior. One nugget tells women to "yield to others; let her put others first, herself last."

In the Song dynasty (960-1279 C.E), a reinterpretation of Confucian teaching called NeoConfucianism stratified the position of women even more. Augmented by ideas of wife fidelity and husband worship brought by the Mongols, NeoConfucian beliefs led to the egregious practices of footbinding, insistence on widow chastity, and the selling of unwanted daughters. Although footbinding illustrates the perceived need to limit female mobility, the practice did not appear until the Song Dynasty and was not universally followed. Women of most ethnic minorities, including Hakka and Manchu women, did not practice it, nor did some peasants who had to work in the fields, nor did women in Japan.

In Japan, the influence of Shintoism lessened the initial impact of NeoConfucian on women's lives. Within Shintoism women held power as mikos, a type of shaman with divination abilities. Before the 8th century, half of Japan's reigning female sovereigns, such as the popular semi-legendary empress Jingu, were believed to have shaman-like powers. Japan's sun goddess Amaterasu, to whom every emperor has had to claim direct descendancy, was also worshiped as a symbol of female mystical power. Her Great Shrine at Ise, cared for by high priestesses, still plays an important role in the lives of the Japanese today.

The more positive influences of Shintoism were weakened by the samurai culture and spread of Confucianism and Buddhism in Japan. Yet, in the Heian era (950-1050 C.E.) women still held relative equity in marriage, education, and property rights. Gender difference in this period favored literate women who were free to write in the expressive, popular vernacular language, while men most often wrote in the more formal, inaccessible, classical Chinese. Both the independence and the gender limits of women of the pampered elite are wonderfully illustrated in the lively, gossipy writings of Shikibu Murasaki, Sei Shogonon, and other Heian female writers.

Women's independence was increasing limited during the long centuries of shogunate rule. Although in the early feudal period samurai women took a considerable role in household management and defense, by the Tokugawa Shogunate (1600-1868), women's rights within the samurai family were practically nonexistent. The oft quoted Three Obediences dictated their lives: "When she is young, she obeys her father; when she is married, she obeys her husband; when she is widowed, she obeys her son." The 1762 treatise called Greater Learning for Women illustrates this NeoConfucian ideal of proper female behavior.

By the late nineteenth, early twentieth centuries, serious challenges to accepted beliefs about gender were mounted in both Japan and China. Although concerns about women's position had been expressed earlier, the concept of women's liberation became a major motivating force within the era's nationalist, reform, and revolution movements. Male nationalists initiated the discussion by arguing that an improvement in the status of women was essential to their country's acceptance by other technologically advanced nations.

A core of educated women in both Japan and China joined the call by speaking and writing in public for the first time. Conservative nationalists and traditionalists in Japan and China at different times reacted by mounting long campaigns against any change in gender roles. Ultimately female activists were labeled unseemly, unfeminine, and too western. An ideal case study of this action/reaction phenomenon is Japan's Meiji Restoration (1868-1912) when the nation's rapid transformation from a feudal shogunate to modern nation opened the door for female public participation. Through speeches, magazines, and within newly formed political parties, a small group labeled Japan's "first wave feminists" tried to raise women's consciousness about their subordinate position.

The phrase "good wife, wise mother" was coined, meaning that in order become good citizens women had to become educated and take part in public affairs. The drive to encourage women to adopt new "modern" ways was pervasive. Woodblock prints were even circulated showing previously forbidden views of women in the imperial family attending public events adorned in western Victorian-era clothes. In spite of these efforts, conservative legislators reasserted NeoConfucian family values by passing restrictive laws, codes, and a new constitution. Women were denied the right to any political participation, including even taking political science courses, and married women lost some of the legal rights they had held during the Shogunate.

The term"good wife, wise mother" was reinterpreted to refer to a woman who sacrificed herself to her family welfare, an ideal that finds some resonance today. The challenge to unequal gender difference was mounted anew in the 1910s when women in Japan's "second wave feminism" set about to oppose the NeoConfucian ideology of "good wife, wise mother." One, Hiratsuka Haruko (pen name Raicho), in 1911 founded the feminist magazine Seito (Bluestocking), where its contributors considered broad social issues such as freedom of love and marriage. Not surprisingly, the magazine was often censored and banned.

Japan's rebellious writers can be compared to those in China where in the decades between 1915 and 1925 a kind of women's emancipation movement also emerged. As young people were drawn into the struggle against imperialism and traditional Chinese society, women in the 1919 May Fourth Movement (also called the New Cultural Movement) experienced for the first time their own emancipation and wrote about social restraints within the traditional authoritarian family system. Using the slogan, "Down with Confucius and his disciples" they sought personal fulfillment and fought for substantial changes in women's legal status.

Throughout the 1920s and early 30s, familial conflicts raged over bobbed hair, coeducation, and freedom in love and marriage. Ibsen's The Doll's House was popular reading as young people thought of their own lives when trying to answer the question, "What happens to Nora after she leaves home?" During China's long revolutionary years the state both promoted and negated new roles for women. The most severe reaction against female activism was the Guomindang's counter revolution, called the White Terror (1927 - 1928), when female activists were accused of being instigators of societal chaos. During Chiang Kai-shek's relentless hunt for Communists, thousand of women were murdered and raped, including those who had simply bobbed their hair.

The Communists, for their part, turned away from what they saw as bourgeois feminist reforms to attack the socioeconomic conditions they perceived as the source of all female oppressions. The idea was that once gender difference was erased, women would be freed to help spearhead the "new society." Mao Zedong coined the phrase "Women Hold Up Half the Sky," and set in motion a campaign to get women out of the home and into the work force. Selections from oral histories collected during the period illustrate his attempts to mobilize the lowest in society, the female peasant, so she could confront "feudal" fathers, husbands or landlords.

Ultimately, the need to develop a sense of solidarity between male and female peasants as both subjects of oppression resulted in criticizing concerns relating to women alone. Such was the fate of author Ding Ling, the most prominent female writer of her generation, whose attack on the sexist attitudes of her comrades resulted in suppression. The state also failed to deal with opposition to the progressive changes embodied in the Marriage Law of 1950, which granted young people the right to choose their own marriage partners, and women to initiate divorce and to inherit property. Female-specific concerns continued to be ignored during the Cultural Revolution when equality between sexes was assumed and class war took center stage.

In China's post 1980 modernization efforts, new tensions have emerged as women are urged to return to their traditional roles at home and at work, and to "feminize" their physical appearance. At the same time, the old ideal of the worker who forsakes even family duties to selflessly contribute to society still holds. A new slogan, coined by a detractor to today's modernization drive, claims that now "Women Hold Up Two Skies!" Propaganda posters dramatically illustrate these shifts from revolutionary times to today when, although over 80 percent of women work outside their homes and some participate in political activities, it is clear that habits established thousands of years ago do not easily disappear.

WOMEN'S WORK

Beliefs in gender difference find reflection in the age-old assignment of women to "women's work," and men to theirs. This can be seen in the predominance of women in the essential work of cloth production. The Zhou (Chou) period (1100-770 B.C.E.) phrase "Men plow and women weave," resoonated at different times throughout China's history. In silk production, so vital to China's trade and diplomacy, rested on the initial labor of women who cultivated the mulberry trees, raised the worms, extracted the silk thread from the cocoons, and spun and wove the cloth. Legends, such as that of Lady Hsi-Ling-Shih who is credited with the introduction of silkworm rearing and invention of the loom, illustrated women's connection to this work as do poems, like the 11th century female poet Ch'ien T'ao's lament that upper class, silken clad "beauties" knew or cared little "of a weaving girl,/ Sitting cold by her window/ Endlessly throwing her shuttle to and fro."

During the expansion of trade during the China's Song dynasty women were heavily recruited to work in the cotton and silk mills as spinners and weavers. In both China and Japan, it was women's work in the textile industries which proved to be the key to industrial success. Japan's burgeoning export trade in silk and cotton textiles, for example, was the result of the women who by the 1880's had formed almost two-thirds of Japan's industrial workforce. Many of the mill workers in both countries were girls who left poor rural homes to live in dorms. Short diary excerpts, songs, work contracts, and charts, dramatically describe the mill workers' hard work, low wages, and attempts to improve their working conditions.

Accounts also reveal that with an independent income, some women began to lead a more self-sufficient life. The unusual marriage resistance movement among some silk workers in South China was a particularly intriguing outcome of this independence. The notion that women "have their place" in textile production persists today. Women are the major workforce in the South China mills and in globalized textile factories and clothing sweatshops world-wide. And the question of whether this sexual division of work marginalizes women, or offers them expanded opportunities, is still being debated.

STRONG LEGENDARY AND REAL HEROES

Counterbalancing beliefs about women's place is the historic veneration of some powerful, albeit exceptional, women. Stories of warrior women such as Hua Mulan and various militant Ninja types appear regularly in classical Chinese fiction. In Japan, samurai women appear, like Tomoe Gozen who supposedly rode into battle alongside her husband during Gempei Wars, or Hojo Masako (1157-1225), wife of Japan's first shogun, who directed armies and in effect ruled the Shogunate from the convent where she had "retired" after her husband's death. Later, bands of women armed with the exclusively female sword called naginata, were called upon to defend their towns or castles. Japanese girls today still learn to use this long sword.

In the modern era, women have been honored for their militant participation during civil wars and the struggles against invaders. In the Taiping Rebellion mainly Hakka women with unbound feet fought both as soldiers and generals against the Manchu government. Women took up arms again in the Boxer Rebellion when young women organized themselves into militant "Red Lantern" groups. During the Cultural Revolution, the militancy of young female Red Guards attest to their willingness to become revolutionary heroes when struggling for what they perceived to be a just cause.

Individual revolutionary female icons who have been held up as powerful figures for women to emulate include China's Chiu Chin (Qiu Jin), who in 1907 was executed by the Manchu government, and Soong-li Ching (Soong Ching-ling), wife of Dr. Sun Yat-sen and champion of social justice and women's liberation, and Deng Yingchao, an advocate of women's rights and wife of Zhou Enlai. The societal admiration of female heroines such as these has helped justify the actions of the women who managed successfully to define new roles for themselves alongside men.

Confucianism was long used as an ideological tool to bolster patriarchal rule. If you take the Venerable Sage's writings seriously, however, there is only one conclusion that is possible: Women, in general, come closer to the moral ideals upheld by Confucius than men. Think about it. What is the most important virtue espoused by Confucius? The Analects suggests caring for parents and elders. The second passage of Chapter I reads:

"Master Yu said: 'It's honouring parents and elders that makes people human. Then they rarely turn against authority. And if people don't turn against authority, they never rise up and pitch the country into chaos. The noble-minded cultivate roots. When roots are secure, the Way is born. To honour parents and elders isn't that the root of humanity?"

That's pretty straightforward; the "root of humanity," the basis of the greatest possible virtue. And when we work on that root, we move toward broader social and political stability from the inside out, progressing from secure family relations to settled national conditions. That is the essence of Confucian thought.

Let's be honest. Who takes on most of the real family work of caring for parents and elders? Is it husbands and sons, or is it wives and daughters? Seems to me that women put more time into family care. And when we factor in caring for children since, after all, Confucius told us to "cherish the young" it is not even close. Women cultivate roots. Men get out of the house for work or less "humane" pursuits. As a man, myself, I know what the first rebuttal is; we have to leave the house and spend time at work to earn the money that keeps the family in food and shelter and other material needs. There's some truth to this.

Yet this is precisely where the real challenge of Confucius can be seen. While he understands that men have to leave the home to do right by the family, limiting their time for care giving, he is very clear about how to resolve what we moderns refer to as "work versus family conflicts." He comes down unequivocally for family. Nowhere is this more evident than in the Confucian demand for a strict period of mourning for deceased parents. In pre-Qin times the Confucians were adamant that bereavement and commemoration continue for three years. The Moists, followers of China's earliest utilitarian thinker Mozi, argued that this was unnecessary and a wasteful interruption of productive work. Confucians countered that expressing such materialistic concerns was unbecoming of a morally educated gentleman.

A three-year period of mourning is obviously impossible in a modern economic context, but if extrapolate this ancient debate to the present, Confucians would argue that men should be willing to limit their time at work to contribute more to the work of the family. Care of the family is everyone's primary duty; it is not "women's work." In advanced industrial societies, traditional gender roles have been challenged and changed. Men are doing more family work, but women are quick to point out that they still carry the greatest burden. Modern Confucians, if they are true to the contemporary implications of Confucius' own teachings, would have to side with the women. And that leaves us with another question. If women are closer to the root of humanity through their family work, and if, as Confucius believes, the humane should rule, then would a modern Confucian have to conclude that women should rule? So much for the patriarchy.

Few intellectual traditions have had a greater impact on women in Asia than Confucianism, in part because Confucian traditions were central not only to China but also to other parts of Asia (Japan, Korea, and Southeast Asia) influenced by Chinese culture. The study of women in these cultures has dismantled basic assumptions about Confucianism: its universality, monolithic nature, and immutability. The study of women has shown many different Confucianisms and has made it clear that the continuity of these traditions is the result of accommodation to social change, not stasis. Scholars of Chinese women's history have, in recent years, moved far beyond an earlier scholarship that focused on Confucianism's role in conceptualizing and rationalizing a patriarchal, patrilineal family in which women were marginalized, victimized, and seemingly left with little opportunity to develop or exercise a sense of their own agency.

Overcoming and supplanting this view has come only through the continuing research of historians who, reading against the grain of the Confucian record, have provided a much more complex picture of women's lives and of Chinese culture. Margery Wolf's work on women in Taiwan represents a rare early glimpse of women developing strategies to increase their power in the family; Susan Mann, Patricia Ebrey, and Dorothy Ko have since demonstrated, in a number of different settings, how important women were as contributors to "Chinese civilization" and how effectively they circumvented the institutional barriers ranged against them.

Elsewhere in Asia, Confucian patterns had less continuity as well as less influence. In the Japanese case, Confucian ideas about the family and statecraft were heavily moderated by existing cultural patterns, even in the two periods when Confucianism is thought to have had greatest influence-the eighth and ninth centuries when the Japanese state was being organized, and the seventeenth and eighteenth centuries of the Tokugawa period. Korea, although thoroughly conversant with Confucianism, was really not dominated by these ideas until well after the fourteenth century, and Southeast Asia, particularly Vietnam, encountered the greatest levels of Confucian influence between the fourteenth and sixteenth centuries.

Recent scholarship makes it clear how difficult it is to walk the tightrope between establishing a history of women in Asia that speaks to their strengths and acknowledges the reality of the constraints they faced. Although historians continue to investigate stereotypical symbols of women's oppression in Asia (sati, footbinding), they do so with a heightened sense of the possibility that Western scholarship "orientalizes" women when it fails to present them as active participants in their own culture, able to find nuanced and effective ways to challenge those constraints.

For a long time China's society has been strongly influenced by the moral and intellectual codes of Confuci-anism. Within the society of classic Confucian values women were treated as lesser beings, completely inferior to their male counterparts. However, as time passed and outside influences began to come into China, other theologies, such as Buddhism and Daoism, began to influence Chinese society. Around the time of the Song dynasty (960-1279) China experienced a renewal of Confucianism in the rise of Neo-Confucianism. The introduction of which was intended to both update the old codes of conduct as well as renew society's beliefs in a Confucian way of life.

For women, the rise of Neo-Confucianism meant a rebirth of many of the doctrines meant to keep them subservient to men. However, although the majority of changes introduced by the Neo-Confucian model were meant to subjugate women they also helped women by opening the door into feminine intellectual discourse by addressing women directly. So, despite intentions or outward appearances, Neo-Confucianism actually aided women in becoming more independent in the male dominated Chinese society. Confucius was a philosopher and scholar who lived from approximately 551-479 BC. He tried and failed to gain a high government position during his lifetime and yet his teachings later on went on to have a profound effect on Chinese politics and society.

The center of Confucian thought was formed when a group of Confucius' disciples decided to compile the lessons they had learned from their teacher. This compilation became known as The Analects. Despite their disorderly compilation, the Analects became the center of Chinese intellectual discourse approximately two centuries after the death of Confucius. Confucian philosophy centered on the belief in the inherently good nature of men. He taught that the Way may be found through discipline and close study of the Classics. Within the lessons taught by Confucius, one key message was that of the importance of filial piety.

In traditional Confucianism, the roles of conduct are directed by in large towards men and the way in which men must pay all respect to their parents, which is how filial piety is defined for the male. However, a Chinese woman must not only be filial to her parents, but to her parents-in-law, husband, male relatives and even to her own sons. For women this meant complete subjugation first to her father, and then her husband, and finally to her sons. Under this subjugated rule women were not allowed the freedom to pursue their own goals in life. Even after the death of their husbands they were bound by the laws of filial piety to remain loyal to him and either live life as a widow or commit suicide. In fact it was considered better for a woman to commit suicide, as this showed a great amount of filial piety towards her husband.

Although women may have been able to find small ways to control their lives, through control over children and servants, for the most part they were always at the mercy of the will of others and society. As time passed, other doctrines, such as those of Daoism and Buddhism, gained importance to Chinese society and Confucianism was no longer the only voice of moral and intellectual law. However, during the Song dynasty, in an attempt to bring back many of the key teachings of Confucianism, adapted for a more modern China; Chinese intellectuals began to promulgate the rise of what the Jesuit missionaries later named Neo-Confucianism.

Neo-Confucianism incorporated newer ideas such as Buddhist transcendentalism into the existing traditional Confucian structure. Neo-Confucians called for people to re-examine their inner self and encouraged people to help society through charitable works. The ultimate goal of Neo-Confucianism was "a means of preserving the imperial order and benefiting while controlling the mass of the people."

Neo-Confucians also emphasized learning and under these guidelines they established many educational institutions comparable to today's liberal arts colleges. But despite these new movements, many of the basic tenets of Confucianism remained the same. Just as in classic Confucianism filial piety was at the forefront of the moral codes of Neo-Confucianism. Within the codes for filial piety a woman's role was clearly subservient to men.

As an example, in the book entitled The Book of Filial Piety for Women, the author, Miss Zheng, describes the way a woman should treat her husband. "From the time her hair is arranged and she meets him [during the wedding ceremony], she maintains the formality appropriate between an official and the ruler. When helping him wash or serving him food, she maintains the reverence appropriate between father and child." Clearly under this model the woman was considered inferior to her husband. Her role in life was to serve him, please him and to bear him sons, so that his family line may continue; thus cementing a woman's place as centered on home and family.

As in classic Confucianism, if a woman's husband died the woman was expected not to remarry and encouraged to commit suicide. "In the Song dynasty the great Neo- Confucian thinker Cheng Yi had declared that it was better for a widow to starve to death than to remarry." Women, under Neo-Confucian rule had little to no personal freedom, to the point that even in death her husband has control over a woman's fate. In a time when in Europe women were beginning to leave the home and family size decreased under rapid industrialization, in China women were becoming even more tied to the home than before, under the control of men.

The only market industry that a Chinese woman could participate in was at-home textile production. Women were allowed, and even encouraged to raise silkworms and weave fabrics which could be sold by men in the market. This was particularly important to widows since women could not claim any inheritance from their parents or husbands and otherwise lived at the mercy of male family members. This made them even more vulnerable to the whims of the patriarchal society. Aside from the basic subjugation of women to me, women were subject to a number of social rules and expectations. In addition to her roles as a child-bearer and homemaker Chinese women were expected to prepare and maintain the traditional ancestral rituals. Ancestor worship was central to the Neo-Confucian household; sacrifices had to be made for all male family members.

The basics of what was expected for the ancestral rites were largely prescribed by Zhu Xi who composed Family Rituals (Zhuzi jiali) and was often considered the founder of Neo-Confucianism. In Family Rituals it is made clear that the primary care taker for the ancestral shrine should be the woman of the house. Because of the great importance of these rites they were time- consuming, tedious and burden-some to the women charged with their maintenance, however they were key to the coherence of a the Chinese Neo-Confucian household. In this way a woman was tied even closer to home and family through her duties to the ancestral shrine.

Around the time of the rise of Neo-Confucianism foot binding also saw a rise in popularity. Foot binding is the practice of binding the feet of women, starting when they are young girls, so that the arch of the foot breaks and the toes are forced under and squeezed together until the entire foot is only three inches in length. This practice was very painful but it became an important status symbol as only those with the money and resources could afford to bind their daughters' feet. The appeal of the bound feet was partially due to the fact that it made women even more fragile and dependent than in their natural state. Because the women with bound feet were unable to walk or even stand without considerable effort and discomfort they became closely tied to their home and family due to the basic fact that they were physically unable to leave the home for any extended period of time.

And despite the way a women might feel about her role in society it was always her duty to instill in her children the same the male-centered Neo- Confucian values she had been forced to life by. Under such a patriarchal doctrine it may not seem as though there would be room for a woman to exercise her mind and better herself intellectually, however in its own subtle way, Neo-Confucianism invited women to do just that. Regardless of the strict rules placed on women under Neo-Confucianism the mere fact that works such as The Book of Filial Piety for Women and Analects for Women, written to teach women in more direct language about their roles in Neo-

Confucian society, have been written shows society understands the need to appeal to women as people capable of independent thought and action. If we look closely at Ebrey's translated version of The Book of Filial Piety and The Book of Filial Piety for Women we can see that the left column, the side which directly quotes the sayings of Confucius, is devoid of any kind of compassion or respect towards women.

In fact, it hardly mentions women specifically; instead it speaks of the roles of fathers and sons, of ministers and officials. This was the way of classic Confucianism. By not mentioning women at all it stripped them of any value they may have possessed. However, under the Neo-Confucian model, women's roles were detailed for their own knowledge as well as the knowledge of men. By publishing texts intended for women, society was recognizing women's capability to think intellectually and morally. These works invited women into the world of intellectual discourse, even if their intent was only to tell women the proper way to serve her husband. In conclusion, we can see that Confucianism has long played a central role in Chinese society so it is not surprising that the rise of Neo-Confucianism had a great impact on society at large, as well as women specifically.

Women's roles under Neo- Confucianism, such as house work and presiding over ancestral rites, kept them closely tied to the home and out of the public sphere. However, despite the fact that the doctrines of Neo-Confucianism attempted to keep women as quite, subservient creatures, molded to the will of men, the manner in which this message was delivered to women helped these women to recognize their own intellectual abilities. By having works published for the express purpose of being read by women, Neo-Confucian women were able to begin their own intellectual discourse, even if it was initially confined to the home.

Confucianism, Taoism and Buddhism constitute the essence of the traditional Chinese culture. The relationship among the three has been marked by both contention and complementation in history, with Confucianism playing a more dominant role. Confucius (Kongzi, 551-479 B.C.), founder of Confucianism, stresses "Ren" (benevolence, love) and "Li" (rites), referring to respect for the system of social hierarchy. He attaches importance to education and was a pioneering advocate for private schools. He is particularly famous for teaching students according to their intellectual inclinations. His teachings were later recorded by his students in "The Analects."

Mencius also contributed a great part to Confucianism, lived in the Warring States Period (389-305 B.C.), advocating a policy of benign government and a philosophy that human beings are good by nature. Confucianism became the orthodox ideology in feudal China and, in the long course of history, it drew on Taoism and Buddhism. By the 12th century, Confucianism had evolved into a rigid philosophy that calls for preserving heavenly laws and repressing human desires. Taoism was created by Lao Zi (around the sixth century B.C.), whose masterpiece is "The Classic of the Virtue of the Tao." He believes the dialectical philosophy of inaction.

Chairman Mao Zedong once quoted Lao Zi: "Fortune lies in misfortune and vice versa." Zhuang Zhou, the main advocate of Taoism during the Warring States period, founded a relativism calling for the absolute freedom of the subjective mind. Taoism has greatly influenced Chinese thinkers, writers and artists. Buddhism was created by Sakyamuni in India around the 6th century B.C. Believing that human life is miserable and spiritual emancipation is the highest goal to seek. It was introduced into China through Central Asia around the time Christ was born. After a few centuries of assimilation, Buddhism evolved into many sects in the Sui and Tang Dynasties and became localized. That was also a process when the ingenuous culture of Confucianism and Taoism were blended with Buddhism. Chinese Buddhism has played a very important role on traditional ideology and art.

Can a Confucian scholar have Buddhist beliefs? Confucius said that it is "harmful to specialize in heresy" and Mencius prided himself with the responsibility to ban wrong theories. It may then be assumed that it must have been problematic for a Confucian scholar to have had Buddhist faith, especially when we consider that the criticism on heresy was reinforced in the Neo-Confucian era. However, part of the intelligentsia with Confucian education held Buddhist beliefs in the late Goryeo to early Joseon periods and have studied Kwon Geun as such an example. As a Confucian scholar who wrote Iphak doseol, a theoretical book on Neo-Confucianism, Kwon Geun was a colleague of Jeong Do-jeon, who wrote Bulssi japbyeon (Array of Critiques of Buddhism).

However, he did not shun Buddhism in his daily life. In the early Joseon period, he participated in Buddhist events as a high government official under royal order. He criticized Buddhism in theory but his behavior was unlike his criticisms. The problem is, however, that the case of Kwon Geun was not unique at the time. Some of the scholars who had received Confucian education during the time of change from Buddhism to Confucianism in early Joseon showed such tendencies, and King Sejong (1418-1450) appears to have had these tendencies too. Theoretically, Sejong had clear knowledge and conviction in Confucianism and Neo-Confucianism. In terms of religion, however, he depended on Buddhism. In other words, while he continued to push forward a policy to promote Confucianism at the national level as a monarch, he turned to Buddhism when he needed it.

He could thus be accused of being inconsistent in theory and practice. However, I came to focus on King Sejong's idea that Confucian and Neo- Confucian knowledge should not clash with Buddhist belief. Sejong ignored the Confucian presupposition that a Confucian scholar could not have Buddhist belief or that Confucian and Neo-Confucian knowledge clashed with Buddhist belief. Instead, he chose both Confucianism and Buddhism according to his political needs, which I believe presents an interesting case. Moreover, given that he was not a simple Confucian scholar but a monarch, the final decision- maker in national policy, his policy and stance concerning politics and religion proves to be an interesting theme for study.

SEJONG'S AWARENESS OF CONFUCIANISM AND BUDDHISM

Was Sejong a Buddhist? To answer this question, it would be helpful to examine the stance Taejo and Taejong, his ancestors, took on Buddhism. Taejo attributed the foundation of Joseon to his belief in Buddhism. He made Monk Jacho, the king's mentor, wangsa (Taejo 1/09/10, jeongsa), and Monk Jogu, mentor of the state, guksa. He allowed the Lotus Sutra to be lectured in court, and was candid with his belief in Buddhism. On the other hand, it is difficult to say that his successor, Taejong, had Buddhist faith. Although he put up tents next to Deoksugung palace and held a Buddhist event with 100 monks, repaired Sarijeon (a place preserving Buddha's relics) at Heungcheon Temple, and dedicated his clothing to the Medicine Buddha (Bhaisajyaguru), all that was done for Taejo.

When the Queen was ill, he gathered monks to recite the sutras and was happy when she was better after prayers. His actions were not, however, out of faith. At every Buddhist event, he claimed that it was done for Taejo. Sometimes he said that it was "because his wife believed in it". There are many other cases when he sought out Buddhism not for religious reasons but for practical needs. In fact, his close officials were well aware that Taejong, who had received Confucian education, did not have Buddhist belief. As such, for Taejo Buddhism was a religion whereas for Taejong it was a pragmatic need. So, how about Sejong? Sejong once called Huang Yan, envoy from the Chinese Ming dynasty, to the inner shrine and gave him Buddha's relics.

He also had the Lotus Sutra written with ink made of gold at the inner shrine (Sejong 2/08/11, jeongmi). He held the Water-Land ritual (suryukaje; a service to console the souls of water and land) for Taejong, had Heungcheon Temple repaired, and sent out the newly printed Daejanggyeong (Great Collection of Buddhist Scriptures) there so that the common people could read it. If Sejong's stance toward Buddhism were only to this level, he would be valued as a monarch who used Buddhism for practical needs just as

Taejong did. However, when he held a celebratory event after repairing Heungcheon Temple, criticisms that emerged regarding his measures were different from the previously.

The bureaucrats were directly pointing out that whereas before Sejong said that he held Buddhist events "not because he revered Buddhism but Buddhism and Confucianism in King Sejong's State Administration 27 because he could not bear to see his ancestors' relics collapse, now he was say- ing that he must respect and hold rituals for Buddha". To such criticism, Sejong refuted, "it is said that the harm of Buddhism is so great that calamity is imminent and it is difficult to be saved." However, it is from here that the debate on Buddhist events began between Sejong and some of the officials. Despite their censure, Sejong allowed a five-day celebratory feast at Heungcheon Temple.

The officials followed Sejong's order in proceeding with the event and Sejong pressed on with the event ordering that "no monk should be stopped within Seoul, even those without their identity certificates." In his th year (1446), he held the memorial ritual for Queen Soheon at a number of temples (Sejong 28/04/15, imja). At this time, too, the bureaucrats pointed out that Sejong had a sutra written in gold and silver and had many more temples built, criticizing overtly that "His Majesty venerated and believed in heresy" (Sejong 28/10/4). To this, Sejong responded openly that he was "already a king who was fond of Buddhism." As the tension between Sejong and the bureaucrats continued, he established a shrine in the royal court despite their concerns (Sejong 30/12/05, jeongsa). Apart from these Buddhist events, Sejong is well known for allowing the publication of a number of sutras.

A special attention should be given to the fact that he ordered Prince Suyang who later became King Sejo to translate sutra into Korean. Considering that several Korean translations of sutras, including Neungeomgyeong eonhae (The Korean Translation of Shurangama) published in the eighth year of Sejo (1462), were initiated under Sejong's order, it seems evident that his interest in Buddhism was more than a political need in reality but rather a clear effect of his belief. Also, it needs to be noted that although the Korean translation of the four Chinese Confucian Classics was attempted under Sejong's orders, it was only actualized in the 1590s during Seonjo's reign. A practical need is to respond passively within the limit of its need, which was the case of Taejong.

However, several publications of sutras and translation works were the results of his religious belief as well as academic purpose. Sejong even composed Worin cheongang jigok (Songs of the Moon's Reflection on a Thousand Rivers) for the memory of Queen Soheon. According to recent research, he also participated in composing the Buddhist music Sari yeongeunggi (Records of Divine Response to Sarira). It certainly seems that his faith was behind his proceedings with Buddhist works as he pushed on despite opposing public opinion. Although he did not openly display Buddhist beliefs, he himself held fundamental belief in Buddhism.

Likewise, although he put forward Confucian moral duties such as loyalty and filial piety as well as his duty to carry out last injunctions and the traditions of his forefathers as his pretext for holding Buddhist ceremonies, it is evident that he was a believer in Buddhism. At the same time, he was also a monarch who had firm convictions in Confucianism and Neo-Confucianism.

He participated more enthusiastically in gyeongyeon, or discussions with scholars on the Confucian and other Chinese classics, than any other kings before him. He was also interested in collecting, printing, and distributing Confucian and Neo-Confucian academic books till his last years.

He sent Xingli daquan (Great Compendium on Human Nature and Principle), Yijing (Book of Changes), Shujing (Book of Documents), Chunqiu (Spring and Autumn Annals), and Shijing (Book of Odes) to the governors of Gyeongsang, Jeolla, and Chuncheong provinces, and had them carved on wooden plates. Each region then published these books and submitted them to Sejong. Sejong read and discussed these books with his officials. He then sent them to other officials and to local hyanggos (county schools).

Amongst these works, the case that proves Sejong's profound interest in the education of Confucianism and Neo-Confucianism was his order to add Hangeul suffixes to the Chinese Confucian Classics. Kwon Geun had added suffixes to Book of Odes, Book of Documents, and Book of Changes under orders from Taejong. Well aware of this, Sejong was concerned of the fact that suffixes to Liji (Book of Rites) and the four Confucian Classics did not yet exist. Adding Hangeul suffixes to the original Chinese text was to provide the basis for interpretation. Sejong was apprehensive of "future scholars teaching their disciples without understanding their original meaning." He said, "if they could teach with these, will it not be of their benefit," and alluded to the need to add Hangeul suffixes to the Confucian Classics.

Sejong thus had such in-depth knowledge of Confucianism and Neo-Confucianism that he was able to understand the issue of education and was convinced about the need for its distribution. Scholars who have studied Neo-Confucianism may emphasize the importance of certain books but when seen from the order of study, Xiaoxue (Elementary Learning) would be first on the list. In Joseon, Elementary Learning was considered as an introduction to the world of Confucianism among scholars. Whenever suggestions concerning Elementary Learning arose, such as including it as a subject of examination for saengwon (successful candidates for the minor civil service examination), increasing its printing and distribution, and reinforcing the education of Elementary Learning, Sejong allowed them without hesitation.

As for rituals, Zhuzi jiali (Zhu Xi's Family Rituals) was also important and Sejong promptly accepted a suggestion to apply Zhu Xi's Family Rituals to rites at court. Hence a man who was devoted to the learning of Confucianism and Neo-Confucianism and the related works also had enough religious faith to write sutras in gold under the directive of Sejong. Sejong once asked the following question to his officials: His Majesty asked his left and right, "Yun Bong said to Choe Seup, "this country adheres to the theory of Confucianism but does not like Buddhist rites.

In China, Buddhist rites are liked by all since Emperor Taizu, especially by Emperor Hongxi, who held the Water-Land ritual (suryukaje; shuiluzhai in Chinese), himself.

It has been a long time since Buddhism has reached China. It is not because there were no Confucian scholars that they did not know people liked Buddhism in China" (Sejong 12/ 11/12, giyu). Sejong was talking about the possibility of combining the knowledge of Confucianism or Neo-Confucianism and Buddhist belief. He was also questioning why Confucian scholars were so strongly against Buddhism in Joseon. To his question, his subordinates answered that "the reason the country's [China's] fate did not last long in China was because they liked Buddhism," but this was not the fundamental answer to his question. Sejong was raising an issue on the thought that equated studying Confucianism and Neo-Confucianism to rejecting Buddhism.

This was not an objection that was raised abruptly by Sejong alone. Taejo had also made a similar comment in his time. He took the example of Yi Saek, a competent Confucian scholar of his time, who was also interested in Buddhism, and remarked that Confucian or Neo-Confucian knowledge and Buddhist belief did not clash. Rather, he reproached that it was wrong to under- stand the relationship between Confucianism and Buddhism as antagonistic. His successor Jeongjong also said, "a Buddhist seeks dao in compassion and non-killing while a Confucian seeks dao in the justice of sparing lives and non-killing. The two are therefore similar to each other," emphasizing the similarities between Confucianism and Buddhism, which initiated a debate between him and his officials who were against this idea.

Concerning this theme, some of the scholars who had studied Neo-Confucianism asserted that Confucianism and Buddhism were ultimately the same in their fundamental spirit. As explained above, Sejong was devoted to the learning and promotion of Confucianism and Neo-Confucianism; he was a scholar as well as a believer in Buddhism. Therefore, for him to raise such a question shows that he was aware of the coexistence between the knowledge of Neo- Confucianism and Buddhist belief. During the Goryeo dynasty, Confucianism as political education and Buddhism as religion coexisted naturally in daily life. Even after Neo- Confucianism was introduced, scholars such as Yi Je-hyeon claimed conformity between Confucianism and Buddhism.

At the same time, monks such as Gihwa who were active during Sejong's era asserted that Buddhism and Confucianism alike helped in politics and everyday life. Despite these arguments that Confucianism and Buddhism could coexist in peace, from a Neo-Confucian perspective, Buddhism was a heresy that needed to be rejected. Why then did Sejong, who must have been well aware of this theory, think that Neo-Confucian knowledge and Buddhist belief should not clash? Don Baker's explanation may be a good reference regarding this question. He argues that before the introduction of Western Christianity in the 1780s, the Western sense of "religion" did not exist in Korea. In other words, religion is a phenomenon that occurred after the introduction of Christianity.

As the Western sense of theo-centric religion did not exist in Joseon, there were no serious conflicts between Confucianism, Buddhism, and Shamanism at a doctrinal level. A religion could only exist in the system as long as it recognized and respected the existing Confucian order. In this vein, it can be interpreted that Sejong thought that Neo-Confucian knowledge and Buddhist belief were not antagonistic. On the other hand, if the introduction of Neo-Confucianism reinforced the tendency to prescribe and criticize Buddhism as heresy, Duncan's explanation is also useful.

Duncan analyzed that from late Goryeo to early Joseon, the difference or change between traditional Confucianism and Neo-Confucianism was not very clear. It is therefore difficult to find a distinct condition of change from traditional Confucianism to Neo-Confucianism at the beginning of Joseon as they gradually changed over a long period of time. If we apply Duncan's observation to Sejong's case, it can be interpreted that in a situation where the tendencies of late

Goryeo when Confucianism and Buddhism coexisted were carried on, Sejong must have followed the trend of the time.

As the religious conflict between Confucianism and Buddhism were weak and as the tendencies of traditional Confucianism remained intact at the time, there is room for interpretation that Neo-Confucianism may have been less rigorous with the rejection of heresy. Sejong's stance on Confucianism and Buddhism can thus be translated as reflecting the trends of the time. However, he reformed Buddhism from a Confucian political perspective and kept his belief as a person in charge for state administration.

SEJONG'S RESTRUCTURING OF THE BUDDHIST ORDER

The theoretical aspects of criticism on Buddhism during Sejong's reign are similar to those raised in Array of Critiques of Buddhism, to which other actual cases at the time were added. The first point to note concerning the criticism on Buddhism that appears in Sejong sillok is an emotional critique on Buddhism. This is found in the sentence at the beginning of an appeal sent by the Office of the Censor-General saying, "Buddha in reality is a Western barbarian who has deceived and tempted good people by suggesting a wizardry of karma between sin and blessing".

It is a contemptuous remark criticizing that as Buddhism came from the West, a barbaric region, it was thus worthless. To those who expected Joseon to rule the eastern region, a religion from the West was meaningless. Next was the otherworldly tendency of Buddhism. It was criticized as "something that has forgotten the affairs of the world and the state" and "a way to turn away from the world and cut ties from mundane life". Buddhism was considered as a religion that renounced or shunned family and the state, which weakened people's duty and interest in political society.

This was reflected in earlier criticism that Buddhism was a religion of no father and no monarch. Such tendencies of Buddhism kept people away from labor, induced them to abandon their family instead of creating one, and ultimately led people to betray the orders of the state and the monarch. Confucian scholars then criticized the way Buddhism encouraged good deeds in order to receive blessings. They contended that it was wrong to lead people to do good by threatening them about the existence of heaven and hell. This is also related to the difference in perspectives on life and death between Confucianism and Buddhism. Since Confucians believed that a person's spirit disappeared from this world upon death, they could not accept the Buddhist view of heaven and hell.

They saw that life only existed once, and so they criticized that the theory of heaven and hell was only a lie to deceive innocent people. As such, most Confucian scholars did not recognize Buddhist teachings in general. At the same time, they thought that Buddhism was dangerous due to its similarities with Confucianism. Buddhism emphasized the discipline of the mind and this seemed similar to the Confucian logic that emphasized the cultivation of mind. In this regard, Confucian scholars severely criticized Buddhism as being adversary to the development of Confucianism and Neo-Confucianism.

The officials and scholars who criticized Buddhism at the time presented as the basis of their criticism such theoretical and historical examples as the critiques on Buddhism written by scholars such as Han Yu and Zhu Xi, the collapse of many Chinese dynasties that adopted Buddhism, and the corruption of Buddhism and Confucianism in King Sejong's State Administration 33 Buddhism during the Goryeo dynasty. Based on this theoretical recognition of heresy, actual issues of criticism on Buddhism can be elicited as follows. First of all, the concern on the monks' increasing political influence should be noted.

Even in Goryeo, which was considered as a Buddhist country, there was criticism on the monks' involvement in political issues. There was wide- spread dissatisfaction with the situation where monks exercised their political power based on their intimacy with the monarch and his family. When Seol Sun, second-rank associate academician (bujehak) at the Hall of Worthies (Jiphyeonjeon), said to Sejong "an evil monk disturbed the political affairs causing the collapse of the dynasty", he had in mind an example from late Goryeo. The officials in Sejong's time were also aware of this possibility but such concern was not so serious after the foundation of Joseon as it was in Goryeo. With the guksa (mentor of the state) and the wangsa (king's mentor) system, there was naturally some room for the monks to exercise influence through official contacts with the king under Taejo's reign.

However, as Taejong got rid of these titles and no longer appointed guksa, political influence from Buddhism lessened. It was only that Sejong and his family showed interest in Buddhism and directly participated in Buddhist activities, which sometimes gave opportunities for a few monks to boast the king's confidence to local bureaucrats and magistrates. However, already in Sejong's time, Buddhist influence had dwindled much from the time of Goryeo. Even those who criticized Buddhism were not so concerned about this issue. The point of contention in the criticism on Buddhism concerned economic and financial issues. In their appeal, officials defined monks as those who never had to work to be fed.

They assessed that the number of farmers would decrease if monks increased in number. Thus they were enraged at monks who "took people's food" when the state finance was facing difficulties. As mentioned earlier, the critique of Buddhism did not believe in the effects of Buddhist events that prayed for blessings, and so they deemed the cost put into Buddhist events as a futile element that wasted state finance. Therefore, they urged that all the Buddhist events be completely banned, or if impossible, be economized as much as possible. At the same time, they could not bear the fact that monks ate good food and wore good clothing. They could not accept the monks in light clothing, eating pastry made of oil and honey, and riding horses. They were also furious that monks drank alcohol.

They emphasized at the beginning of their critique on Buddhism that it should be a religion clear of greed and that Buddhist practice should be like an ascetic in the snowy mountains, criticizing the monks' extravagance and lamenting that Buddhism had lost its true spirit. The focus of criticism from the economic aspect was the management of land and slaves owned by temples. These lands and slaves were related to the problem of decreases in labor responsible for military service and corve labor. As previous research pointed out, "the expansion of the temple economy at the end of Goryeo" was one of the reasons for disorder in land laws and subsequent intensification of issues concerning land reform. Thus, the reform of the Buddhist order was an urgent issue demanded by state finance, and land was at the core of this reform.

In this context, there were continuous demands for reform of the land owned by temples during the reigns of Taejo and Taejong, and Taejong successively limited temple-owned land and slaves. Also, by enacting institutions such as docheopje (certification of monkhood), he made it more difficult to become a monk in order to maintain a substantial number of citizens and a strong army. Even Taejo, who was in favor of Buddhism, consented to such measures. From Taejo to Taejong, the general trend was the restructuring of the Buddhist order through measures such as reorganizing the size of lands owned by temples and imposing tax on them. As a result of such process, the status of Buddhism was weakened. Restructuring continued on an extensive scale under Sejong's reign.

The proposition submitted by the Office of Protocol concerning Buddhist reform on April 5, 1424, the sixth year of King Sejong's reign, suggested reorganizing seven sects to two denominations of Zen and non-Zen Buddhism, and banning the Seungnoksa (office responsible for Buddhism-related affairs). Heungcheon Temple and Heungdeok Temple were to be responsible for the execution of these measures, with their names being changed to Seonjong Dohoeso and Gyojong Dohoeso, respectively, which were to take charge of managing matters related to monks. These measures entrusted the management of monks to the organization of monks, which decreased the importance of the task.

If we look into the specifics of the unification of two denominations, previous sects Jogye, Cheontae, and

Chongnam were put into Seonjong while Hwaeom, Jaeun, Jungsin, and Siheung were put together as Gyojong. At the same time, it was suggested that 36 temples should be selected and subordinated to denominations in Seoul and other regions. Subsequently, 4,250 gyeol (a unit of measure for land) were allocated to 18 temples under Seonjong and 3,700 gyeol were given to 18 temples under Gyojong, thus reducing the size of land and the number of monks that were to be allocated to each temple. Sejong took measures to reorganize the Buddhist order following the criticism and public opinion on Buddhism raised by officials and Confucian scholars.

He also allowed criticism on heresy and accepted parts of their argument, depending on the circumstances. Examples of such measures include the closing of the shrine in Munsojeon, moving the Buddha of Great Benevolence and sarira to Heungcheon Temple in the 15th year of his reign (1433), and stopping accepting felicitations from the monks, who belonged to five sects from both denominations. Sejong agreed to the suggestions made by officials and the contents of appeals on rejecting Buddhism submitted by Confucian scholars. Responding to their opinions, he managed the Hall of Worthies and participated in discussions with scholars on the Confucian and other Chinese classics more enthusiastically than any other kings before him. The way he collected, printed, and distributed academic books to other regions were all measures that reflected the direction of his policy.

Along with these academic works, he continuously promoted enlightenment policy to lead the people toward the world of Confucian ethics. Publications such as Samgang haengsil (The Three Bonds and Actual Examples of their Practice) are the reflections of such a will. At the same time, he assented to restructuring the Buddhist order so as to improve state finance.

Unlike his kind measures that protected the monks and ordered no imposition of severe control over them, against the officials' request to punish monks when they committed petty crimes, he was very clear about policies related to economic issues. And as his forefathers had done, he maintained docheopje that limited the ways to become a monk, restricted the construction of new temples, and had parts of temple-owned land and slaves returned to the public.

As such, Sejong restructured the Buddhist order. When we look at the contents of restructuring, however, it was not a policy that denied the existence of Buddhism itself. The oppression of Buddhism under Sejong's reign was to reduce the external size of Buddhism and limit its secular power or influence so that it could remain as a religion, which was its original role. In spite of doing this, Buddhism was still allowed to remain and function as a religion in the world of Confucian politics. And, it was also because he had noted its value and necessity in everyday life from the perspective of state administration.

REASONING AND JUSTIFICATION

There were diverse opinions concerning the issue of Buddhist reform in Sejong's era. An appeal submitted by jehak (first-rank associate academician), Yun Hoe, and others at the Hall of Worthies reflected opinion that strongly asserted the rejection of Buddhism. Based on general theoretical criticism on Buddhism at the time, they defined Buddhism as the "law of barbarians" and urged the destruction of pagodas, burning of sutras, and laicization of monks. They also demanded the editing of Zhu Xi's Family Rituals into a simpler form so that it could be easily distributed to the public and practiced. Following this appeal, Sin Cheo-jung and 101 other scholars at the National Confucian Academy (Sungkyunkwan) also submitted an appeal on March 12, 1424 (the sixth year of Sejong), which maintained a similar tone.

They also criticized staunchly the Buddhist theory and teachings on life and death and listed historical examples of harmful Buddhist influences, all the while demanding a strong response from the king. Their demands included forcing the monks to return to their hometowns and allocating them to the regional military, turning their residences into ordinary housing, burning the sutras, assigning land at temples to the military in order to increase provision, distributing temple-owned slaves to government offices, turning the vessels used at temples over to official use, printing carved wooden plates on paper, and subordinating temples in Seoul to government offices and those in the country to post houses in districts and counties or to village schools. While they were adamant in the eradication of Buddhism, they proposed Zhu Xi's family rituals as an alternative to Buddhist rites.

Sejong said that he accepted their outspoken advice but by claiming that "it was difficult to reform everything at once", he did not follow their suggestions. On the other hand, there were those who approached the issue from a realistic point of view, in a more flexible way. They suggested a scheme to control Buddhism by decreasing the vice of Buddhism. They were aware that although Buddhism and Confucianism in King Sejong's State Administration Buddhism was defined as heresy and its abuses were talked about, it could not be eradicated all of a sudden. On May 9, 1423 (fifth year of Sejong), daesaheon (minister) Ha Yeon and others at the Office of the Inspector-General (Saheonbu) appealed that in order to decrease the harm from Buddhism rather than eliminating it entirely, a measure should be devised to render Buddhism to devote itself to its religious role of practicing the dao, of purity.

In other words, they wanted Buddhism to return to its original place of religion, to which Sejong answered that "it was not something to be reformed abruptly," thus accepting their opinion. This in fact was the basis of Buddhist policy during Sejong's era. With more officials agreeing to the gradual reform of the Buddhist order, Sejong was able to control the speed and content of the reform. As he implemented slower reform than suggestions of complete rejection raised by scholars and officials, he could be evaluated as being passive in his response to Buddhism, although there were also times when he even defended it. What then was the reason behind his attachment to Buddhism, which was being ousted by public opinion?

There still was a demand on Buddhism during Sejong's reign. Monks were summoned for various national events at the time, and in Veritable Records of King Sejong, a number of records state that monks and shamans took part in the ritual for rain, something that continued before and after Sejong's reign. As one drought continued, it was the officials who proposed gathering the monks to offer a ritual for rain. If it did rain after the ritual, the monks would ask for recompense. Suryukjae, a full-scale Buddhist event, took place for the first time at Jingwansa and was held annually from the fourth year of Taejo (1395) until the tenth year of Jungjong (1515).

Sejong also held a grand Water-Land ritual (suryukaje) to honor the memory of his forefathers; the ritual commemorating the first anniversary of Taejong's death was also held at Jingwansa. Several temples were officially constructed to pray for the welfare of the royal family and they were also supported by the royal family. This situation was not so much different for ordinary people. Buddhism persisted in everyday life and big part of Buddhist propagation to the people also persisted under political silence. As Buddhism had a certain role in politics and everyday life as a religion, it could not be banned all at once. Confucian scholars and officials were undoubtedly complaining that the "monks are of no benefit to the state and only cause trouble to the world" and that they must eradicated but it was impossible to ban Buddhism so abruptly.

Buddhism could be banned but there was no alternative. The alternative, naturally, were Confucian and Neo-Confucian rituals but the spread of Zhu Xi's family rituals were still at its initial stage. Even if rituals such as Zhu Xi's family rituals were disseminated throughout society, they could not entirely replace Buddhist rituals or activities. The leading trend may have changed but to completely replace Buddhism was very difficult in the real world. Therefore, to enforce the eradication of Buddhism as a way of realizing the ideology while disregarding actual condition was also unreasonable.

It needs to be noted that monks could have been regarded as a labor force in reserve for emergencies. When the officials advised Taejo to rule wisely, they also advised that "public service need to be stopped." The king and his officials proclaimed such people-centered politics found it burdensome to mobilize people for various construction works. In circumstances where it was difficult to mobilize farmers during the farming season, monks, though they may not have been an alternative, could have been regarded as a complementary labor force. It was naturally the monks of low rank who were mobilized. There was, however, a case in the second year of Taejo's reign (1393) when the king demanded participation from Buddhism and Confucianism in King Sejong's State Administration monks in the construction of the new capital to Jo Saeng, who was the head monk at the Naewondang (private shrine for prayers and meditations in the royal court).

Considering also the remaining records that state the mobilization of monks to the construction and repairs of palaces during the Japanese Invasion of Korea in 1592, Sejong must have also considered monks along similar lines. There is some research that suggests monks were in charge of special tributary payments. They were mobilized for paper manufacturing and printing in particular and even delivered local specialties.

Sejong had special interest in the distribution of Confucian and Neo-Confucian books and he sometimes ordered local governments to produce these books and also sent them the books. During this process, according to the record written on January 26 (giyu), 1428 (tenth year of Sejong's reign), which concerns the report from the governor of Gangweon, in publishing and pre- serving Sishu daquan, "monks who volunteered were put to work building the Court Book Depository (Jangseogak), and they were paid when their service was done."

As temples were involved in the publication of books until late Joseon, the role of monks must have been taken into consideration. Although more research is needed, there is a possibility that monks were put to military purposes during Sejong's reign. It has already been pointed out above that monks were mobilized in the constructions of palaces, and existing records state that they were also responsible for defending the citadel. More clearly, when we consider that monk soldiers such as Hyujeong were active during the Japanese Invasion of Korea in 1592, Joseon likely also used monks for military purposes.

The relationship between foreign affairs and Buddhism needs to be taken into consideration. In Veritable Records of King Sejong, it is recorded in detail how often Japan requested books such as the Lotus Sutra. In Taejong sillok (Veritable Records of King Taejong), it is recorded that "when a messenger sent by So Sadashige (who was the de facto ruler of 15th century Tsushima province) asked for the Lotus Sutra" (Sejong 12/05/28, sinhae), Hwang Hui, minister of the Office of Protocol, said that even though it was rare in Joseon, he made efforts to find it as So Sadashige wanted it earnestly.

Afterwards, Japan kept requesting for the Heart Sutra, and Joseon sent it when they could find it (Sejong 11/03/28, gapsul), and if they could not, they sent some- 40 The Review of Korean Studies thing else as a gift. The fact that Emperor Ming also had favorable tendencies to Buddhism cannot be ignored. The envoy from Ming during Sejong's reign requested goods related to Buddhism, and the Emperor protected monks from Joseon who had taken exile to China. Such an external environment may not have been the main aspect that encouraged Sejong to actively protect Buddhism at the time.

However, it must have acted as a positive environment to protect the Buddhist order. Among these aspects, Sejong appears to have taken the first aspect, that is, Buddhism's function as a religion as a particularly important factor. It must have been difficult to simply prohibit Buddhism when there was a clear demand for it. Considering these circumstances and tendencies, it is understandable that Sejong held on to Buddhism with a controlled level of intensity, despite opposition from officials and scholars. Under such circumstances, what logic did Sejong present as he protected Buddhism while appeasing the oppositions from officials and scholars? Also, how did he solve the conflicts between the consolidation of Buddhist religion and Confucian politics, and how did he succeed in combining the two?

Sejong emphasized his justification in that he was respecting the decisions of his forefathers. Even Taejong, who did not hold positive belief in Buddhism, thought that he had to maintain the Buddhist tendencies in his time as it was his father Taejo's faith. Therefore, he built a temple at Geonwolleung, forged and hung a bell at Gaegyeong Temple, and repaired the Buddha's relics(sarira) shrine at the Heungcheon Temple, (Taejong 11/03/30, gyeongin). Sejong also established that he was "following the will of the forefathers" and justified Buddhist events.

At the same time, he also used Confucian ethics and logic such as loyalty and filial piety in his justification for Buddhism, as follows: In ancient times a man asked Zhu Xi "if the father liked Buddha and his son did not, when the father dies, should the son hold the ritual for his father or not?" Zhu Xi answered, "it is appropriate that the son talked of Buddha's harm to his father in order to abandon misguided beliefs when he was alive. If the father did not follow, it is then proper to hold the ritual for the father." Heungcheon Temple was established by Taejo and was entrusted to Taejong. Although Taejong did not believe in heresy, he continued the works of Buddha rather than banning them because it was Taejo's will.

With this Sejong ordered the construction of a pagoda at Heungcheon Temple. Afterwards when Heungcheon Temple was repaired and the Tripitaka assigned there for preservation, he refuted the resistance from the officials saying that Heungcheon Temple was built by the previous king. Next is the logic in the same vein as above. Sejong used to state that "it can not be changed suddenly as it is a tradition". However, it was not simply because it was a tradition that it could not be changed abruptly, rather Sejong was concerned with the consequences that could occur when things that had been rooted deeply in everyday life were changed suddenly.

Confucian scholars were criticizing that Buddhism was heretical but Sejong understood that it was not easy to convince people of the issue of heresy. It was not that he wanted to maintain it simply because it was tradition.

Rather, it was impossible not to consider the subsequent issues of such measures.

Officials who asserted the eradication of Buddhism also agreed with Sejong on this point, which is why they suggested controlling and tuning Buddhism so that it's perceived negative influence of engaging in politics and concerns with money would not be excessive, rather than taking measures to oust Buddhism overnight. Due to his Buddhist beliefs, Sejong tended to defend Buddhism. However, as seen above, he understood that Buddhism was needed in reality at a national level.

He accepted this and used Buddhism in state administration. There were anti-Buddhists who viewed the relationship between Confucian politics and Buddhist beliefs in terms of confrontation, but Sejong admitted and embraced the value of Buddhism at a political level. To him, Confucian politics and Buddhist beliefs were theoretically in a conflict relationship but they could also be combined according to the needs in reality. As seen so far, Sejong was a monarch with Buddhist beliefs. He was also a king 42 The Review of Korean Studies who had studied the classics diligently, participated in gyeongyeon (devotedly, and concentrated on the works of Confucian and Neo-Confucian education.

Seen within a Confucian framework of expulsion of heresy, he may not appear to have been consistent. However, considering that Taejo and Taejong had also held similar thoughts and that there were many officials who agreed with his thoughts, his case was not so peculiar at the time. His reign was caught in the time of change from Buddhism to Confucianism, and when it came to Buddhism, various tendencies coexisted, such as adamant anti-Buddhist to moderate ones, and to those who even talked about the coexistence of Buddhism and Confucianism.

In such an era, despite his belief in Buddhism, Sejong agreed on the political and economic abuses of Buddhism, and accepted suggestions that Buddhism needed to be restructured in order to solve the issues in state finance. In his later years, he established his personal shrine and showed his interest on the religious level. However, he distinguished his belief from the purpose and need of state policy. This is why he was able to make decisive changes to the Buddhist order so as to facilitate political needs. At the same time, though the advice from officials criticizing the abuse in Buddhism may have been aggressive and given in critical manner, he did not punish these officials.

He kept open the communication route that was related to heresy. And following their advice, he limited civilians from becoming monks as much as possible, reorganized the number of temples, and moved part of temple-owned land and slaves to public offices. The reason Sejong restructured the Buddhist order was to overcome the problems subsequent to the secularization of Buddhism, not to deny Buddhism itself. It was in this point that he differed in opinion from the officials who argued for the expulsion of Buddhism concerning the reform of the Buddhist order.

The reason Sejong established such Buddhist reform was because he believed that Confucian or Neo-Confucian knowledge and Buddhist beliefs were not confrontational. Sejong's personal belief, recognition of possible coexistence between knowledge and religion, and a comprehensive awareness of the religious needs that existed at the national and social levels all appeared in his mixed response and attitude toward Buddhism. Trying to bring Buddhism back to its own place on the basis of recognizing Buddhism at the core of his policy on Buddhism, he was able to accept the religious role of Buddhism that had long since been practiced. He was not willing to ban Buddhism, the religion that he himself and a number of people depended on, simply because of some Neo-Confucian scholars' criticism.

The basis of his Buddhism and Confucianism in King Sejong's State Administration 43 policy on Buddhism was to recognize the religion. In addition to the religious role of Buddhism, there were other more realistic and concomitant reasons Sejong held on to Buddhism, such as the possibility to mobilize monks as laborers in an. National and social rituals or events that Buddhism was responsible for were reduced as

Confucianism and Neo-Confucianism spread throughout the society. However, Sejong recognized the value of Buddhism at the religious level.

Meanwhile, he promoted Confucian or Neo-Confucian learning and ethics education. He reinforced academic functions such as those of the Hall of Worthies and the gyeongyeon, and based on this, he published and spread various Confucian and Neo-Confucian books and aimed for a Confucian state while agonizing over the details of education. In the time of ideological change when Confucianism and Buddhism coexisted and when diverse opinions and conflicts could be expressed, Sejong, rather than openly expressing his belief in Buddhism, maintained a conviction that Confucian and Neo-Confucian knowledge could coexist with Buddhist belief.

And while listening to diverse voices concerning the ideological issue, he controlled the speed and content of Buddhist reform. As he possessed Confucian and Neo-Confucian knowledge, he was able to balance his thoughts in policy making that concerned the Buddhist issue. By responding to the issue of Buddhist belief in a flexible and realistic way with clear knowledge and conviction, Sejong was able to minimize confusion at the beginning of state foundation, and was later appraised as the king who laid the foundation for Confucian and Neo-Confucian politics and culture to develop in Joseon.

The first struggles between the two religion/philosophies, Buddhism and Confucianism, to survive and thrive in post-Han China marked the beginning of considerable evolution for them both. Confucianism, discredited after the fall of the Han, still provided the ethical base of China's population. Buddhism, largely an alien and confusing religion, had to absorb more than a little of Chinese culture in order to survive. This took a considerable amount of time; Buddhist priests were living in China for centuries before they managed to firmly establish their religion. Eventually, during the "Golden Age" of the T'ang, Buddhism was the most commonly practiced faith in all China. By this time Buddhism had been made quite distinctly Chinese.

This was accomplished mainly by the emphasis (and frequent insertion) of Confucian ideals, virtues, and morals into the traditional Buddhist literary canon and the modification-during-translation of that canon to appeal to Chinese readers. Buddhism, though ultimately more sophisticated than any belief system in China at the time of it's introduction, seemed to the average Chinese to be more like a Taoist mystery cult than a serious religious alternative. Buddhist missionaries quickly realized that this reluctance stemmed primarily from the fact that Buddhism lacked any kind of emphasis on values a typical Chinese would consider vital. The best example of this is the absence of filial piety as a theme in the Buddhist sutras.

A quick glance through the Confucian Analects will reveal almost the exact opposite – it's hard to find an analect that doesn't touch on filial piety at least obliquely. To the Chinese of the time, the most important relationship in the world was the one that they had with their parents. Buddhism, which evolved in a land where one's caste was more important than one's parents, had only a few isolated stories with this theme. These few, such as the Jataka, which told the story of a son who so loved his blind parents that he dressed in a deerskin to go into the forest and obtain the fresh deer milk they required, were all quickly translated and distributed.

In this particular tale, a lord out hunting accidentally shoots the son, and upon realizing his error, swears to see that the boy's parents are taken care of. The boys parents were so overcome with grief they uttered the Act of Truth (a powerful Buddhist prayer) with such emotion Sakka himself descended and restored the boy to life. Another traditional Buddhist sutra that appealed to the Chinese was the Yu-lan-p'en-ching, in which a son, Mu-Lien, upon attaining arhatship after his death, wished to repay his parents for the love they had given him. To his dismay, he found that his mother was banished to the Avici Hell, tormented forever for her greed in life (which she had kept hidden from him).

Mu-Lien then appealed personally to the Buddha himself on his mother's behalf. The Buddha instructed Mu-Lien to prepare a great feast including the hundred delicacies, and on the 15th day of the 7th moon to offer it to the monks of the ten quarters on behalf of his ancestors (specifically his mother). This was done, and Mu-Lien's mother was released from the Avici Hell. Such stories were not common in India, due to their lack of popularity, but the Chinese loved them. Soon, it became apparent that traditional Buddhist scriptures did not offer enough of these stories of filial piety to compete with Confucianism. Sutras began circulating that, suspiciously, seemed to have no Indian counterpart prior to their "translation." These forged sutras helped close the gap considerably between Buddhism and China.

One of the best known forged sutras is the Fu-mu en-chung ching (Sutra on the Importance of Parental Love). This sutra appears in a multitude of variations and titles, and appears almost like a Confucian analect at it's beginning: "the Buddha said, 'In this world our parents are closest to us. Without them, we would not be born...'" The sutra goes on to describe how being a good Buddhist is a really good way to show your parents that you love them. Though this sutra, and others, were forgeries, they still became part of the canon of Chinese Buddhism. This is one major way in which Confucian thought and practices directly influenced the evolution of Buddhism.

Another way in which Buddhism was subtly altered during the attempt to make it more appealing to the Chinese was the adaptation of the five Silas (or Cardinal Precepts) of Buddhism to match the Five Norms of Confucianism. The Cardinal Precepts are not to lie, steal, kill, commit adultery, and drink intoxicating beverages. The five Norms are human heartedness, righteousness, propriety, knowledge, and trust. The correlation between these two sets is described in another blatantly invented sutra, the T'i-wei Po-li-ching: "Not to kill is paired with human-heartedness, not to steal is paired with righteousness, not to commit adultery is paired with knowledge, to not drink intoxicating liquor is paired with propriety, and not to tell lies is paired with trust."

One Chinese scholar (Chih-I) even assigned the Chinese five elements and five directions to the five Silas, further weaving Buddhism into Confucian Chinese culture, and vice-versa. Another major way in which Buddhism was modified was in the translation of the Sutras themselves. This was more troubling that it might at first appear. First of all, Sanskrit and Chinese are different in almost every way, and many different characters in Chinese seems to mean the same thing to foreign interpreters but carry entire loads of different connotations for the Chinese. Also, the original sutras tended to be rather matter-the-fact, telling what happened and why and what can be learned, with a minimum of frills and poetic language.

A direct translation of such sutras would certainly not appeal to the detail and metaphor loving Chinese. Also, there was a lack of characters available to describe Buddhist concepts, so dharma often became Tao and nirvana became Wu-Wei due to the lack of any other way to present them. Also, the sutras were modified to emphasize control of women rather that the slightly more respectful status they sometimes earned in Indian society. Due to it's growing appeal in the masses of China, and also to the weakened state of Confucianism after the fall of the Han dynasty, Buddhism became the dominant belief during the Six Dynasties period. When the Sui reunited China in 581 Buddhism was commonplace, and when the T'ang took over in 617 It became practically a state religion.

With the near disappearance of Buddhism in India, its evolution in China is of the utmost importance. Nowhere else on Earth was the Buddhist tradition being carried on by a powerful, civilized culture. The changes that the Confucian tradition imposed, however unintentionally, on the religion modified virtually all sects of Buddhism, and are vital for us to understand it as a religion today. A Comparative Look At Buddhism, Islam, and Confucianism Throughout history, great civilizations and people have risen and fallen, and during their fleeting existence, religious activities have assumed important functions in those societies.

Confucianism, Buddhism, and Islam, are three legacies left by great men, which still have a profound affect on society. Like with all human inventions, though, these three philosophies are all relative to each other: They are comparable in their simplicity of beliefs, the emphasis they placed on the role of women within their society, and the transformation into different sects in later years; but differ from each other in their emphasis in each field respectively. The basic doctrines of these three philosophies can be readily compared with each other. They each carry their tenets in a basic, simple format which is easy to understand and follow.

Their beliefs also provide an ethical code encompassed within their beliefs, and each has an objective to attain through simple means. In Buddhism, the fundamental beliefs are to recognize life as cycle of birth and rebirth, and to overcome this cycle to attain Nirvana. The fundamental beliefs of Buddhism are contained in The Four Noble Truths, which are:

Life is suffering,

Suffering is caused by desire,

The way to end suffering is to end desire,

The way to end desire is to avoid the extremes of a life vulgar materialism and of self-torture, and to follow the Middle Path(Eightfold Path).

Following the Middle Path, to Buddha is the way to overcome the painful cycle of life, and are relatively simple practices. They are thus:

- Right understanding, or views: recognizing that material security does not bring peace of mind and that rituals do not erase the effects of pass acts;
- Right motives: the quality of the drive behind the thinking and being free from carnal thirst, malevolence, cruelty, etc...;
- Right speech: not indulging in cruel and harsh talk, thereby being able to establish a link between 'right motives' and 'right action';
- Right action: any actions that proceed from an unobstructed mind. This also includes abstaining from unwholesome actions and performing those which are beneficial;

- Right means of livelihood: the idea of not harming living things through any means, and to abstain from indulging in anything which would cloud the mind;
- Right effort: efforts taken to encourage the development of of the other paths and to discourage any hindrances;
- Right mindfulness: to prevent the excessive development of of one path at the expense of another;
- Right meditation: to quiet the mind and present true pictures to the mind of any hindrances to the Middle Path.

The Middle Path, as seen above, is an ethical code for a relatively simple life of performing good deeds, not harming yourself and others, and maintaining ethical thoughts and frame of mind. By following the Middle Path, a person would eventually reach enlightenment and be able to achieve Nirvana. To the Buddha, Nirvana is the extinction of self hood and a final reunion with the Great World Soul. Similar to Buddhism, Islam is also a simple faith with simple teachings, with an easily obtainable objective. Islam's beliefs though are held in a monotheistic framework,and in what is known as the Five Pillars of Islam.

The supreme deity of Islam is Allah and obeying the will of Allah is done by following the Five Pillars of Islam. They are thus:

- Every Muslim must utter There is no God but Allah and Mohammed is his prophet;
- Every Muslim must pray five times a day and publicly on Friday at noon;
- Every Muslim must give alms(charity) to the poor and unfortunate;
- During the holy month of the Ramadan, every Muslim must fast from dawn to sunset; and
- Every Muslim must make a pilgrimage to Mecca at least once in their lifetime.

Along with the Five Pillars, Muslims(followers of the Islam faith) must also abstain from eating pork, gambling, drinking alcoholic beverages, and engaging in dishonest behavior. These rules are the basic laws a Muslim must obey, and they do not require too much effort from the individual or put a strain on the individual. By following them and by obeying the will of Allah, a Muslim is guaranteed a place in an eternal paradise filled with sensual delights. This eternal paradise is the objective of those who are faithful to Allah and Islam. Confucianism is also similar to the others, in its simplicity in teachings and adherence.

First Confucianism deals with the rational cosmic order and the organization of worldly affairs. Confucian belief is that all humans were endowed with their own Dao(Way), which was dependent on their role in life, and it was the individuals duty to live accordingly to their Dao, and not to ignore it. And by following their Dao accordingly, then their own affairs and those of the community would prosper. From this philosophy comes the concept of duty and humanity. In the concept of duty, the individual sacrifices his personal interests and desires for the good of the family, community, and state. With the concept of humanity, this consists of compassion and empathy for others.

These are the central concepts of Confucianism, where the objective of its followers is for the affairs of the state, community, and individual to be prosperous and harmonious. Though Buddhism, Islam, and Confucianism share the common ground of simplicity in teachings and adherence, they differ from each other sharply. First is the emphasis of each philosophy. Buddhism is sometimes called a reinterpretation of Hinduism, but is not a religion. Buddhism does not emphasize a god, nor the need to worship a god, but the adherence to an ethical lifestyle. On the otherhand, Islam is a religion(called a Religion of The Book) and emphasizes a supreme deity, Allah, and the need to obey his will. Whereas Confucianism as a philosophy, does not emphasize a higher metaphysical order(other than the Dao), nor does it emphasize the necessity to worship a deity.

Confucianism is also not a reinterpretation of the some other religion or philosophy, either. Confucianism can be seen as a political philosophy, because Confucius' philosophy took shape during China's Spring and Autumn Period- a period of quarrelling and fighting among regional political leaders.6 Confucius looked to the Golden Age of Zhou, in lamentation and inspiration of his philosophy. He is quoted to have said: The practice of the Great Way, the illustrious men of the Three Dynasties - these I shall never know in person. And yet they inspire my ambition...... Thus each philosophy's emphasis is the difference, in the similarities of each one. With Buddhism, its emphasis is on a mere ethical lifestyle. With Islam, it is obedience to and adhering to the will of a deity, Allah.

And finally with Confucianism, emphasizing the greater good of the state and community. Another difference between Buddhism, Islam, and Confucianism, is the ultimate objective(or salvation as some may have it) of each philosophy. In Buddhism, the ultimate goal is to defeat the painful cycle of life and attain enlightenment(Bodhi). On attaining bodhi, the individual can reach the final reunion with the Great World Soul(Nirvana). This is not like a heavenly salvation, nor an eternal paradise. Nirvana is likened to a dreamless sleep or to a 'blowing out'(as of a candle). Islam, on the otherhand, does not emphasize a heavenly salvation, nor an eternal sleep nor a Great World Soul. Islam does, however, offer the hope of attaining a place in an eternal paradise of sensual delights, through devotion and worship of Allah.

The sensual delights probably consisted of pleasures not found in the geograhical region of the Arabian desert. Thus, Confucianism is totally different from both Buddhism and Islam. Confucianism does not offer a reunion with the Great World Soul, nor does it offer an eternal paradise of sensual delights: It does offer to the individual, if one lives according to his Dao, the hope to have the affairs of society(state, community, and individual) to be in order and prosperous.

In all, each philosophy does emphasize an objective,or form of salvation, though each one differs dramatically: Buddhism, with its abstract Nirvana; Islam, with an eternal paradise; and Confucianism, with the secular prosperity of the state, community, and individual. Another similar aspect which

Buddhism, Islam, and Confucianism share is the vulgàrization,or sectionalism, each experienced later in the centuries.

Each underwent a transformation, years after the founding individual had died. For Buddhism, it was the division into the two sects, Mahayana and Theravada (Hinayana). Later the Mahayana sect became further transformed into four other sects. Like Buddhism, Islam also underwent a transformation into two factions, the Shi'ites and the Sunnites. Confucianism, like Buddhism and Islam, underwent a form of modification into Neo-Confucianism. With Neo-Confucianism, two new schools appeared. The School of Reason and School of Mind. Their transformation, though, affected each one differently. For Buddhism, Islam, and Confucianism, their shared aspect of modification is also the differences between them, as to how it affected each one individually.

For Buddhism, the modification of the belief became a complete vulgarization of Buddha's original belief. Buddhism went from an ethical philosophy to a Salvationist religion. Buddhism split into two sects Mahayana and Therevada (Hinayana), with Therevada maintaing the traditional beliefs and Mahayana becoming the Salvationist religion of Buddhism. It emphasized the worship and devotion to Buddha as a God, Nirvana as a heavenly salvation, and the worship of bodhisattvas(those who achieved bodhi) as saints. Mahayana was furthered divided into four sects which further degenerated Buddha's original message: Chan-emphasized meditation could bring enlightenment instantly; Pureland-emphasized Nirvana as a form of heavenly salvation; Tantrism-emphasized the use of special gestures and symbols to call upon mystical powers; and White Lotus-emphasized the second coming of the Buddha and and to rebel against existing regimes.

These beliefs along with the Mahayana completely altered Buddha's original message. For Islam, it did not undergo such a dramatic change as Buddhism. For Islam, the religion divide into two sects: The Sunnites and the Shi'ites. The two factions retained the original teachings of Mohammed, but struggled over who should lead the Islamic nation, after the death of

Mohammed. Like Buddhism and Islam, Confucianism also underwent a change and appeared as Neo-Confucianism. With Neo-Confucianism, the nature of thinking and learning changed. The School of Reason and the School of Mind were the two current sects of New Confucian thinking.

The School of Mind emphasized instrospection and self-learning,while the School of reason emphasized education for all and investigation into all matters, but both were abstract and enjoyed a fleeting popularity. Thus the changes to Buddhism, Islam, and Confucianism were very different in the effects each had on the ideology. Another shared principle between Buddhism, Islam, and Confucianism, is the endorsement of the inequality of the sexes. Specifically, the low social status that the women procured in each society. In Buddhism, though women could join the monasteries, there was a secondary(if not menial) status of women.

As Buddha had written to one of his followers, Ananda: Women are soon angered, Ananda; women are full of passion, Ananda; women are envious, Ananda; women are stupid, Ananda. That is the reason, Ananda, that the cause, why women have no place in public assemblies, do not carry on a business, and do not earn their living by any profession. In Islamic society, women were no better off than their earlier Buddhist counterparts. Islamic culture encouraged the cloistering of women at home and prohibiting the social contacts with males outside the family. Also, the women were often required to dress in a custom, which would cover their entire body.

This is probably due more to custom than religion, because in the Koran men were admonished to treat women with respect and women were allowed to own property. They were, however, better off than their Buddhist and Confucian counterparts. Confucianism also did little to encourage the equality of men and women. Confucius did not belittle or denigrate the importance of the woman's role as a mother and a homemaker, but it is evident that in his hierarchal Five Relationships, that he acknowledged that women took a secondary status in society.

His Five Relationships are:

- Emperor to subjects Father to son
- Husband to wife
- Elder Brother to younger brother
- Elder Friend to younger friend.

From Confucius' Five Relationships, it is obvious that women had a role of little importance in the daily rituals of society. For Buddhism, Islam, and Confucianism, the shared ideology of the lowly stature of women is common to all three, though custom more than religious ideology affected the status of women in society. Buddhism, Islam, and Confucianism are legacies left by three very great and very different individuals. Each philosophy, though different, shared certain aspects between each other: Simplicity in beliefs and adherence as an ethical philosophy, the emphasis of the low status of women in each society, and the fact that each became modified, or vulgarized, to suit the needs of its followers. But their shared aspects are also what contrast each of them, in that each emphasized the different needs of man and his society.

5

Women in Pre-Modern Asia

Patriarchy was already well established before the dawn of the last millennium. But the outcry against it goes as far back as when it first arrived. It was only in the last century that feminism made it possible for women and men to conceive of equitable human relations between the sexes. Almost all women are feminist by social circumstance, insofar as they have to suffer the subjugation specific to being female. There is no single feminist understanding. Feminism ranges from the conservative to the radical, and can be informed by a variety of political philosophies.

In the "Asian" context, feminisms have coalesced to give birth to the "modern Asian woman". She is the girl or woman who is gainfully employed in non-agricultural jobs, even if she earns less than three quarters of the wages of men. The core distinction of this new woman lies in her formal education which enables her to hold "modern attitudes". The modern Asian woman exists in relation to the image of Asian women as victims - such as the "Chinese" woman with bound feet and the "Indian" widow who burns to death in her husband's funeral pyre. Such representations of the Asian women fuelled the wrath of reformers, like India's Manmohan Roy (1774-1833) and China's Kang Youwei (1859-1927).

Not surprisingly, the prototype of the "modern Asian woman" has its roots in the "modern girls' schools" set up between the early 1800s and 1900s all over Asia. Some wealthy families engaged private tutors, and even sent their daughters to the West to ensure their modernisation. These new women became symbols and active participants in nationalist movements. Indonesia's Radeng Ajeng Kartini (1879-1904) was one example. She was a strong champion of women's rights but, nevertheless, declined a scholarship to study in the Netherlands, and ¼6 became the fourth secondary wife of an elderly man. Ms Kartini's case clarifies that modernity in Asia may have liberated women, but it also subjected them to the demands of romanticised domesticity.

Thus, while liberal reformers welcomed the new woman, they were also ever watchful that she was never so overly modern that she lost her "culture" - femininity as defined by patriarchy. The "Asian" quality that the modern Asian woman was supposed to preserve was related to the idea of women as "natural" service providers, first in private, and then in public. Nowhere is this assumption clearer than in contemporary discourses which distinguish the "good" Asian and the "bad" Western modern woman. The good women could be role models, while the bad silenced. Formulations which emphasise women as wives and mothers, however, do have a long history in Asia.

For instance, the idea of service to father, husband and ruler in China is located in Liu Hsiang's Biographies Of Admirable Women, which re-emerged in the Han Dynasty when his The Mother of Mencius was treated as a classic of Confucian piety. Asian modernity has indeed been critical of the exploitation of women, and it has, indeed, made certain crucial gains for women. But even as it changed women's lives for the better, it did so within a patriarchal order. Today, a number of urban Asian women struggle with anorexia and bulimia. Global culture affords goods and services manufactured by women working in sweat shops, to benefit billion-dollar enterprises engaged in selling to modern women.

"Because you are worth it," says an advertisement for a brand of beauty products, re-defining the "modern" woman as narcissistic: She does what she does because she, and only she, wants it. Yet, the advertisement works only because the ideal of beauty it invokes is that produced by the male gaze. It is important to recognise that the modern Asian woman is inherently feminist. But it is important to recognise, too, that the consciousness of the modern Asian woman remains conservative because it is still subject to the workings of a misogynous culture and political economy. That the modern Asian woman continues to be oppressed is the problem not only of women, but also of patriarchy.

This recognition is mirrored in the United Nations' Convention on the Elimination of All Forms of Discrimination Against Women (Cedaw), which states "the full and complete development of a country, the welfare of the world and the cause of peace require the maximum participation of women on equal terms with men..." A thousand years ago, inequalities were believed to be divinely ordained, or given by nature. That Cedaw exists today signals that where women are concerned, they will only be equal if patriarchy is displaced. In 1949, when China became a communist country, Chairman Mao Zedong's famous slogan "Women hold up half the sky" became part of state ideology.

Finally women were being recognized for their contributions both to the communist victory and to society in general. They were now supposedly free from many outdated traditions and laws. But Chairman Mao forgot to mention that women, besides holding up their half of the sky also had to juggle education, marriage, absent husbands, child and parental care, work, political meetings and other duties. So even then, freedom for women came at a price. The situation remains difficult for women. China is the only country in the world where more women commit suicide than men.

Every year, 1.5 million women attempt to take their own lives and 150,000 (one woman every four minutes) actually succeed. Many seem to feel that there is no way out of an abusive marriage and often no one to turn to, no money and not enough education to find a job in order to be self-sufficient. But ask many Chinese women who are now in their 20s and

30s how their lives compare with that of their mothers, and they would likely tell you that they are much better off. The lucky ones work in air-conditioned offices or factories, even if in mostly secretarial, clerical and assembling positions, have more spending power, the ability to travel and run their own businesses without having to toil long hours in the fields as their mothers and grandmothers once did.

Some savvy city women now even sign prenuptial agreements and are permitted by law to sue their husbands for divorce, although getting a divorce is still difficult because most judges are men and they often side with the husband, who is allowed by law to keep the family home after a divorce. According to the Chinese government's 2000 census, people with university educations rose from 1.42 percent in 1990 to 3.61 percent. But there is no official figure on how many of these are females and what subjects they are studying. By contrast, in Hong Kong, more than 70 percent of college students are women.

China also has another problem a shortage of women. The "one-child" policy that came into force in 1975 and China's traditional preference for male children over females means men between the ages of 21 and 36 are finding it difficult to get married. The government census of 2000 showed that the country has 20 percent more boys than girls, aged 0 to 4 years. That is, four boys will be competing for the hand of one girl in the future. Some men might not be able to find a bride at all. Since China opened its market to outside investment, thousands of village girls have moved to coastal towns to work in factories.

Even though their wages are meager and living condition harsh they have become their family's sole breadwinners. The girls go home sporadically, perhaps once a year, before the start of the Spring Festival, or Chinese New Year. So what is the roadmap for Chinese women? More social, political and economic changes are needed - promoted and instigated by women. But real power still lies in the hands of men. China's ruling Politburo consists only of men. Women hold political jobs in the third and fourth tiers, but these are not decision-making positions. Unfortunately, this trend is still true in most Asian countries.

In Thailand, only 1 percent of women is in politics or holds a government post. In the entire world, only 3 percent of women are in public office. The same is largely true in Cambodia, China, Laos, South Korea, Singapore, and Vietnam. Even in a developed country such as Japan, women are not keen to become entrepreneurs, let alone government servants or politicians. They do, however, control the family's finances and husbands are given a weekly allowance. This is because, according to Asian tradition, women who step out of the box are often viewed as scandalous, immoral, outrageous and often evil.

A chaste woman does not flaunt herself in public, be controversial or have different views than those of her husband. Also, women do not tend to view active participation in politics as a means to better their lives. Another example of women's reluctance to be in the public eye is the otherwise modern island republic of Singapore, where very few are women represented in government. Ho Ching, executive director of Temasek, the powerful investment arm of the Singapore government, is one of the few exceptions. Forbes magazine in 2005 named her as "the second most influential woman in the world outside the United States". But then, she is married to this island state's Prime Minister, Lee Hsien Loong.

For years, the number of internationally known women in China was very few -Soong Ching Ling, the wife of Sun Yat Sen and her sister Madame Chiang Kai-shek Soong Mei Ling head ed a short list that also included the infamous Madame Mao, the gang of four leader Jian Qing. However, just this month the paper-recycling tycoon Zhang Yin was named as China's richest person - not woman - with a fortune estimated at US$3.37 billion. Ms. Zhang, 49, went from 36th to first by buying scrap paper in the United States and recycling it for use in China.

In Malaysia, only a handful of women have played political roles. One woman who has is Dr. Wan Azizah Ismail -who spoke out and campaigned against the politically inspired 1999 imprisonment of her husband, Deputy Prime Minister Anwar Ibrahim. Another is Puan Rafidah Aziz, who has been in the Malaysian cabinet for decades and is now Minister of Trade and Industry. The United Nations International Development Fund for Women (UNIFEM) noted in the year 2000 that women accounted for more than half of the work force in Asia, but their careers remain concentrated in social areas (14 percent), legal (9 percent), economics (4.1 percent), political affairs (3.4 percent) and executive (3.9 percent). Only 13 percent of women are in managerial and administrative posts, although experts recognize this as a significant increase in the past 20 years.

No statistics exist on how many Asian women are entrepreneurs and or run their own businesses. No statistics exist either on how many women from Thailand, the Philippines, Malaysia, Sri Lanka, India and Nepal are migrant domestic workers around the world, although collectively they remit billions of dollars a year to their families and their countries. In Hong Kong, it is the women of the "baby-boomer" years whom I believe have benefited the most from education, employment opportunities and healthcare. Women in here have made massive strides. In 2002, women comprised slightly more than half the Hong Kong population. More than half of university graduates are women. Women make up 43 percent of the labor force.

There are many reasons why so many Hong Kong women have achieved "boardroom success." For example, it could be because with the right education and or the right family connections many found better jobs, equal pay and financial independence. Many working mothers are able to employ full-time live-in maids to look after their children and help run their households Grandparents often play an active role in looking after or keeping an eye on the grandchildren. Also, many women have credited their spouses for being supportive, allowing them the opportunity to go out to work and to compete.

In spite of strong traditional views still held by many Asian societies, the advancement of women continues but these women are multi-tasking often logging very long working hours, bringing work home and even working on weekends and public holidays. After all, it is still a man's world with many men desperately holding onto traditional views of what a woman's role in society and the home should be. Also, many women continue to rank themselves third in importance, behind the husband and children. Women in Hong Kong still put in 63.3 hours a week of office work, (men 66.1 hrs), not including looking after the children, relatives and housework.

But success often comes at a price – young, educated Asian women are now finding it more difficult to get married or are marrying later and having fewer children. With better education come higher aspirations and many successful women refuse to marry down. Men, on the other hand, often are afraid of marrying a woman who is smarter, better educated, has more earning power, who talks back and most important of all, is not keen on motherhood. As a result, many educated women opt out of the marriage game, to stay single and live either with their parents or in their own apartment. An example is Singapore.

With a falling birthrate, the government has for years arranged "Love Boat" cruises for single, well-educated professional men and women to find love and marriage and produce more babies. But with all the freedom and choice – marriage to a person of their choice, able to go to college and find high paying jobs - come new worries - health, life after retirement and how to continue to play an active role in society. In Asian countries where there is still one-party rule or where conflict and civil unrest is rife, the lives of many women and children continue to be at risk. They lack shelter, food, proper health care and education.

And finally, Asia's most famous political prisoner is a woman -Myanmar's Aung San Suu Kyi, the country's pro-democracy leader. This Nobel Peace Prize winner (1999) has been living under house arrest off and on for more than 16 years. So, clearly, it is safe to say that the majority of women in Asia still have a long way to go.

"Asian women" is an ambiguous category; it seems to indicate a racial as well as a cultural designation. The number of articles or books on being Asian or Asian-American is on the rise in other disciplines, but in comparison to the material on black or Hispanic identities, Asians are largely missing from the field of philosophy of race. Things Asian in philosophy are generally reserved for those who study Asian philosophy or comparative philosophy, but that focus usually excludes reflections on Asian identities as such.

This lack in the literature prompted me to start my own reflection with such questions as: Why do Asians not take an active interest in discourse on race? What does the category "Asian" designate? What contributes to their invisibility in general? Is this a stereotype? Are they simply "white-identified?" Are Asians responsible for their own invisibility, or is there some other factor? What is the relation between Asian philosophy and being Asian, if any? Is there any interesting connection between being Asian and feminism? As a Japanese woman philosopher who is also interested in feminism, these questions seemed natural.

This chapter is an attempt to clarify some of these issues in the light of my experience working in the profession of academic philosophy. The first contributing factor to invisibility is thus the very category of "Asian" itself. However, beyond fragmentation, the term "Asian" does seem to indicate a set of certain cultural characteristics which is often stereotyped.

Asia covers a vast geographical area encompassing the following: In the north and the northeast, Mongolia, parts of Russia, Korea, Japan, China, and Taiwan; in the south and the southeast, the Philippines, Malaysia, Thailand, Indonesia, Vietnam, Cambodia, Laos, Singapore, and Myanmar (Burma); and the Indian subcontinent and the surrounding countries of Sri Lanka, Bangladesh, Nepal, Bhutan, Tibet, Pakistan and Afghanistan. It includes numerous languages, ethnic traditions, and religious practices, and national historiographies.

Some of these traditions share very little, others have been in direct conflict with one another for centuries. There are vast differences in the degree to which the regions are Westernized or modernized. Sometimes the intra-Asian differences are greater than the so-called East-West differences. Needless to say, there is little unity; the only thing which brings any of these cultural traditions together is the fact that they are located in certain parts of the Earth. If by "Asian" we mean individuals from any of these regions or nations, then the use of the term is perhaps not too controversial as a description.

However, that is usually not the sense in which the category is used or understood. "Asian" is supposed to be a racial, ethnic, or cultural category indicating in some vague sense "non-white." (The color of choice is yellow or brown, to which are added physical features involving short stature, slanted eyes, and straight, black hair.) Asian is also "non-Christian," which may mean innocuously Buddhist or Hindu. But often, Asian means "heathen," "barbaric," or "evil." Asian is also "non-Western," which is to say Eastern or Oriental (with the sense of distance, opacity, insignificance, or at best, exoticism).

The connotations of the category "Asian" are often used in combination, and they are often problematic, especially when used in conjunction with "women." When Asian-Americans are classified together with those who are from Asia (the first-generation Asians or Asian-Asians) under the category of "Asian," then the term is used predominantly to indicate a racial grouping. People are often classified in terms of racial appearance and grouped together by its perceived similarity. This is why, for instance, many people might assume that a first-generation white-Argentinean immigrant is more American at first sight than a third-generation Chinese-American, although the opposite is likely to be true.

There might be nothing in common between a 19-year-old third-generation Korean-American woman growing up in the suburbs of Los Angeles listening to hip-hop and a 60-year-old Malaysian woman who has lived in the U.S. for three months, but they are both Asian females. Many Asian-Americans speak only English, especially if they are third- or fourth- generations, and have little knowledge of Asia. They often learn about Asia in the same way other American children learn about it. Those who come from Asia, on the other hand, learn English as a second language; experience America as a foreign country (often with the expectation that it is the "best in the West") and struggle to make sense of it as immigrants, long-term residents, or visitors.

To this extent, "Asian" and "Asian-American" are indeed distinct categories, although often they are conflated because of the supposed racial unity implied by the term. The sense of Asian as "non-Christian" is perhaps outdated today, but it is a part of racist cultural experience of the United States. For instance, Chandra Mohanty notes that during the era of yellow peril, the "morality of Asian women" was used as a basis of exclusion under U. S. immigration policies. The ideology of yellow peril was of course used extensively during W.W.II, the Korean and Vietnam Wars, and in the 1970s U. S. relation to China before Nixon reestablished diplomatic relations.

The depiction of "sneaky, evil Orientals" in the early 1960s James Bond movies ("Dr. No") portray them as immoral technocrats out to destroy the world. Such a depiction preyed on xenophobia about "Godless" ones, and while it often targeted Communism, there was something especially menacing about the Asian version. Asian women today continue to be stereotyped as sex slaves, man-pleasers or playthings, who are passive and lacking moral character. For many American servicemen who served in the Pacific War, Korean War, or in Vietnam, their first or only exposure to women in Asia was in the context of prostitution near overseas bases.

These associations of Asian women with sexual pleasure as corrupt or morally dangerous are often made by those who have puritan sensibilities. The sense that Asia is definitely the uncivilized "other" is often rooted in the fact that except for the Philippines and to some extent Korea, the dominant cultures in Asia are not Judaeo-Christian. That is a cause of suspicion in cultures which conflate moral sensibilities with religious beliefs. When the term "Asian" is used in conjunction with a broader historical, cultural, or intellectual category, as in Asian philosophy, Asian religion, Asian art or Asian food, then often "Asian" is supposed to indicate one of the "non-

Western" elements on the multicultural map; in this sense the connotation usually excludes "Asian-American."

At first sight this use of the term may appear rather neutral as in the case of designating a geographical region, but it raises a threefold problem. First, when the term is combined with a further classification such as philosophy, religion, art, or food, then there are as many philosophies, religions, arts, and kinds of food as there are varied traditions and practices all over Asia, even within a seemingly unified region such as Japan. One really would have to specify a particular kind of philosophy, food, etc., and the general designation of "Asian" becomes rather empty.

Second, be it literature, food or religion, the broad category of "Asian," when displayed alongside other ethnic categories such as "African," "Hispanic," or "Native American," it gives people the false sense that they have understood something about Asia, when in fact no such category is adequate. This is a version of the trap which Stanley Fish calls "boutique multiculturalism." Diversity is for the consumption of those who feel they should be knowledgeable about "other cultures" - though superficially - much as they enjoy ethnic restaurants. Third, and most seriously, the notion of "non-Western" is often not neutral but heavily normative in a way that favors being Western as the measure of legitimacy. So, if "Asian" is supposed to mean "non- Western," then it is not an innocent designation.

This is the problem of Eurocentrism, and it is this use of the term which becomes problematic in the understanding of Asian philosophy. In sum, upon examination, the category of "Asian" is often either racist or it simply falls apart, much like other essentializing categories such as "woman," "Hispanic," or "poor people." "Asian" does not cover a politically unified racial platform, culture, linguistic group, class, or tradition. Most immigrants from Asia tend to identify themselves with particular national identities ("I am Taiwanese") or ethnic groups (Hmongs or Sherpas).

Many Asian-Americans tend to identify themselves with a specific ethnic background to the exclusion of others ("I am

Chinese-American, not Japanese!"). Moreover, intra-Asia conflicts, such as between Korea and Japan, Tibet and China, or Indonesia and East Timor, are often so hostile that the idea of being put together in one group may be passionately resisted. This fragmentation results in the invisibility of the category of "Asian," especially among the immigrants. In fact, "Asian" is often not a category at all in the discourse on race, which is most visibly demarcated in terms of black/white.

Yet, the term has practical or political applications, such as establishing academic departments (Asian Studies) and forming a group for strategic purposes such as economic empowerment (pan-Asian organizations) or fighting against racism. Moreover, most people, including people from Asia as well as Asian-Americans, do have a sense that the term has some vaguely unified cultural meaning. But beyond vague generalizations, is there any recognizable content? And if so, how does it operate in our social consciousness?

CULTURAL ELEMENTS

The stereotype of Asians (in whichever sense one may take it) includes the idea that they are docile, withdrawn, and happily resigned to the status quo, never challenging or demanding anything. As a result, although racism against people of Asian descent is an unending reality, politically they are often either ignored, unrecognized, or worse, praised as the well-assimilating model minority. The so-called positive stereotyping of Asians exacerbates the problem; they are studious, smart, cooperative, hard-working, and therefore do not require protection.

Many of them are middle-class, have access to education (sometimes better than that of whites) and are in other respects privileged. They are perceived to be doing just fine without receiving special attention, just like all the other middle-class Americans. If they are assimilated, they are invisible as a group in the dominant culture as well as to the oppositional, racial minority cultures. There are other cultural factors which contribute to invisibility. Some of these are psychological (or "internal") and these are especially pertinent to women.

Others are sociological (or "external"). In addition to the complexity of being Asian, the category of "woman" or "women" has its own history of contested meanings. Need not review here the history of feminist thought, but there is one relevant way in which the category of "Asian women" is stereotyped, which is related to the connotation and use of the term "Asian" in general and contributes especially to the invisibility of Asian women. Let me focus on the Confucian tradition to illustrate how it has helped form the Asian stereotype, especially with respect to women.

This is the dominant cultural tradition in countries such as Korea, Japan, Taiwan, Singapore, and among Chinese immigrants who often become the dominant class in other parts of Asia and elsewhere. For both men and women, the ideals of Confucian virtue include obeying authority, yielding to others, always making sure the others' needs are met first, never calling attention to yourself, one should always know one's place, and "he who speaks out destroys the harmony." In addition to these general human virtues of jen, or "humanity," Confucianism designates gendered virtues (such as a wife's duty to her husband, a son's duty to his parents) in explicitly patriarchal ways.

These ideals are very much a part of the culture in these countries, in the same sense that Christianity or individualism is a part of the culture in the U. S., permeating through gender, class and race. For the sake of brevity and for my purposes, let me use the term "Asian" in the remainder of this section as designating "those whose living culture is based on the Confucian tradition." The images of obedience, respect, and orderliness, when combined with women's position in the tradition, contribute to the stereotype of Asian women as docile, obedient, quiet, intuitive, or timid.

Asian female stereotype is either characters exhibiting passivity or the sexualized, exotic image (there is no middle ground). In other words, the designations of the traditional notions of femininity and Asianness more or less coincide; an outspoken, aggressive, independent Asian woman (or a man) is often seen as an unwelcome exception, so "un-Asian," even a threat or embarrassment, among many women themselves in Confucian Asia. For instance, for many women in Japan even today, maintaining Confucian virtues of "self-effacement," harmony with others and enjoying the presence of silence and quietude" is an ethical as well as aesthetic way of life, often regarded even as an ideal in the sense used in virtue ethics.

Throughout the educational system children are taught that calling attention to oneself is a form of self-indulgence. It may be false consciousness (as I often try to point out), but the ideology nevertheless functions as a strong psychological component internally enforced by the women themselves. In a culture where "repose" and "respect for others" amount to the same thing, the last thing they would want would be visibility, especially if it were perceived to come from their own agency; that is "too undignified" (as my aunt might point out). Note also that in a cultural setting where the majority of the people speak softly and pay much attention to others to begin with, one does not need to raise one's voice or act in such a way as to call attention to oneself. One is already visible enough.

The conflation of femininity and Asianness applies even for males in that "Asian male" remains a feminized category; even if they are "martial arts experts" (another stereotype) their nimbleness and skillfulness make them much more feminine than, say, an American football player, who is archtypically masculine. This is not to mention another stereotype of "those Asian engineer nerds" who will be good workers because they will yield and obey orders. So the problem of the feminization of the non-Western, so-called colonized peoples raised in the feminist literature applies especially to the category of "Asian."

It is not only a reality in the practical senses but also an explicit ideology of choice among those in the Confucian tradition themselves; not to have an independent or critical voice is not just a female virtue, but a virtue of cultivated personhood. In this context, it becomes almost impossible for a woman to speak up without feeling extremely awkward about her sense of place and her own self-worth as a person of integrity and cultivation.

An Asian woman is in this way doubly submissive in Western contexts, first as a woman, and second as an Asian. Yet, the very category of "submissiveness," if it is meant to have a negative connotation, escapes her own consciousness; she is simply being her mature self.

Sociologically the invested drive to fit in and "be a part of the whole" is often closely associated with the phenomenon of Asian assimilation among immigrants from Asia into the dominant white middle-class American culture (especially into the value system of puritan work ethic). The first thing many of the immigrant parents do is force their children to learn English, then to excel in school, and get a profession. This almost non-negotiable drive for upward mobility requires diligent assimilation.

Self-pity, victim consciousness, and separationist self-consciousness are deadly to the process toward success. Not only are they excessively self-indulgent, but they are also a waste of time and energy, and therefore not allowed. As a result, many children of immigrant parents from Confucian Asia explicitly reject their own identity as Asian or Asian-American, or member of a "minority culture," contributing further to the invisibility problem. In their view in fact, invisibility is not a problem at all; if anything, it is a sign of success. Being white-identified is not a bad idea, if it leads to a more prosperous lifestyle. It is not unusual to see such assimilated Asians developing racism against blacks and Hispanics, adopting exactly the racism prevalent in white middle-class culture.

The irony of course is that they are often targets of such racism themselves, yet they continue to think of themselves as being lucky that they are still "more white" than the other groups. They come to believe that what they have to do is to further separate themselves from other minority groups, as if they could be tainted by association with darker color. Here the invisibility problem takes a pernicious turn-the dominant discourse of racism has won all the way, obliterating the last remnants of resistance through assimilation.

LOCALIZING THE ASIAN: MODERNITY, EUROCENTRISM, AND ORIENTALISM

Turn now to the issue of "Asia" in a broader historical context in order to examine the third contributing factor to invisibility. The assimilationist ideology of white-identification among Asians has another important source, and that is the problem of colonialism. In the 19th-Century European consciousness, it was taken for granted that the West represented the "universal."

For instance, European philosophers have always raised the question of truth about the human mind. As exemplified by Hegel, history was a linear temporal progress, from the premodern past to the modern present, culminating in the techno-scientific culture of Europe and America. Since both systematic philosophy and science developed primarily in Europe, the notions of "truth," "universality," "modernity," and "being Western" came to be conflated in the minds of intellectuals.

In this framework, thought that was "non-Western"- a geopolitical designation - was either simply "false" or conceptualized as "backw ards" in the temporal progression. The assumption was that once "primitive" cultures developed, they would begin to manifest the European forms of culture and consciousness. The place of legitimate culture was Europe; though "exotic," Asia, Africa, South America, and anywhere else untouched by European modernity were culturally marginal and insignificant. It is worth noting, however, that this form of Eurocentrism was not so prevalent before the period of European expansion.

Even in philosophy, Leibniz, for instance, studied Chinese thought and valued it highly. The influence of Hinduism on Schopenhauer is also well documented. The extent and type of the actual European colonization in Asia varied, but the idea that Europe was the center of modern civilization became a kind of pervasive cultural understanding in most of the Asian countries since the late 1800's. These cultures were colonized to the extent that the legitimate point of cultural reference was taken to be European civilization. In Japan, for instance, the terms "Westernization" and "modernization" were often used synonymously; for the past 100 years, viewing the world in terms of "West vs.

East," which amounts to "modern vs. traditional," became a cultural paradigm, affecting everything from politics, educational reform, fashion, and the idea of what should be valued. In this dualistic paradigm, the West represented what is new, advanced, and forward-looking; the traditional, on the other hand, was old, backward, primitive. Since the Europeans and Americans who came to Japan around the turn of the century were Caucasians, the perception of "white people" was associated with "modern civilization."

To be modern, then, would be to act and "be" like white people: sit on a chair rather than a mat on the floor; use silver instead of chopsticks; wear blouses and skirts rather than kimonos; eat bread and meat instead of rice and fish; don't get too much tan or else your skin will become dark. Although today the culture in Japan is a hybrid of Japanese, American, European, and other Asian influences, the "West vs. East" paradigm in which the "white West" symbolizes advancement is far from forgotten. In this context, even within the consciousness of those in Asia, "Asia" became the "other" of Europe.

This is the problem of self-alienation and internal oppression in colonized consciousness, but with respect to Asia, in particular, it is a part of the problem of "Orientalism." Since its publication in 1978, Edward Said's Orientalism profoundly changed the way in which the issues related to East and West are discussed. Said's main thesis is that the very category of the "Orient," a sweeping category applied to all Asiatic cultures, was a European invention produced in order to "contain difference" in the era of colonial expansion.

Either by way of rejection or exoticism, the category of the "Orient" served as a representational tool for Europeans to bring the "unknown" under control; it was by definition an aspect of European imperialism. The category of "Asia" or the "Far East" (east of Europe, of course) was a part of this Orientalist discourse; the region was "so different," mysteriously far, opaque and insubstantial. When such representations are adopted by those who are in the "Orient," they produce a self-alienated, colonized consciousness. In India in the early part of this century, many Indians themselves came to believe that it was "for their own good" that the British ruled them, since modernity, the culture of the British, would ultimately liberate them from the premodern past.

Many Indians came to see their own culture as obscure and backwards, and the "new" and European lifestyle and values as better and more cosmopolitan. In reality, of course, despite its "good intentions" of modernizing India, the colonial administration systematically advanced a particular imperialist agenda. The real power of colonization is the ability to achieve this willing participation by transforming the colonized subjects' own point of reference from the native culture to the Western one.

The point of a "postcolonial critique," as well as Said's idea of a solution, is to abandon the very categories of "Orient" and "Occident" altogether and to expose the inherent forms of domination and subjugation. The ultimate irony is that the methodology of critique as well as the theories themselves is basically European in origin. The very idea of "theoretical empowerment" for fighting oppression, which privileges knowledge, is often alien to the real victims of this whole process-women and ethnic minorities in these Asian countries who have virtually no access to education nor political power to begin with.

Those who can speak on their behalf are speaking, but the experience ultimately remains alienated and the promise of a good life seems unreal. In East Asia, moreover, the historical situation was complicated by the fact that the history of colonialism did not neatly fit into the "Europe vs. Asia" paradigm because Japan was itself a colonial power over Korea, China, the Philippines and parts of Indonesia. The "colonized women" in Korea, for example, endured a three-fold oppression-Japanese imperialism, the West, and their own patriarchal system.

This history contributes to today's fragmentation of the category of "Asians," as mentioned above. However, despite such complexity, to most of the European as well as American intellectuals Asia still remains one localized "other" in the Far East or "on the other side of the Pacific." Despite the fact that in American academia the critique of Eurocentrism is by now a near-standard procedure and dominant discourse in some departments, Eurocentrism, or in the case of philosophy, Anglo-centrism, does remain a persistent reality, both in the U. S. and elsewhere in the West as well as the non-West.

As Dipesh Chakrabarty laments, "That Europe works as a silent referent in historical knowledge itself becomes obvious in a highly ordinary way...Third-world historians feel a need to refer to works in European history; historians of Europe do not feel any need to reciprocate." Needless to say, in philosophy the case is similar, if not worse. The study of philosophy often excludes anything outside of Western philosophy, and this is true even if one studies philosophy in Asia.

In Japan, the academic discipline of philosophy (tetsugaku) generally does not include Japanese philosophy nor any other Asian thought; "philosophy" means, as a subject, the study of thought from the pre-Socratics, the Greeks, medieval thought, the modern period, the Enlightenment, 18th- and 19th-Century European thought, then contemporary European philosophy including postmodernism, and analytic or Anglo- American philosophy.

In other words, in Japan the conception of philosophy is thoroughly Eurocentric; what is called "Asian philosophy" in the West is studied in Japan under Eastern thought (toyo shiso), often a separate discipline altogether. Thus, the problem of invisibility with respect to Asian thought is aggravated not only by the Eurocentrism and Orientalism of most of the European and the majority of American intellectuals, but also by Asians themselves. In addition to the already-existing Confucian ideology of "fitting in" and "not making a case for oneself" - a particularly feminine mode of having a self - the Asian colonized consciousness which adopted Eurocentrism/

Orientalism as its own culture, compounds the problem further by identifying the point of legitimacy outside itself, thereby making itself even more invisible and acknowledging that invisibility is the way it ought to be.

In sum, Asians are invisible as a category because of the following reasons. First, upon close examination the category itself tends toward fragmentation rather than coherence. Second, the Confucian cultural influence, especially for women, promotes invisibility, as it is idealized as an ethical or aesthetic end.

Third, Eurocentrism and Orientalism contribute not only to the European or American ignorance toward Asia, but also to produce the self-alienated colonized consciousness among Asians, which shifts the reference point of self-understanding to that of European consciousness. This self- alienation and assimilation render the "Asian self-consciousness" invisible even to Asians themselves. I would like to turn now to some of the specific problems in philosophy as an academic discipline in the light of these contributing factors to invisibility.

CLAIMS OF PHILOSOPHY

The discipline of philosophy can itself be an object of critical analysis. What are its boundaries, and how should that understanding be reflected in the curriculum? Apart from politics and turf wars, there seems to me to be a variety of conceptions about. what philosophers regard as the proper topic and method of philosophy as a discipline. From broader to narrower conceptions, here are some of the ways in which "philosophy" seems to have been defined by academic philosophers: Philosophy as defined by the type of questions it asks which define the subdiscipline within philosophy.

Examples are: "What is a good life?" "What is reality?" "What is knowledge?" "What is the 'self?" These are all philosophical questions to the extent that they are considered legitimate questions about basic human reality and beyond. This broad conception often includes the notion of philosophy as reflection, contemplation, and analysis about the human condition. Sometimes material from literature or other disciplines are used to articulate a point of view. Often introductory philosophy textbooks are organized around such questions and it is not unusual today to see some inclusions of writings from other disciplines.

Philosophy as a rational system of thought, as opposed to mythic storytelling or in contrast to other endeavors in the humanities or social sciences. Apart from literature, religion, psychology, sociology, anthropology, etc., philosophy in this sense takes a meta- position with respect to the production of knowledge itself and concerns itself with theory-building about the fundamental questions such as reality, justice, and personhood.

Philosophy as the History of Western Philosophy

This is the conception mentioned above-the study of thought from pre-Socratics to contemporary European or Anglo-American thought. By definition, anything outside of this tradition is not philosophy proper.

Philosophy as a Critical Method of Argumentation

In this conception philosophy is strictly about constructing sound arguments and effective counter-arguments. The methodology adopts a "scientific method" of weeding out the propositions which are falsified. This is often a presupposition in analytic philosophy. In this view contemporary European philosophy is "not philosophy" because "it doesn't have arguments" or contains propositions which can be neither true nor false. By the same token, any form of thought, if it does not have arguments of the kind studied by these philosophers, is not philosophy proper.

At its narrowest conception, this approach may exclude not only contemporary European philosophy but also philosophies of any other tradition, ancient and medieval philosophy, feminism, environmental ethics, and many others which do not belong to the parameters of contemporary Anglo-American philosophy. Often, Asian philosophy or comparative philosophy is included in the discipline under 1, the broadest conception. Many of the multicultural philosophy textbooks include not only Asian thought but also the philosophies of other traditions. Certainly, all of these philosophical questions have been asked and analyzed in detail in Asia over the past 2500 years, if not longer, and various systems or coherent schemes have been produced.

Conception could certainly include some Indian philosophical systems, Buddhist metaphysics, or aspects of Japanese philosophy (e.g., Nishida's theory of "place"), but perhaps not others, such as Taoist thought. Conception 3 excludes Asian philosophy because it is outside the Western tradition. Conception 4 again should accept some forms of Indian metaphysics or Buddhist dialectic, such as the Middle Way of the Madhyamika school which is highly technical in its logicism, but in common practice the particular conception of argumentation in question (and therefore the notion of philosophy) often must be based on the "scientific method" of the Anglo-American analytic tradition, so anything outside this tradition is excluded.

If one's field of specialization includes Asian philosophy, one is always nervous because she or he must be prepared to explain why anything Asian should be considered philosophy at all, sometimes to a rather unsympathetic audience which subscribes to conceptions 3, 4 or even 2. This kind of experience is also all too familiar with anyone specializing in feminist thought in philosophy. But in fact even those who narrowly conceive of philosophy as 2, 3, and 4 all agree that conception 1 is indeed a legitimate way to understand philosophy as a discipline. So yes, on the one hand, Asian philosophy belongs to philosophy to the extent that proper questions are being asked, but no, on the other hand, it's not really philosophy because the questions are not being analyzed or answered in the proper way.

Often the inquisitor is unaware of the fact that he or she has switched meanings. But if one grants conception 1 as the legitimate subject-matter of philosophy, as most people in the field of philosophy indeed do, then endorsing 2, 3, and 4, while at the same time excluding Asian philosophy, requires a further justification. This is where the sticky questions of legitimacy, prejudice, exclusion, and power claims enter in. One such prejudice is indeed Eurocentrism and the associated problems discussed above. For those who hold conception 3, it is a matter of definition that there is no such thing as a "non-Western philosophy." But if so, they must be claiming either those other traditions do not ask questions such as "what is a good life" or "what is reality," or that only the Western versions of those questions and answers are legitimate.

The former proposition is empirically false; the latter position is ethnocentric (in this case Eurocentric, but in essence no different from other cultures claiming that theirs is the measure of truth). Why should the philosophical answers arising out of a particular geopolitical history claim monopoly on the world's philosophical insights? Or on any group, including one's own, for that matter? However, the source of Eurocentrism is deeper; it is not that Europe as such is privileged (ethnocentrism), but rather that this privilege is justified-that this intellectual history contains in itself something which is universal and true, by which other traditions may be judged. This is what drives conceptions 2 and 4.

The measure of truth is scientific thinking broadly conceived; it is an Enlightenment, "modern" methodology which employs critical thinking, verification and accurate abstraction, as opposed to simply relying on beliefs or authority, a "pre-modern" ways of thinking. It may be that European thought is just as contingently related to the "universal" as non-European thought, but it was nevertheless in Europe that science first flourished and technology was first developed on a large scale.

This is why, so it is believed, Europe enjoys the culture of modernity which is defined by the triumph of rationalism over mythic or religious beliefs, and universalistic thinking over local knowledge. So properly speaking, this form of Eurocentrism is a kind of "scientism" or "modernism," and not only is this method used to critique non-European forms of thought, but even within Europe it is used in order to critique its own "dark ages," for instance.

Subscribing to the belief that scientific modernism has merits is in itself not Eurocentric, nor is it automatically scientistic. The belief that Europeans are superior because they developed this culture is Eurocentrism, and the claim that anything that does not fit the criteria of scientific method is not knowledge or false knowledge, is scientism. Asian philosophy is often excluded on both accounts, either because it is already deemed inferior or too foreign, i.e., not made by Europeans, or because it is prejudged to lack the right criteria of knowledge.

Exclusion based on Eurocentrism is prejudice, a version of Orientalism. The scientism objection is trickier (apart from the bigger question of whether the very method of science is ethnocentric, universally justified, or objective). Even if one grants its framework, and the formal features of science or methods of critical thinking can be abstracted from European intellectual history, scientific thinking can still be employed to understand ideas from other cultures, or by people in such cultures themselves.

If it is universal, then by definition it is not a property of Europe and there is no justification for exclusion prior to a scientific investigation of non-Western thought. So exclusion without serious investigation is also prejudice; as noted, there are systems in Asian thought which fit the description of "scientific" if one is patient enough to go through different modes of presentation (as in Indian or Buddhist metaphysical texts). The critique of scientism itself is a separate discussion developed in postmodern literature and science studies.

INCLUDING ASIAN WOMEN

Finally, there is a more subtle form of exclusion which actually appears within the language of multicultural inclusion, often addressed as the problem of tokenizing and ghettoizing. This is where the stereotyping of Asian women becomes a practical issue. I grant that the language of multicultural inclusion is a big step in the right direction, but it still has a long way to go. Often, scholars from India or China are proud of their own long tradition and philosophy and believe that they can make some contribution to philosophy in the West.

However, much to their disappointment, they discover that their "inclusion" is not in itself a sign of engagement from outside their own group. They are ghettoized, with no apparent connection to the rest of the academic community. Often the only way the engagement might occur is if they conform to the methods of Western philosophy, using European or Anglo philosophy as a framework to explain their own ideas, thereby enforcing the Eurocentrism that discredits them in the first place.

Women and minorities are "included" for the sake of diversity, but anyone who is a woman or a minority philosopher knows very well the experience that her ideas may not actually be taken all that seriously or that her merit appears already to be in question. Because of the racial sense in which the term "Asian" is used, if one is from Asia or is an Asian-American, almost without exception one is expected to know something about Asian thought and is thereby given some authority. An Asian woman may feel especially that she should indeed study Asian philosophy, so as to be able to offer some kind of a "bridge to the mainstream."

Or she may expect that her outsider status is only natural, that it is "her place" to be doing some "non-mainstream" philosophy, due to her colonized consciousness and her self-understanding that she should not be presumptuous. Yet at the same time she may feel disqualified because the whole field is marginalized. This is a case of triple-marginalization-being Asian, woman, and teaching or doing research in a field which remains invisible. Asians are in this way often tokenized to do Asian philosophy in the same way women are somehow expected to include feminism as one of their areas of competence, only to find themselves located outside the "mainstream."

An Asian woman may face a further obstacle. The particularly feminized characteristics of being an Asian woman may pose a problem within the feminist discourse itself, especially in the United States where the standard of respectability is strongly tied to the notions of autonomy and independence. Apart perhaps from feminist ethics, traditional feminist consciousness has focused predominantly on the notions of oppression, subversion, and revolutionary change. Across the variety, the notion of oppositional agency (to patriarchy, capitalism, male-domination, injustice, disempowerment) is an essential component of the feminist movement.

This confrontational model is indeed quite alien to many of the women in Asia, especially among the strongly Confucian countries. An immigrant woman from Taiwan may feel that her cultural self is not only unappreciated, but even cast in a negative light as a victim of false consciousness (and therefore patronized as being "in need of help"). Worse, she may be labeled "anti-feminist" to the extent that she may be perceived as actually willingly seeking the passive, dominated status. She may thus come to feel condemned and ashamed in the eyes of "liberated women," that her own "backward" culture "denigrates women."

She may struggle to be more liberated, more American by forcing herself to be more aggressive, only to worsen the experience of self-alienation in the process of assimilation. Yet, an Asian woman also may be well aware of the fact that Confucian patriarchy has done much damage to the women in this culture and wishes for a change. This is a catch-22, a doubly-alienated self-consciousness. Further problems may include the fact that calling attention to his or her "Asianness" may be the last thing a particular person from Asia might want - a student from Asia may be seriously interested in studying Aristotle.

Or, the personal experience of being Asian may be quite alien to an assimilated fourth-generation Chinese-American person. The contradiction again is that, whether first- or fourth-generation, one is often expected to express Asian ideas, but only through "legitimate" Anglo-American or European means and with the result of finding oneself thereby further alienated. In addition, despite formal inclusion, the whole attempt at inclusion may have little to do with genuine interest; it may be for the sake of endorsing the political ideology of multiculturalism, which may be a very localized agenda of particular departments or individuals.

Because the discourses of race and diversity are distinctly American, most scholars from abroad - even Europe - find "foreign" the very idea of politicizing academic discourse in that way. This is why many of the scholars from Asia either specialize in Confucianism, Indian philosophy, or comparative philosophy, with little political interest on race, or else they forgo any scholarship on culture or politics altogether and specialize narrowly in logic, epistemology, or metaphysics. If the former, then ghettoization is a problem.

If the latter, then they are perceived to be assimilated and therefore invisible qua Asian. Granted that often the "privileged access" to the consciousness of women, minorities, immigrants, etc., is actually appreciated and the interest in this access is genuine, but one should be vigilant about the latent exclusionary move - the stamp of "otherness" which makes Asians, especially Asian women, invisible within the inclusive language itself.

If philosophy as practice has a role to play in this issue, it should, at a minimum, critique its own assumptions and methodology and eliminate claims which are unfounded - - such as automatic prejudice against any non-Western thought - so that a critical investigation and reflection on these issues can move forward and a path for real engagement and understanding can be articulated. What I had hoped to accomplish in this chapter was to provide one perspective on being an Asian woman in philosophy. In sum, the difficulties she may face are several.

First, given the culture in which the norms of behavior does not particularly encourage visibility, oppositional agency, and subversive action, an Asian woman may miss the very vehicle which may be necessary for exposing injustice and creating change. Yet at the same time, even if she were to become conscious of the need for visibility and agency, the transformation of her own consciousness to such a stance may produce self-alienation. Second, if she were to become "visible," because of her perceived Asianness, she must then face the further problem of Eurocentrism or Orientalism and the associated prejudice.

Third, there is a doubling, tripling, or even quadrupling of the cultural negotiation problems in that not only an Asian woman faced with the problem of being a woman, but also the problem that the Asians are feminized to begin with. In addition, she may further face the problem of feeling internally compelled to take up the already-marginalized field of Asian philosophy (or feminism, or whatever else she may perceive as "more appropriate" in terms of the idea of service to the discipline) and she may face problems even within feminism due to the often negative connotation given to the "feminized."

Including Asian women, then, involves a multi-layered task: one is called to be self-critical of one's possible prejudices against Asians, women, non-European or American thought, and ways of being a woman other than those set by Euro-American standards. In conclusion, let me say that I would, however, resist the categorization of philosophy as such as by definition Eurocentric and "white-male." Although these crude mind-sets do exist rather commonly and should be resisted, philosophy's critical method should not be abandoned because it is what makes critique possible in the first place.

Resistance and vigilance should always be there to expose illegitimate grounds for dominance and marginalization, regardless of where it occurs. Claims to legitimacy must always involve a self-critique of its own foundation, and our inquiry must be guided by a genuine spirit of understanding. Many economists and economic historians assume that there is a positive relationship between economic growth on the one hand and well functioning markets for labour, land and capital on the other. They also assume that these factor markets need the backing of an institutional framework vested in the state.

Evidently, Western Europe is an area for which these links have been and are being demonstrated, going back as far as the Pre-Modern Period, but there is mounting evidence that these relationships can also be demonstrated for Japan, for (parts of) China prior to 1800 and possibly for (parts of) India before 1750. The 'discovery' of such links for Asian countries appears to coincide with their high rates of economic growth during recent (China) or fairly recent (Japan) decades.

This might one lead to expect that Southeast Asia, with very satisfactory growth rates during the decade or so preceding the 1997 financial crisis, is now on the brink of being discovered as another example of the above-mentioned links in more remote periods. Those who started reading this chapter with that expectation in mind will have to be disappointed however, although I have to admit that there are recent studies that suggest that economic developments in Southeast Asia came much closer to the Western European pattern than is usually believed.

This is quite a departure from the traditional point of view that Southeast Asia, prior to the colonial experience, was mired in some kind of eternal Middle-Ages. In much of the literature published before the 1980s, the countries of Southeast Asia were regarded as 'hermit states', as they were supposed to have done their utmost to keep outside influences at bay. New research shows convincingly that population growth and international trade led to many changes in the region between, say, 500 and 1850. This is a correction that was long overdue Nevertheless, we should not go overboard on this.

Although statistics for many areas of Southeast Asia are absent or dubious for everything prior to c. 1950, I have collected a number of data that may be assumed to reflect the area's level of development and that can be used in a comparison with other Eurasian countries. Productivity of labour expressed in millions of (net direct) calories per adult male agricultural labourer around 1800, Java and selected European countries.

Java, therefore, was doing as well as Portugal in terms of labour productivity, and came fairly close to Finland. These were the most economically backward European countries for which such data can be produced. In comparison to the United Kingdom, the most advanced European country at the time, Java's labour productivity was evidently very low.

Therefore, assuming that the labour productivity of Java was not lower than that of most other Southeast Asian areas, Southeast Asia cannot claim to have been at par with the more developed European areas. Looking at both indicators - productivity of land and labour - the conclusion appears to be inescapable that during the nineteenth and early twentieth century Southeast Asia was not at the same level of economic development as were the most advanced areas in Eurasia. This is in keeping with the more anecdotal evidence we have on features such as the level of technology, the scale of enterprise, and the fact that the non-agrarian sectors of the Southeast Asian economy were relatively small and unsophisticated.

Moreover, compared to Western Europe, Northern India, Southeastern China and Japan, Southeast Asia was relatively sparsely populated, and it seems to be an almost universal rule that in Pre-Modern societies the highest rates of economic growth were to be found in densely populated regions. All this implies that we cannot expect high rates of economic growth in Pre-Modern and Early-Modern Southeast Asia. If the assumption is to be confirmed that there is a link between levels of economic development and the functioning of factor markets, we should find labour, land and capital markets in Southeast Asia that were not functioning as well as they did in the more highly developed parts of Eurasia. This assumption will now be tested.

LABOUR

As many people associate slavery with Africa and America, it may come as a surprise to many that slavery, or rather bonded labour, used to be quite important in parts of Asia as well. It may also come as a surprise that slavery - in contrast to America, but not to Africa, where slavery was, and sometimes still is, indigenous - was not introduced there by Europeans. My impression (as a layman in the field of South and East Asian history) is that it was much more important, say, around 1500 in Southeast Asia than it was in either South or East Asia.

Bonded labour, which includes serfdom, debt peonage, and people with heavy corvée (statute labour) obligations, was widespread in Southeast Asia during the Pre-Modern Period (and therefore prior to European influence), probably particularly in the core areas of the early states. Although it is usually assumed that there is a negative link between population density and slavery, with bonded labour to be found particularly in societies where people were scarce and land abundant, within such societies bonded labour appears to be connected to those core areas where a monarch rules over a sedentary peasant population, with a moderate population density.

The sparsely populated marginal upland areas, where the state's authority is absent or weak, home to 'acephalous', 'tribal' groups of foragers and swidden agriculturalists, do not appear to be important slaveholding regions, though our information on these areas is not as good as it should be. At any rate, although it should not be assumed that there were no slaves among tribal groups (there were, at least in the nineteenth and twentieth centuries), their territories do not appear to be the main slaveholding regions in Pre-Modern and Early-Modern times.

However, the tribal areas were important as sources of bonded labour for the core states, perhaps increasingly so as time went by. Wars with or raids into the marginal areas produced prisoners of war who were often settled as bonded labour in a core states. Such states became stronger after 1500 through trade with China, India, and European powers, which not only enriched the core areas - and particularly the monarchs who monopolised most of the trade - more than it did the peripheries, but also provided the rulers with modern European firearms, sometimes including European mercenaries as instructors.

This is not the time and the place for a debate about the many gradations of servility in these societies, but the question is valid whether every person with labour obligations towards the ruler should be regarded as bonded. If, as was often the case, these obligations amounted to six month per year, the answer clearly should be positive. But what about those with a corvée obligation of only one month per year? After all, most of us pay taxes of more than 12% per year, and nevertheless we do not regard ourselves as bonded. On the other hand, the government tells us, taxpayers, only how much we have to pay, and not how to earn the money we owe them. As long as such obligations were not commuted to monetary payments, one could arguably regard it as bonded labour.

However, if that is bonded labour, there were many Southeast Asian regions were not much labour was not-bonded. If, for instance, we would regard everyone with corvée obligations in eighteenth-century Thailand as bonded, there would be hardly any free people left. Be that as it may, there were sufficient people left with a genuinely bonded status to enable us to say that bonded labour was quite important in Pre and Early-Modern Southeast Asia. Looking into the causes of bonded labour, mention should be made in the first place of a basic ordering of society in countries such as Burma and Thailand during the Pre-Modern and Early-Modern Periods.

Here we encounter a basic division of commoners (usually peasants) into those groups (often entire villages) who owe corvée labour to the monarch, and those who don't. Most other villagers were either paying taxes or owed labour obligations to the nobility or the clergy. Labour obligations to the crown were often quite heavy, but they could also be regarded as an honour, such as having a high rank in the military or serving in some other non-menial capacity at court. As we have seen, being a war-captive or a victim of a raid was one way of becoming a true slave or serf.

As their status was usually hereditary, their offspring were slaves as well. Bondage could be punishment meted out by the ruler or a magistrate, or it could be the result of a fine that had been commuted owing to an inability to pay. An important category of true slaves and serfs, particularly during the Pre-Modern Period, were bondsmen and women of religious institutions, often called glebe slaves in the literature. Laymen, including the king, donated large amount of land to

Hindu and Buddhist temples, stupas, monasteries, etcetera, often together with the people to till the soil. Glebe slaves had a hereditary status as well.

Another road to serfdom was debt, or perhaps one should say poverty. There is a thin line between those who after one or two very bad harvests (owing to natural disasters such as droughts, floods and epidemics, and/or manmade disasters such as wars), voluntarily became slaves of a more well-to-do patron, and those who after a bad period had to borrow money or produce which they could not repay, either immediately or ever. There are several points to be made regarding the link between debt and bondage.

Although it has been assumed that in the past a Southeast Asian peasant, once in debt, would hardly ever get out of it, it is important to remember that debt peonage, in principle, was a temporary affair. In some Southeast Asian societies – which were often more literate than we historians have been aware of – contracts were drawn up, stipulating the amount borrowed and the conditions of the loan. Redemption was in principle possible, and it is far from certain that it was as rare as we may have assumed. Such debts could also be transferred, and we have contracts and registers testifying that this actually happened fairly frequently.

Such data suggests that debt peonage might have been a regular means of hiring oneself out as a labourer, switching to another employer by having him take over one's debt. It is even possible that those becoming debt bondsmen or women were not destitute but just needed money for an investment, for which they had to conclude a debt peonage contract as they had no other security than their own labour power, for instance because they had no land or only usufruct right on land. Hypothetically, therefore, part of what appears to have been a labour market really may have been a capital market.

Finally it should be pointed out that being perpetually in debt, and therefore having to work at least part of the time for a creditor, although seemingly the epitome of abject poverty, had its upside too. Debt bondage also meant that some well-to-do patron had a stake in keeping the debt bondsman or woman alive, tying them over during lean periods. In a world in which weather anomalies were all too frequent occurrences, and where the state institutions were lacking that could have cushioned the blows of nature, such an arrangement must have meant the survival of a great many people.

Of course we would like to know what proportion of the population was actually entirely 'free', here defined as tax paying but not subject to servile obligations. I have the impression that in some societies this number might have been very small. One group of people, though, appears to have been free everywhere in Southeast Asia. It is well known by specialists and non-specialists of the region alike that Chinese migrants played an important role as merchants, petty traders and moneylenders, but it should not be forgotten that most Chinese migrants arrived in Southeast Asia as coolies, owning nothing but their labour power (and often in debt to boot).

In Java, perhaps most but certainly many of the workers hired by the Dutch East India Company (VOC) in Batavia (now Jakarta) in the early seventeenth century were Chinese. The Chinese in Thailand constituted a reliable source of wage labour from c. 1800 onwards. Later in the nineteenth century the state increasingly switched from statute labour carried out by Thais to wage labour performed by Chinese for infrastructural works such as the digging of canals. By 1900, many labour obligations due to the crown had been commuted to taxes in money. It is also likely that those – often tribal – groups that lived too far away from the core areas, or that could not be easily reached for other reasons (e.g. because they lived in forests or swamps) paid only token homage to a ruler.

They were probably expected to send small amounts of produce or gold as tribute, but it is unlikely that they were called upon for corvée labour. In principle, therefore, they were free to do with their labour as they saw fit. However, for the same reasons that the state left them alone, one can hardly expect them to have been available on a routine basis for the labour market. Although even hunter-gatherers often spent some of their time collecting commodities for the (international) market, their economy was almost entirely geared towards subsistence, and the economic necessity to present themselves for wage labour would have been restricted, at best, to difficult times and to those occasions that income had to be generated for ceremonies. So although the majority of these people in principle would have been available for wage labour, they were usually just not interested.

Therefore, in the nineteenth century, when under colonial rule Western enterprise was opening up 'waste' lands in tribal areas, local wage labour was often hard to get, and entrepreneurs had to import (indentured) labour from elsewhere. In some countries there were also groups of commoners living in the core areas (not tribals or foreigners) that were not supposed to perform compulsory services, and were therefore 'free' as defined earlier. The artisans and traders (athi) of Early-Modern Burma appear to have constituted such a group. It is likely that these – usually urban – groups would have been exempt from corvée labour elsewhere as well, although they would have been called upon to practise their trade for free for the monarch on special occasions.

However, many such people would not be expected to be available on a routine basis for wage labour – they should be regarded as independent entrepreneurs and their apprentices. Finally, data for Java suggests that at least from 1650 onward there were always some unskilled wage labourers – usually called coolies – available in and around the areas where the VIOC had established itself. We are probably talking about small numbers of people who, for various reasons, had left their village societies. They were an unruly lot who appear to have spent most of their income on gambling, whoring, drinking and opium. They figure prominently in reports about criminal activities. Here, apparently, we find a genuine proletariat in the making.

Data on wages between 1650 and 1800, although not abundantly available, suggest that there was a downward tendency, which implies that the supply of coolies was increasing. However, around 1750 there are signs in Java that this development towards a full-fledged proletariat was rivalled by another tendency. This was the appearance of what in Java was called a bujang, a young, unmarried male (occasionally a female), who was temporarily looking for work outside his village. Of course such people had always existed, but their presence in larger numbers in the 'Western' sector of the economy appears to have been a rather novel phenomenon.

We are talking here about temporary migrants, who came looking for work during one or two seasons, perhaps more, but who eventually intended to go back to their villages and get married, for which they should have been saving part of their income, in order to be able to pay the brideprice. It is no longer assumed by most historians that Southeast Asia prior to European influence was a moneyless region. On the contrary, most core areas were familiar with coinage of one kind or another (minted gold and silver coins or unminted but standardised lumps of these metals) by 1400. Chinese copper coins circulated in the area as well, and also baser coinage of a much smaller denomination (caixas, picis). Nevertheless, this was not a fully monetised society when the Europeans arrived on the scene. After 1500, the region received large amounts of (American) silver from Europa, while Japanese silver may have played a much larger role than many of us have been aware of. It has been suggested that increased monetisation initially may have led to more rather than less debt peonage, which comes perhaps as a surprise to those who would have expected 'more market' to have led to more free labour.

Nevertheless, market influence in the end appears to have been the undoing of corvée labour. Between 1700 and 1900, service obligations in many Southeast Asian countries (Birma, Thailand, Vietnam, Java) were being gradually commuted to monetary payments, or they were reduced and finally abolished, while work for the state was increasingly being paid for. This happened more or less at the same time as the substitution of monetary taxation for taxes in kind, and no doubt for the same reasons – more money had become available, more people were willing to work for wages.

The development of slavery and serfdom is a somewhat more complicated story. Full-fledged slavery - as a proportion of the total labouring population - may never have been very important during the period we are discussing, as so much statute labour was available to the state and to the nobility. However, many elements of the population could not dispose of corvée labour, and as wage labour was difficult to get, slavery was often the only solution for non-noble entrepreneurs, perhaps mainly merchants, and in the less populous areas even for the nobility. There is also evidence that rulers and nobility of ports-of-trade availed themselves of slaves, perhaps partly because they could not mobilise sufficient corvée labour, but perhaps also in order not to be outdone in conspicuous consumption - an important feature of slavery - by (foreign) merchants.

Slavery was often also the only solution for resident foreigners looking for workers. Slavery then, far from being (only) a 'backward' mode of production, was almost certainly stimulated by the growth of international trade and the increasing importance of production for export. This applied perhaps in the first place to ports-of-trade, but this mechanism made itself felt in the rural hinterlands as well. Indigenous pepper production in Sumatra prior to 1860, for instance, depended largely on slave labour, and so did the However, in the densely settled core areas of Java and Northern Vietnam for instance, slavery was rare in the indigenous countryside, and largely restricted to the ports-of-trade.

When the influence of European powers increased during the nineteenth century, and solidified into formal colonialism, slavery was slowly but surely phased out. Thailand, although not under colonial rule, but certainly apprehensive that slavery could constitute a pretext for the colonial powers to intervene, followed suite. Slavery in Southeast Asia was not abolished for economic reasons by the colonial powers, but for humanitarian ones. The motives for the ending of the slave trade and slavery did not have much to do with the situation in Asia. They were largely connected to the discussions then going on in Europe about plantation slavery in the Americas.

However, it coincided conveniently with the increasing availability of free wage labour in the region.

Nevertheless, slavery persisted in many Southeast Asian fringe areas into the twentieth century, and in the late 1940s Condominas encountered a few slaves when he was doing fieldwork in a tribal upland area in Vietnam. The upshot of all this appears to be that free (wage) labour had always been available in small numbers, but that during the Pre and Early-Modern Periods various forms of bonded labour were predominant. For a time the supply of various kinds of free and unfree labour was increasing due to the influence of the international market, possibly from 1400 onwards.

However, from the late eighteenth century locally, and during much of the nineteenth century across the region, corvée obligations and full-fledged slavery were being increasingly abolished, while free wage labour took their place. This development was linked to three factors - population growth, the continuing growth of international trade, and measures taken by the colonial rulers.

LAND

Rights to land in Southeast Asia are undoubtedly a hot topic, and this has been the case for much of the twentieth century. It is also a topic that has generated many studies, in which assumptions were often made about the development over time of such rights. Nevertheless, there do not appear to be many reliable historical studies concerning this issue, based on empirical data. It is still possible, as Glenn May (2004) did for the Philippines last year, to write an article based on actual research of the primary sources, in which the received wisdom about the historical development of land rights is stood on its head. Therefore, much of what I am going to say here is very preliminary and impatiently awaits further research.

Moreover, to generalise over a number of countries, each of which has a long history of dealing with landed tenure arrangements, thus creating its own particular brand of tradition, with which my familiarity is almost by necessity rather limited, I will almost certainly be adding erroneous statements of my own. Nowadays, many students of land tenure arrangements distinguish four types of land rights – unowned or open access land, state land, common property, and individually owned private property. During the nineteenth century most colonial regimes assumed that the indigenous rulers of Southeast Asia were the owners of all the lands in their countries, a notion that certainly existed among the ruling elites of these states.

The colonial states regarded themselves as the successors to such rights. This explains for instance why Thomas Stamford Raffles, the British Lieutenant-Governor of Java during the so-called British Interregnum (1811-1816), could regard all Javanese cultivators as 'renters' from the state, and why he called his taxation system the Land Rent System. However, since the early twentieth century, the view has been gaining ground that it was not the ruler or the state, but the village or the clan in which land rights ultimately vested. In this view, land was the common property of the villagers, for which terms such as communal rights or customary rights are often used. Such rights were often no longer in evidence, so the argument went, because the indigenous or the colonial state had usurped them.

However, in stateless societies, village rights to land could still be encountered. Both opinions – the king as the original owner of all the land or all rights to land originally vested in the local community – can still be encountered in the recent literature. Usually, those who cite the former version are interested in the densely settled core areas of the Southeast Asian states, while supporters of the latter hypothesis are interested in the sparsely populated tribal margins. In fact, therefore, these views are not mutually exclusive. It is also generally assumed that these rights have changed drastically since the colonial state took matters in hand and introduced individual private rights to land.

The general trend, therefore, suggested implicitly or explicitly by many scholars writing about At a much earlier date (16th century), the king of Spain had declared himself owner of all the lands in the Philippines by right of conquest. Based on the same right the VOC regarded themselves as the owners of Batavia and its Environs (Java) after 1619. This view was pioneered by the Dutch scholar Cornelis van Vollenhoven, founder of what is often called the Adat Law School. The term he used for such village rights was beschikkingsrecht.

This has been translated variously as rights of avail and rights of disposal, but nowadays the term residual rights appears to be used by most scholars. Southeast Asia, is that land rights were transformed from state or common property to private property as a result of colonial intervention. This is not the place for a long and detailed discussion about land rights in Southeast Asia in Pre and Early-Modern times, and a few comments on the views mentioned above will have to suffice. The main point to be made is that individual ownership of land certainly predates the colonial experience in Southeast Asia.

Perhaps the best documented area in this respect is tenth-century Java, where epigraphic evidence strongly suggests that land could be bought and sold on a freehold basis, pawned and leased. Irrigated rice land in particular appears to have been held at this early date in hereditary individual private tenure. Individual hereditary private property in land prior to 1500 or 1600 is also to be found in Burma, Vietnam and the Philippines. Thailand appears to have been the country where the claim that the king was the sole owner of the land appears to have been taken more seriously than elsewhere.

Here, private individual rights to land were weakest prior to the late eighteenth century, and those who cultivated the land could not claim more than usufruct rights. Even around 1800, when land could be sold and bequeathed by the cultivator, it was not in general used as collateral. My impression is that the areas where hereditary private tenure of land predominated were to be found mostly in the densely populated core areas of the indigenous states, in and around capital cities and/or ports-of-trade. Here, land had become scare and therefore valuable at an early stage, and had therefore become 'commodified' even if its legal status may have been that of regal domain land. It is also clear that many other forms of landed tenure could be found in Southeast Asia prior to colonial rule. It is not an either or question.

Not much discussed in the literature it the size of privately owned lands, with the exception of the situation in the Philippines, where large ecclesiastical and private estates came into being after the arrival of the Spaniards. When the literature mentions private tenure as introduced by Europeans, should it not be specified what the size of these holdings was? One assumes that a society largely based on large landholdings is quite different from one where smallholders predominate everywhere. A few words, then, should be said about size, before and after the arrival of the Europeans. One of the most conspicuous features of Pre-Modern (but much less of Early-Modern) Southeast Asian landholding was the presence of many large ecclesiastical estates.

Unless one regards such holdings as a category all by itself, in addition to the four mentioned earlier (and there is much to be said for that), this would be an example of privately owned large landholdings. In principle, however, they could not be alienated, and in that sense they do not meet the criteria of private ownership. Large estates of the nobility are mentioned in Pre-Modern Vietnam, but around 1500 rulers actively sought to discourage such latifundia, which were seen as competition for the monarch.

Large landholdings came into existence after the clearing of large new areas for agriculture, as happened in the Mekong delta in Vietnam in the 18th century and the Irrawaddy and Chao Phraya deltas in Burma and Thailand respectively during the nineteenth century. In such areas absentee landlordism and tenancy became the rule. There does not appear to have been much difference in this respect between indigenous and colonial rule. The new lands had in common that it was impossible for individual smallholders to clear these swampy deltas. This could only be undertaken as a large-scale enterprise by people who could dispose of large fortunes. It seems therefore that environmental circumstances dictated the land tenure arrangements.

In the early twentieth century medium sized properties were found in the Red River delta in northern Vietnam. Locally, they were called large landholdings, but in comparison with for instance the large holdings in the Philippines such a term appears to be inappropriate. In Vietnam, the properties under discussion measured a few tens of hectares. They were often the end result of many small transactions, perhaps mainly lands that had been given as collateral for a loan and that had to be forfeited when repayment proved impossible. Such properties were also to be found in some areas of Java, but here the proportion of the land in the hands of owners of medium sized holdings was much smaller.

Does this imply that the land market in northern Vietnam was working better than it did in Java around the same time? In my view, this discussion leads to two main conclusions. Individual tenure often predated the arrival of the Europeans, and statements about private property should specify the size of the lands concerned. Common property or communal tenure, also termed customary tenure, is now often regarded as the form of tenure historically to be found in stateless societies. Many anthropologists writing about tenure and environment seem to feel that it is private property, introduced by alien forces (the colonial state, Capitalism), that is to blame for many of the environmental problems of today.

In their view, customary rights to land would be better suited to sustainable exploitation of the natural environment. There are a number of problems with these terms. In the first place, they suggest that all 'primitive' or 'tribal' communities owned land in common. This appears not to be the case. This, at least, is what could be concluded from research by well-known Borneo scholars such as Derek Freeman (1955) and Bill Geddes (1954) among the Iban and the Land Dayak respectively around 1950.

The claims created here by the individual by clearing the land are admittedly not identical with our 'individual tenure' in the usual sense of the word, but neither is it communal tenure - the village or the longhouse do not appear to have had residual claims. However, there are many instances in Borneo of stronger communal claims on the land. The second point is that there is another phenomenon called communal tenure, which has nothing to do with the 'pristine' arrangements mentioned here.

It refers to the fact that in villages of sedentary peasant-agriculturalists, often located in long-settled, densely populated wet-rice growing areas, part or all of the arable lands did not have permanent individual owners. These lands were distributed by the village head among all families (Java), or among a section of the villagers, often, but not always, the landless and/or the 'dwarfholders' (Vietnam). Redistribution could be annually or after more years. This phenomenon was to be found in Java and northern Vietnam around 1800 and later. As a rule, such communal holdings could not be alienated.

Another point that is not often discussed is whether the colonial masters were indeed as interested in introducing private property as many scholars seem to think. In the first place some colonial powers appear to have preferred concessions to outright property, at least for large-scale Western enterprise. Ever since the Agrarian Law of 1870, plantations in the Indonesian Archipelago had to depend entirely on the acquisition of leases, usually for a period of 75 years. Such a period was sufficiently long for banks to accept leasehold land as collateral. In Java, the situation had been more complicated between 1820 and 1870.

Between those years no non-Javanese had been permitted to buy land. The planting of crops for the world market by Western enterprise could only be undertaken on arable lands hired from villages. These arrangements were part of the so-called Cultivation System. In the Philippines, Spanish legislation during the nineteenth century worked in favour of the creation and expansion of haciendas, but this was done at the expense of small private holdings. Even as late as 1914, under US rule, the legislation stimulated the acquisition of large landholdings by the high and mighty, which went to the detriment of smallholders, who became tenants on the properties they once owned.

The state, therefore, encouraged the growth of the number of large private holdings, but they also encouraged the disappearance of smallholdings. There are also indications that colonial powers during certain stages of their presence in Southeast Asia were in favour of communal holdings. The Spanish crown, for instance, gave land grants to Philippine villages in the late sixteen and early seventeenth centuries, thus creating communal holdings out of the royal domain. But even during part of the nineteenth century the Dutch colonial state actively encouraged the growth of communal holdings in Java, as it was convenient for the sugar industry and for other aspects of the Cultivation System.

Whatever the connection between the arrival of the colonial state and the origins of private rights to land may have been, we can be certain about one thing – between c. 1800 and 1940 almost all forests in Southeast Asia were declared property of the state. Before 1800, most forests in the more remote areas had been open access resources, while in the more densely settled areas they had been regarded as part of the village commons. Forests as private property, well known from Europe, must have been rare or even non-existent in Southeast Asia, both before and after 1800.

Furthermore, in my opinion the literature – that on the Philippines excepted – on rights to land might be too much concerned with the formal arrangements of landed property (private or not), while it could be argued that it is of equal importance whether such lands are owner- operated or being worked by tenants. It is generally accepted that tenancy – probably mainly share tenancy – has increased considerably during the last 100 or 150 years or so. It has been estimated that by the 1950s around 50% of all farms was tenant operated.

This means that a large proportion of all cultivators will not be able to put up the land they are cultivating as collateral. This makes them dependent on 'improving landlords' (while most landlords are better known for their rentier mentality) or moneylenders who charge usurious rents in order to compensate for the risk they are running, unless the state is willing to shoulder this burden. Finally, after all the exceptions and counter currents mentioned here, it is undoubtedly true that most colonial states attempted from the late 19th century onwards to improve the registration and therefore creation and recognition of private property in land.

Most countries – but not the Netherlands Indies – introduced the so-called Torrens system, where the registration of title deeds was coupled to cadastral surveys and an exact positioning of the relevant plots of land. However, this attempt was fraught with many difficulties, of which the main ones were the lack of trained personnel and the endless disputes over conflicting claims. The pace of registration was therefore excruciatingly slow, and the process was far from finished at the end of colonial rule.

Summarising all this, we must conclude that the notion of unidirectional development from communal property to individual property under the influence of the colonial state does not seem to reflect very well what happened, while it is, furthermore, not sufficiently specific to tell us much about the social and economic effects of changing land tenure arrangements. First and foremost it should be pointed out that individual private tenure has existed for ages in many areas of Southeast Asia. The occurrence of this form of tenure appears to be related to population density and the working of the international market.

As the areas where private property of land was the rule, appear to coincide with those areas where slavery and serfdom were absent or rare, it is tempting to posit a connection between the two. Is it plausible to assume that investment in land became more attractive when investment in people was no longer possible? Not all land tenure arrangements among marginal (tribal) groups should be regarded as 'communal', while the term 'communal rights to land' has been used for village communities in the populous core areas as well. Many European regulations between 1570 and 1870 were not aimed at the creation of private property in land, and in various cases they led to distortions of private property already in existence.

Even after 1870, there are many instances of colonial states preferring long leases for Western enterprise instead of private holdings. In the case of forests the option of private property was never contemplated, the forests being declared sovereign domain instead. However, various colonial regulations have, indeed, facilitated the creation of private landed property since the late 19th century. In many instances, however, this was not conversion from communal land into privately owned land, but from open access and state land. The production of title deeds has also harmed many smallholders who could produce no proof of their claim, and thus favoured large holdings over small ones, both subcategories of private property.

These regulations have also facilitated the creation and growth of a class of tenants, whose titles to land may be insufficient for the acquisition of cheap credit. Finally, the point should be made that up until today the existence of so many property regimes that have succeeded but not replaced each other - indigenous, colonial, post-colonial - is a source of incredible confusion and uncertainty as regards titles to land. Many peasant-cultivators are now working on plots that used to be parts of a concession, or a plantation no longer in existence, but as the status of the land is unclear, they are regarded as squatters and cannot get title to the land they are cultivating. Thus, they are easily swindled out of their land by those in authority.

A similar point could be made about lands being expropriated for large-scale projects undertaken by the state, but that has more to do with the lack of appropriate legal institutions than with tenure arrangements. We will talk about institutions presently.

CAPITAL

Asia has always had the reputation of being a money-poor, cash-hungry and debt-ridden part of the world with very high interest rates, a sink of imported specie and bullion. This is easily illustrated – at least for South and Southeast Asia – for the period between 1600 and 1900, when we have quantitative data on interest rate levels. The lowest interest rates in the indigenous sphere to be found in Southeast Asia during this period, both in legal texts and in actual practice, appear to have fluctuated between 25 and 35% per year. In a number of cases it is clear that such rates were only applicable if some sort of collateral was present (e.g. livestock). In Java, Europeans who lent money to Chinese sometimes charged somewhat lower rates during the 17th and 18th century - 16 to 18%. However, much higher rates were to be found in many cases.

Occasionally, the laws set limits to the amount of interest to be charged, but we do not know whether people actually paid any heed to such injunctions. Given the structure of authority - which will be discussed- it is unlikely that the state actually upheld such rules, although occasionally a 'just' ruler may have attempted to do so. Be that as it may, in indigenous legal texts maximum rates of between 80 and 150 are to be found. In some texts the principle is formulated that the repayment of a debt cannot be more than double the original sum that was burrowed, which, therefore, after one year would have been an interest rate of 100%. So even if such maximum legal rates had been adhered to, repayment must have been an enormous burden on Southeast Asia's commoners, often people living on the edge of survival.

There are indications that the highest rates were paid on the smaller sums, both according to the law and in actual practice. This was still the case in colonial times. Pierre Gourou, writing about northern Vietnam in the 1930s, presents the example of people borrowing 1 Piaster, for which they had to pay an interest of 1 sou a day, or an interest rate of 100% for a hundred-day period (and therefore 365% after 1 year). Such amounts of money are in our eyes very small beer indeed, but seen from a Southeast Asian peasant's perspective this was serious money (often because any cash was serious money).

Therefore, particularly those with the smallest margins were paying the highest rates, and could easily get into trouble, by losing their land or having to enter into debt peonage. Interest rates were lower in 17th -century India, at least if loans made available by local merchants to the VOC can be used as an indication.

The rates were also decreasing during the century, no doubt as a result of large silver imports from Europe. The lowest rates were to be found in Surat, where they dropped from 12 to 7½%, those in Bengal were somewhat higher, dropping from 15 to 10, while the highest rates occurred in Coromandel, decreasing from 24 to 12%. All these rates were charged for very large amounts, so rates for smaller amounts would have been higher. Finally there are data for the European-dominated centres in the 17th -century Indonesian Archipelago, Batavia and Ambon.

Here, interest rates paid by the VOC to private persons, probably mainly Europeans and European institutions (such as the orphanage) varied between 6 and 9% per year. This was getting very close to rates charged in the Netherlands during the same period, at that moment the most advanced financial centre in the world, where interest rates varied from 3½ and 5% for large loans to the state or the VOC. The most plausible explanation for these differences in interest rates appears to be a combination of the different degrees of penetration of European capital and the different levels of economic development. India's economy – or at least the economy of areas such as Gujarat, Coromandel and Bengal – was of a more complex nature than the indigenous economies of Southeast Asia, and larger amounts of European capital were imported in India than in Southeast Asia.

Only places such as Batavia and Ambon, where the European element was numerically and economically dominant, were doing marginally better in terms of interest rates than Surat, the Indian city with the lowest rates. Why were interest rates so much higher in Southeast Asia than they were in Europe? I will mention a number of factors, or rather complexes of factors. Pre-Modern and Early-Modern Southeast Asian societies were characterised by status based on ostentation (conspicuous consumption) and reciprocity. Status could be acquired by organising large ceremonies, which had to be reciprocated by competing status seekers (competitive feasting). For a Southeast Asian of a certain standing, wealth had no meaning unless it could be shown.

Those organising a ceremony for a funeral, a wedding, a circumcision, a shamanic performance to get rid of an illness, or a purification ceremony to atone for sins or crimes, often had to go into debt as they had to present their numerous guests with liberal quantities of meat and alcoholic beverages. Such ceremonies occurred at all levels of society. Being indebted owing to conspicuous consumption was not regarded as morally wrong. This cultural feature may have played a role regarding the alleged proclivity of Southeast Asians for gaming and gambling, in particular for cockfights, where huge sums of money could be wagered. A second factor is the scarcity of money. Although, as was mentioned earlier, many Southeast Asian countries did have various types of coinage since the Pre-Modern Period, minting coins came much later than it did in Europe.

This phenomenon might be related to the fact that the proportion of the economy that was market oriented was small in comparison with more advanced countries, which, in turn, appears to be related to the relatively simple and unsophisticated nature of Southeast Asia's Pre-Modern economy and society. Low levels of population density appear to have played a role here, which might ultimately be linked to environmental factors. Within Southeast Asia there were huge differences, and one could find barter economies not too far from the monetarised core areas.

The scarcity of money may have been stimulated by the often reported proclivity of Southeast Asians to 'hoarding'. Beside the well known fact that gold and silver coins were taken out of circulation and turned into jewellery, there are many instances to be found in the sources of treasures being buried. A third factor is that of natural and manmade hazards. Of course, natural risks are present in every society, and most Pre and Early-Modern societies did have few buffers against such disasters.

It seems likely that Southeast Asian societies were even more at risk than others because of the hazards connected to the ENSO (El Niño-Southern Oscillation) phenomenon, which hits the region harder than other areas, causing droughts and floods with sad regularity in addition to the weather anomalies that are to be found in other regions as well. It has also been argued that tropical areas are more subjected to all kinds of diseases, which would make Southeast Asia, a region entirely located in the intertropical convergence zone, more risky in this respect too.

Finally, Reid (1988) has been argued that Southeast Asia was characterised by a more than average level of conflicts. Even if all these factors would only make a marginal difference in comparison with other parts of the world, taken together they are likely to have made a big difference, which would imply more risk and therefore higher interest rates, all other things being equal. Finally, high rates also may have been caused by high transaction costs. Gourou argued that in Tonkin (northern Vietnam) moneylenders would never get their money back if they were not supported by a local Mandarin, and Mandarins did not come cheaply.

In many areas of Southeast Asia moneylenders were aliens (Arabs, Indians, Chinese), and it is well known that particularly in times of economic crisis, recouping their loans would be very difficult, to put it mildly. They needed bodyguards-cum-enforcers to stay in business, or, occasionally, to stay alive. Particularly in Indonesia authors have complained about the lack of trust that would contribute to an adverse business climate, and thus to high levels of interest. Finally the lack of contract enforcement should be mentioned, a factors that belongs to the institutional factors to be dealt with presently.

One question that should be researched further is whether the possibility to make someone who defaulted on a loan a debt bondsman should not have brought interest rates down. It should equally be investigated whether the possibility to foreclose on landed property in the case of a defaulting debtor would not lead to lower interest rates. As we have seen in the cases of Batavia and Ambon, the presence of Europeans with lots of cash led to lower interest rates in the seventeenth century.

We should study the development of interest rates in Southeast Asia from, say, the 1870s onward in order to find out whether such developments took place across the region. However, lower interest rates would not automatically make for less indebtedness. One could even argue that, on the contrary, cheaper credit would make for more people willing to take out loans. One should also consider the arrival of more shops with credit facilities in the Southeast Asian countryside during the same period. But that would go far beyond the scope of this chapter.

INSTITUTIONAL FRAMEWORK

The low interest rates in Batavia were not only the result of the presence of more cash, but also, one assumes, with the will and the means to enforce contracts. Thus, we arrive finally at the institutional factors, which will be dealt with briefly. Although it is no longer fashionable to speak of 'Oriental Despotism', one is hard put to find another equally evocative term to describe the behaviour of Southeast Asian power holders. They were certainly Absolute rulers by the fifteenth century, and income and firearms acquired through trade with Europeans strengthened their position.

Evidently, Southeast Asian society prior to 1850 was not a civil society. The king could do as he damn well pleased, and he was certainly above the law (as the laws themselves show us convincingly). The states we have been dealing with in this chapter had subjects, not citizens. There was a generally high level of insecurity among commoners and nobility alike. One of the reasons people were hoarding is that they would not show too much of their wealth, lest they made the monarch jealous. Rulers were known to make unexpected and unreasonable financial demands.

These factors have generally been held responsible for the lack of an indigenous stratum of well-to-do (non-royal and non-noble) large-scale merchants. Rulers preferred to deal with Chinese, Arab, Indian or European merchants, as these, in their eyes, could never pose a threat to their position. The fact that much of Southeast Asia's commercial transactions was thus in the hands of strangers might be an additional explanation for the eternal shortage of cash in the region, as these merchants repatriated a (large?) proportion of their earnings. Next to the role of the monarch, the quality of the legal framework within which a society operates is of great importance for the issues we are dealing with.

Written laws were present in most Southeast Asian countries from an early age onward. These laws contain clauses about property, financial transactions, written contracts, bondage, and punishment for crimes. We do not know how much of this was ever put into practice (some of it surely was – we know of instances that debts were registered for instance), but the general impression is that might was stronger than right, and that it was fairly easy for someone with money to pervert the course of justice. There were doubtlessly many just kings and good judges, but there were also many examples to the contrary, and there were no institutional constraints to keep a bad king from doing things he shouldn't.

The rule of law did not apply where the monarch was concerned. Finally, it should perhaps be pointed out that there are no traces of self-governing bodies, such as the cities in Europe, or of representative bodies in which commoners held seats, such as the parliaments in many European countries. With free labour not abundantly available, landownership often burdened with residual rights, capital scarce and expensive, and an institutional framework that is not conducive to economic growth, one is hardly surprised to find lower levels of economic development in Southeast Asia than one does in Japan and Western Europe during the Pre and Early Modern Periods.

For further research, it would be interesting to concentrate on the more advanced areas, where free labour, individual rights to land, and relative large amounts of money were available (and, one assumes, lower interest rates). These were the ports-of-trade, sometimes also the capitals of the various core areas. It is in these areas that slavery and debt peonage were also reportedly of great importance, an anomaly worthy of further investigation.

6

Women, Colonialism and Nationalism

This chapter necessarily deals with the way and manner in which religion, ethnicity and the state interact in Sri Lanka with consequences which have affected the country as a whole. The concept of State is invested with certain significations which are hard to dispense with in any discussion of the state of any country. There are two perspectives which need to be articulated. The first approach puts forward a series of ideological and political factors - such as the pressure exercised by the economically dominant classes upon the state and society and how the ideological affinities build the strength of the state for action by class collaboration. The second view holds that with or without the ideological congruence, the state ensures the accumulation and reproduction of capital.

The state, it would appear, in this perspective is constrained by and subordinated to external pressures. While the former view implicitly argues for the coercive function of the state, the latter does not. The latter takes away all the autonomy of the state, which is perceived to be all powerful and coercive. We take the view that while enjoying a certain relative autonomy - because of its power - and while being coercive by the nature of possessing the military, navy and police forces, it serves the interests of the dominant classes. There is a partnership of ideological affinities between those who control the state and its powers, and those who own and control the means of major economic production and activities. In democratic societies, the consent is achieved not by coercion alone - as is evident by the instances of political violence during election times - but also by the consent given through the ballot boxes.

Similarly, ethnicity is a broad concept; implicit in its usage are a number of factors, which are used to distinguish and differentiate people of one group from another. Significant among them are race, language, religion and sometimes the colour of the skin. Ethnicity does not remain passive or dormant as a social marker. It assumes a political force, politicising itself into sometimes passive social movements and sometimes into violent political movements. Theories are replete as to how the transformation takes place. Ethnicity is purposely used to mobilise groups into political entities with claims of exclusivity (Donald Harowitz, 1985; Joanna Pffaf-Czarnecka, 1999: 43; P. Brass, 1991). The question of identity in terms of language, religion or culture looms large in the way ethnicity is actualised.

The state's involvement by design in the process of the transformation of political ethnicisation is a major factor, which has caused havoc in many countries (Nepal, Sri Lanka and India). The interesting phenomenon that needs to be underlined here is the state's collaboration not with the dominant classes (economical) but how this collaboration is transformed into one with dominant ethnic groups (socio-political factors). Sri Lanka is a typical example of this ethnic collaboration. However, this is not to totally ignore the economic argument. The minority communities' resentment arises out of a series of oppressive experiences, both socially and economically, where the state has legislated them out of employment or deprived them of economical activities.

Often the argument is that the cake is not large enough to divide economically among the various groups- whether ethnic or any other, which brings about the understanding of the phenomenon of identity formation and political mobilisation. This is contested on the ground of a thesis of economic reductionism, which takes away the issue of social marginalisation that the groups suffer. There is an abundance of literature on the history of the ethnic conflict and the responsibility of the Sri Lankan state and its governance patterns. In terms of how the Sri Lankan government handled the ethnic conflict, there is much to be desired. But proportionately its policy towards the manner in which it handled the religious question of the people is much less discriminatory.

However, the fact that religion is tied to ethnicity among the Sri Lankans, has its implications for an overall lack of an ideology of pluralisation. The manifestation of this implication is very well captured in the phrase: Sinhala Buddhist Nationalism. The rise of Sinhala Buddhist nationalism too, has been documented by various scholars. This phraseology has an in-built sense of exclusivity in a multi-ethnic society, especially when the state is the chief protagonist in the promulgation and an adherent of the ideology through legislation. The principle of democratic secularism has been eroded.

The Sri Lankan state made Buddhism the state religion and introduced clauses in the Constitution which provided, amongst others, the clause that Buddhism should be protected by the state, thereby giving a privileged position to Buddhism, the religion of the majority Sinhalese. As far back as 1939 a future prime minister of independent Ceylon was to make a speech that 'we (the Sinhalese) are one blood and one nation. We are a chosen people'. The Sinhalese, it is believed, are a chosen people because of the religion they practice, i. e, Buddhism, which according to a myth in a chronicle was specially bestowed by the Buddha. This kind of political rhetoric further contributed to the idea of the tyranny of the majority to which the state was socially and politically held responsible.

THE LEGACY OF COLONIALISM

As everywhere else in the colonial empire, the British employed a strategy of divide at empera in Sri Lanka as well. If we go back into pre-colonial history there is evidence of state patronage for religion, culture, literature and art. The temples were governed by the state. The modern concept of secularism, democracy and pluralisation are new to governance systems from the pre-colonial times. The Portuguese, the Dutch and later the British, continued with the ancient practice of patronage in their governance patterns. When the British introduced representative governance, unfortunately the old ideology prevailed. Representation of communal, ethnic and religious interests, were adhered to in the state machinery.

The legislative council of Ceylon in 1860 had three Europeans, one Sinhalese, one Tamil and one Burgher - so to say the local Sri Lankans were treated on the principle of inferior equality while the Europeans enjoyed superior privileges. Apart from the racist superiority that is played upon, the Sri Lankans were seen and treated as an ethnically or communally separate bloc and it was believed that they cannot represent each others' interests in governance. This should be seen not merely as a practice, but also as an ideology of ethnic exclusivity - the construction of the other in terms of ethnicity, language and religion.

This pattern was continued and adopted for further polarisation, when in 1889, the number of councilors was increased to eight-it extended another division, that of the low country Sinhalese and Kandyan Sinhalese, while the Tamil, Burgher composition continued and the Moor as a new inclusion was instituted. By not simply subscribing to any conspiracy theory, though there is relative truth in that, we should also look into the historical circumstances that have motivated this ethnic-oriented governance style of the British. There is evidence to show that the British were cautious - the following quote is symptomatic of the trends that were to follow:

'In a community composed of different races who are attached to ancient customs ...... it is indispensable that changes in law should not be adopted precipitately'. Besides, Earl Crewe, the Secretary of State for the Colonies, adopted the view that the Governor should retain the Executive Council in its present as there is 'the necessity of the maintenance of the principle of racial representation'.It would seem that there is a historical continuity. The British, not surprisingly, subscribed to the main argument of orientalism which took the view that the Asiatic communities were static, they resist changes and that they are conservative and similar in structure and ideology. The orientalist discourse gained further currency with the race theory intervening to construct an otherness of the colonial societies (Said 1979). Dynamic and progressive characters are denied to the colonies.

The Sri Lankans are divided by ethnicity, 'race' and religion. The modern representative governance, which essentially should be on the principle of political representation, picked up the natives from their ethnic and religious backgrounds. This had serious implications and consequences for the future politics of Sri Lanka. It extended an ideology of ethnic, race and religious exclusivity, created a sense of otherness towards other communities and groups, and created a working political ethics according to which the governors of the Sri Lankan polity could represent only group interests and work for the interests of that particular community from which they hailed; they were, thus, responsible merely for that community. Religion is usually tied to ethnicity in pre-colonial societies, but conversions by the conquerors have changed this scenario. In Sri Lanka, we have three major ethnic groups but five religions.

Traditionally, the Sinhalese were Buddhists, the Tamils were Hindus and the Muslims followed Islam. However, after the arrival of the Portuguese, Dutch and British missionaries, a few of the Tamils and Sinhalese have been converted into Catholicism and Christianity. Mercifully, there are no violent religious conflicts in Sri Lanka, though in nationalist parlance the Sinhala Buddhists is a popular political term. There are indeed Christian-Buddhist conflicts at the level of ideology and we hear of a Christian conspiracy and unethical conversions which are posited and posed as a threat to a pan-Sinhala Buddhist identity. The Sri Lankan state did not intervene so violently against the church as it did against the ethnic minorities except to appoint a Buddhist Commission to enquire into the religious grievances of the Buddhists.

The attitude of the state is simply due to the fact that more often, some of the more influential members of the ruling elites of the state, happen to be Christians. Sinhala nationalism and Sinhala chauvinism are invariably connected with Buddhism, though many of the Sinhala nationalists are not necessarily Buddhists. A strange phenomenon though it is, the Buddhist monks in Sri Lanka are not only members of political parties, but are involved in active politics, championing the cause of Sinhala Buddhists and often exert pressure on the state to follow a particular agenda.

Ethnicity and religion, therefore, are very much implicated in Sri Lanka in the state formaticn and in the manner it functions. Though religion has lost its salience in the minority ethnic groups such as the Tamils and Burghers, amongst the Muslims and Sinhalese religion is a major political marker and sometimes a virulent factor. However, even among the other communities, religion plays a major role, but only as a social and cultural determinant. Through revival of various types of rituals and cult formations are familiar sights, they are not politicised but remain dormant at the socio-cultural levels, influencing merely the religio-social lives of the people.

Language as the marker of ethnic groups is the major divisive factor in Sri Lanka. The refusal by the state to give parity of status to the Tamil language has led to claims being made now by the Tamils that they belong to a distinct society with an ancient and rich language. Tamil nationalism, however, does not include a religious fanaticism in its ideology or practice. It has a semblance of a secularism with no claims to religious exclusivity. However, the Sri Lankan state has been characterised as a failed state due to the discriminatory politics that the state indulged in since 1948, when Sri Lanka got independence from British rule.

THE HANDLING OF ETHNIC AND RELIGIOUS FORMATIONS

Sri Lanka is a typical example of how contemporary categories such as religion, tradition and modernism contribute to interlocking processes in state formation first, and then into state structures and functions. Anthropological scholarship interrogates the connections between religion and knowledge, religion and power, and religion and subjectivity. In an era when we discourse about modernity, nation states, enlightenment and rationality, how does religion intervene, interact and disrupt certain processes of righteousness? It is an interesting exercise to show how, and to what extent, religion and language are used as markers of ethnic identity in constructing the nation state, law and legislation, in an era of late modernity in Sri Lanka.

After it gained independence in 1948, Sri Lanka, till the present era of ethnic conflict, has been in the dual process of the ethnicisation of politics and the politicisation of ethnicity. The state effectively came into being managing and serving not only the common affairs of the elite but also the common affairs of the majority community. In the manner that the state turned into an instrument of legitimising the tyranny of the majority, it also turned into a coercive agency. The state in its desire to satisfy the demands and aspirations of the majority community used both coercion-repressive state apparatus such as the military, and the police-and the consent of the people-through the voting system. Hegemonic groups gave their consent.

The modern state that came into being in Sri Lanka, which inherited certain legacies of the colonial state, also inherited from other agencies certain other ideologies, such as caste groups, ethnic groups and religious groups, which have claimed exclusivity and have a constructed image of an 'other' with regard to other communities. These processes are reflected in a very strange manner when the subjects who have now become citizens start to play their roles politically. Power came to be vested in the state through a process of ethnic majority collaboration. The majority ethnic and religious community was very smoothly elected into power through the party system.

The political parties have ethnic name boards and had policies and plans to carry out a particular agenda. The state was in fact trapped into action. Conversely, the state is also seen as very powerful with powers vested in it. It has the power to pass laws, regulate the lives of the people, form and create public opinion by exercising control over the state media and also to create a willing and consenting citizen. When one single party did not get an absolute majority, coalition governments were formed with other parties who could be ideological partners in the state formation. Does this mean that the state, invested with various powers, has become a necessary evil? Has democracy failed by itself or has it been made to fail? The answers to these questions are again loaded and necessarily signify the constitutional guarantees and safeguards for such pitfalls of functioning democratic structures.

The post independent Sri Lankan state has had many reversals in its management of ethnicity and religion. Abandoning the principle of secularism, Buddhism, the religion of the majority Sinhalese, was made the state religion with special clauses in the Constitution for its propagation and protection with special privileges. In a country which is multi-religious with three other major religions, this act has alienated the rest of the people making them second class citizens, feeling a sense of abandonment. If, on the contrary, the state had adopted a policy of administrative indifference to all religions, there would have been no community which would have felt either favoured or neglected.

The pre-modern function of the state to protect religion has been ideologically instituted into modern state formation. Another insight that we get from the modern state is the shift of the hegemonic class collaboration to hegemonic ethnic collaboration, which essentially is the majority community. Our modern history is replete with historical instances of how the Sri Lankan state has handled ethnic and religious conflicts. The first encounter of the Sri Lankan state's attempt to see Sri Lanka as a Sinhalese country was soon after independence in 1948. It passed the Citizenship Act which rendered 975,000 Tamils of Indian origin, who were brought by the British to work in the tea plantations in Sri Lanka without a home. The Act required that they must have proof of three or more generations of paternal ancestry in Ceylon.

This is an ethnic question as well as a working class question. Seven years later, Prime Minister S.W.R.D. Bandaranaike, who was known for his liberal policies and who once championed the cause of federalism and supported the rights of the minorities, came into power on a Sinhala Buddhist nationalist (chauvinist) platform with a loud pronouncement of 'Sinhala only' - as an election slogan. This was the beginning of the prolonged ethnic strife. This rendered the Tamil speaking people, including the Muslims, as second class citizens. It was a violation of a fundamental right of a section of the citizens. This piece of legislation can be read purely as an attempt to appease majority chauvinistic aspirations.

The modern Sri Lankan state, ironically viewed the English language as a remnant of colonialism and felt that the Ceylonese should revert back to the ancient cultural symbols through their language by a cultural revival. This became the predominant ideology of post colonial Sri Lankan nationals. There is no history of a Ceylonese war of independence. There was no nationalist struggle - either political or cultural against colonialism - during the colonial period in Sri Lanka except the Youth Congress movement in the North of Sri Lanka, which did not survive for long. Hence the true nationalist struggle started in Sri Lanka, after decolonisation.

It was a war of independence against the remnants of colonialism. That the nationalist dress, nationalist religion, the nation's language, culture, literature and art had to be revived in the name of Sri Lankan nationalism was the predominant ideology of the nationalists. As we have argued, the national, however, was not inclusive of the other minority culture.

The nationalist movement, unfortunately, started too late and with dangerously sectarian interests riding rough on the aspirations and rights of other communities the Tamils, Muslims, Burghers and Europeans. The modern state picked up symbols of pre-modern life styles to build up a coherent ideology. This was essentially a Sinhala nationalism exclusive in its character which was reflected in the state policy of post-independent Sri Lanka.

It left out the non-Sinhala nationalists in the game of the independence struggle of the Sri Lankan nation and there evolved strategies to construct two nations - a Sinhala nation and a Tamil nation. The centralised Sri Lankan state became coercive and made many more laws to punish the dissidents. The Prevention of Terrorism Act and the 6th Amendment which outlawed the Tamil Members of Parliament from the Parliament is an example of some draconian laws. The state failed to intervene creatively and positively, and failed to accommodate minority rights and aspirations through a regressive notion of a centralised state which refused to delegate power in the form of regional autonomy.

In 1958, immediately after the Sinhalese language was made the official language communal riots broke out and many Tamils were killed and their properties were destroyed. The state was passively inactive and intervened too late. It delayed imposing a curfew and gave time to the looters and the killers to go on rampage. The Sri Lankan state was instrumental in causing the first migration of its people. The Burghers migrated to Australia and the Europeans to the United Kingdom and some of the Tamil elite professionals migrated to various countries. The fact that in 1959, the Prime Minister of the country - the highest executive of the state - was murdered by a Buddhist monk, in collaboration with the other Buddhist clergy and a minister of the Cabinet, has a significance with a multitude of meanings.

The murder was committed because the Buddhist clergy felt that the control and power it had on the Prime Minister, was declining. His ascendancy to political power which captured state power, was largely due to the active support of the Sinhala Buddhists who were led by the clergy. He was installed in power so that he would protect the Sinhala Buddhist interests to the exclusion of others.

When it felt that their power on him was waning, it decided to put him to death. This act is symbolic of political terror to such an extent that the state with its enormous power structures was stilled into silence momentarily till the legal course of action identified the culprits. The extension of the ethnic differentiation of the state has manifested in the way the racial riots of 1958 and 1977 were handled by the state and the repressive state apparatus; the police and the army looked on passively on the terror inflicted on the common men and women and the destruction of property of the minority ethnic group.

In 1958, 1977 and 1983 (the last was worst and is referred to as the ' pogrom'), the riots against the minority Tamils were engineered, planned and activated by the close collaboration of the State, which purposefully delayed the declaration of emergency and the imposition of curfew. Rather provocatively, the state passed the 6th Amendment to the Constitution, which effectively outlawed the advocacy of secession, which meant that the Tamil political parties were denied representation in the legislature. This was a move to placate Sinhala chauvinism. With this move from 1983 - 1988, the North-East of Sri Lanka was denied any political representation. It was clearly a policy of blaming and punishing the victim - the ethnic minority.

What went wrong with the Sri Lankan state? Little recognition was given to the fact that Sri Lanka is a multi-ethnic plural society. In Sri Lanka, we have the Sinhala majority which constitutes 74 percent of the population, which is predominantly Buddhist, but Christians and Catholics also form a part of it, forming part of the religious minority among the Sinhalese. Among the Tamils there are three denominational, cultural, groups: the Tamils of the North, the Tamils of the Eastern Province and the Tamils of the upcountry, who were brought from India to 'Ceylon' as indentured labourers by the British. Christians and Catholics are minority religious groups amongst the Tamils. Muslims are either Tamil speaking or trilingual.

The Burghers, the descendants of the Dutch and Portuguese, are a politically neglected group. They do not figure so much into the political discourse of ethnicity. However, cultural and political discourse over the centuries has posited a particular detrimental ideology on the consciousness of the majority that Sri Lanka belonged to them - they inherited the land - it is the Dhamma Deepa, the chosen land of the Buddhists, where Theravada Buddhism has to be preserved. History was mythologised and mythologies were historicised. This exclusivist ideology was represented fully in the centralised state. The state came to represent a territorial unity which denied administrative or political decentralisation and achieved a centralised legislature with judicial power vested in it.

The notion of a centralised state came to protect Sinhala interests and defined itself in opposition to other interests of ethnic and religious minorities. Significantly, the notion of a centralised state with control over the legislature and judiciary, coupled with the idea of protecting exclusively the interests of the majority ethnic groups, has resulted in very violent and bloody struggles for over two decades in Sri Lanka.

This whole process questions, unambiguously, the notion of representative democracy, which essentially functions on numerical strength. In plural societies, majority rule can very easily turn into ethnic or religious majority rule, and not necessarily into political or ideological majority rule. Such shortcomings should necessarily lead one to creatively look towards the principle of regional autonomy, decentralisation and the devolution of power, and the Lijphartian notion of consociationlism (1977:25) Perhaps Sri Lanka should work towards these goals.

INTERNAL COLONIALISM IN CHINA

In an earlier chapter, it is suggested that the categorization and taxonomization of all levels of Chinese society, from political economy, to social class, to gender, to ethnicity and nationality represents a wide-ranging and on-going project of internal colonialism. Though now long subsided, the debate provoked by Michael Hechter's (1976) history, Internal Colonialism: The Celtic Fringe in British National Development, 1536-1966, had an interesting history of its own. While a few articles had been written on the subject in the mid-1960's and early 1970's, which mainly concerned themselves with the continuing political-economic effects of former colonization in Mesoamerica, Hechter's book was the first to formulate a theoretical approach that had wide application to existing post-colonial Western urban societies.

Hechter (1975:8) draws an important theoretical connection between Lenin's The Development of Capitalism in Russia and Gramsci's The Southern Question, arguing that international relations are tied to internal social relationships. In this regard, Hechter suggests that the channeling of certain peoples into "hierarchical cultural divisions of labor" under colonial administrations led to the development of ethnic identities which superseded class (Hechter and Levi 1979:263). This "internal colonialism" is predicated upon the unequal rates of exchange between the urban power-centers and the peripheral, often ethnic, hinterlands. In his study of The Celtic Fringe, Hechter traces the national development of the post-colonial British state, as though these areas were still under economic colonial exploitation.

Hechter's elaboration of the theory of internal colonialism proved incredibly fruitful for studies outside Britain, particularly in post-colonial and socialist societies. An onslaught of over 40 articles and at least two books appeared in the mid-1970s with the phrase in their titles, culminating in a special issue of Ethnic and Racial Studies devoted to internal colonialism in 1979. Internal colonialism was found to be applicable to South Africa, Thailand, Sudan, Wales, Brittany, Quebec, Austria-Hungary, Scotland, Bangladesh, Cherokee Native Americans, Chicanos in America, the Palestinians in Israel, and the original intent behind and reason for the success of Stalin's nationalities policy in the Soviet Union.

The majority of these examples stress the exploitation of the many ethnics, who are less culturally literate in the dominant tradition, by the few urban power elite who trol access to and distribution of capital. Interestingly, though the theory was later criticized and generally abandoned for being too general and too widely applicable, it was never applied to China. Nevertheless, I would argue that recent shifts in China's policy makes the approach even more relevant for understanding China's colonial politic at the end of the twentieth century.

It is quite ironic that while the People's Republic was founded on an "anti-imperial nationalism", in the current post-colonial world, at a time when most nations are losing territory rather than recovering them, China is busily making good its claims on Hong Kong, Taiwan, and the Spratleys. In spite of Beijing's claims to the contrary, the removal of the British colonial administration from Hong Kong in 1997 does certainly not mean its liberation. There is something that rings true when one states that Tibet is literally a colony of China, despite any definitional problems with the theory of internal colonialism.

UYGHUR ETHNOGENESIS AND INTERNAL COLONIALISM

The following statement was told to me by a Uyghur tour guide at the ancient Astana underground tombs outside of Turfan. First heard in 1985, this widely believed Uyghur historiography was repeated on subsequent trips in 1990, 1992, 1994 and 1996: "The Uyghur people are the direct descendants of a high civilization of Central Asian nomadic people who had a kingdom based here in Turfan. The elegant paintings and wrapping in this tomb date to the Han Dynasty (206 B.C.-220 A.D.) and are comparable in beauty and sophistication. A mummy in the Xinjiang Provincial tombs also found in this area dates over 6 000 years old and proves the Uyghur people are even older than the Han Chinese".

Chinese histories notwithstanding, every Uyghur firmly believes that their ancestors were the indigenous people of the Tarim basin, now know as Xinjiang. This land was "their" land. Nevertheless, I have argued elsewhere the constructed "ethnogenesis" of the Uyghur (Gladney, 1990). In his popular history of Xinjiang, Jack Chen (1997 : 100) noted the re-introduction of the term Uyghur to describe the Turkic inhabitants of Chinese Turkestan. While a collection of nomadic steppe peoples known as the "Uyghur" have existed since before the 8th century, this identity was lost from the 15th to 20th centuries.

It is not until the fall of the Turkish Khanate (552-744 C.E.) to a people reported by the Chinese historians as Hui-he or Hui-hu that we find the beginnings of the Uyghur Empire described by Mackerras (1972). At this time the Uyghur were but one collection of nine nomadic tribes, who initially in confederation with other Basmil and Karlukh nomads, defeated the Second Turkish Khanate and then dominated the federation under the leadership of Koli Beile in 742 (Sinor, 1969 : 113). Gradual sedentarization of the Uyghur, and their defeat of the Turkish Khanate, occurred precisely as trade with the unified Tang state became especially lucrative. Samolin (1964 : 74-5) argues that the stability of rule, trade with the Tang and ties to the imperial court, as well as the growing importance of establishing fixed Manichaean ritual centers, contributed to a settled way of life for the Uyghur tribes.

Sedentarization and interaction with the Chinese state was accompanied by socioreligious change : the traditional shamanistic Turkic-speaking Uyghur came increasingly under the influence of Persian Manichaeanism, Buddhism, and eventually, Nestorian Christianity. Extensive trade and military alliances along the old Silk Road with the Chinese state developed to the extent that the Uyghur gradually adopted cultural, dress and even agricultural practices of the Chinese. Conquest of the Uyghur capital of Qarabalghasun in Mongolia by the nomadic Kyrgyz in 840, without rescue from the Tang who may have become by then intimidated by the wealthy Uyghur empire, led to further sedentarization and crystallization of Uyghur identity.

Indeed, it is the Uyghur nationality of Gansu today, not the Uyghur, who fled the Kyrgyz to Central China who are thought to preserve much of the original Uyghur history in their contemporary religious, linguistic, and cultural expression. One branch that ended up in what is now Turfan, took advantage of the unique socioecology of the glacier fed oases surrounding the Taklamakan and were able to preserve their merchant and limited agrarian practices, gradually establishing Khocho or Gaochang, the great Uyghur city-state based in Turfan for four centuries (850-1250).

Reflecting the earlier multi-ethnic, multi-langual, and multi-religious traditions established in Qarabalghasun, this is "Uyghuristan" described by Oda (1978) to which contemporary Uyghur separatists refer today. Most of the Uyghur separatists who are devoutly Muslim would not wish to resurrect the wide variety of religious and ritual practices found in the former Uyghuristan. The gradual Islamicization of the Uyghur from the 10th to as late as the 17th centuries in Hami, where according to Kahar Barat one could still find Uyghur Buddhists (Barat, personal communication), while displacing their Buddhist religion, did little to bridge these oases-based loyalties.

From that time on, the people of Uyghuristan centered in the Turfan depression who resisted Islamic conversion until the 17th century were the last to be known as Uyghur. The others were known only by their oasis or by the generic term of Muslims. With the arrival of Islam, the ethnonym "Uyghur" fades from the historical record. Instead, we find the proliferation of such localisms as "yerlik" (persons of the land), "sart" (caravaneer), "taranchi" (agriculturalists from the Tarim basin transplanted to Ili under Qjan-long), and other oasis-based localisms. Under the Manchu Qjing dynasty (1644-1911), the region was first brought under direct control from Beijing due to Manchu efforts to defeat the Zunghars, and it was only in the late 18th century that is received the name "Xinjiang" (new border or new dominion) in Chinese.

During the Republican period, Uyghur identity was marked by factionalism along locality, religious and political lines. Forbes (1986), in his detailed analysis of the complex warlord politics of Republican Xinjiang, finds important continuing distinctions between the three macro-regions of Xinjiang : the northwestern Zungaria, southern Tarim basin, and eastern Kumul-Turfan ("Uyghuristan") areas. Rudelson (1991 and 1992) confirms this persistent regional diversity along three, and the insightfully proposes that there are four macro-regions, dividing the southern Tarim into two district socio-ecological regions.

The Uyghur were recognized as a nationality in the 1930s in Xinjiang under a Soviet-influenced policy of nationality recognition that contributed to a widespread acceptance today of continuity with the ancient Uyghur kingdom and their eventual "ethnogenesis" as a bona fide nationality. This nationality designation not only masks tremendous regional and linguistic diversity, it also includes groups such as the Loplyk and Dolans that had very little to do with the oasis-based Turkic Muslims that became known as the Uyghur.

While rebellions by Yakub Beg in the late 19th century, and the short-lived establishments of the Eastern Turkestan Republics (TIRET) in Kashgar in 1933 and Yining in 1944 (Benson 1990), indicated Uyghur attempts at resisting expanding Chinese colonialism, these efforts failed just as those of the Uzbeks and Tadjiks in Csarist and Soviet Central Asia.

In the second half of the 20th Century, Xinjiang was occupied by the communist Chinese state in what was regarded as "peaceful liberation", in that, like Tibet, the People's Liberation Army did not have to fight its way into the province, but were welcomed by local leaders. "Minoritization" of the Uyghur became objectified when they were recognized by the Chinese state in 1950 as the Uyghur nationality, and the region was recognized as the Uyghur Autonomous Region in 1956. Chinese practices of "integration through immigration" has meant the in-migration of Han Chinese since the 1950s, with populations increasing from an estimated 5 percent in 1940 to 38 percent in 1990.

The expropriation of Xinjiang's vast mineral and petrochemical resources, with processing of petroleum products in the interior, primarily Lanzhou, further fits the internal colonialism model. Finally, the development of the tourist industry in the region as a "silk road" destination follows the line of touristic developments in the minority areas of the southwest that Oakes (1995) and Schein (1996) have analyzed as "internal colonialism" and "internal orientalism" respectively. The widespread diversity and factionalism found today among the Uyghur reflects a segmentary hierarchy of relationality common among all social groupings. Uyghur are divided from within by religious conflicts, in this case competing Sufi and non-Sufi factions, territorial loyalties (whether they be oases or places of origin), linguistic discrepancies, commoner-elite alienation, and competing political loyalties.

In addition, it might be argued that resistance to the Chinese state has also contributed to factionalism among the Uyghur, particularly among exile communities, as Ortner (1995) has argued for the complex and internally contested nature of resistance movements elsewhere. It is also important to note that Islam was only one of several unifying markes for Uyghur identity, depending on those with whom they were in significant opposition at the time. For example, to the Dungan (Hui), the Uyghur distinguish themselves as the legitimate autochthonous minority, since both share a belief in Sunni Islam. In contrast to the nomadic Muslim peoples (Kazakh or Kyrgyz), Uyghur might stress their attachment to the land and oasis of origin. In opposition to the Han Chinese, the Uyghur will generally emphasize their long history in the region.

The indigeneity of the Uyghur poses an alternative to Chinese historiographies of the region, which is consonant with "internal" colonizing regimes seeking to assert power in a region not previously their own. By moving the clock back far enough, any regime can claim the land as inoccupied. Claims of indigeneity always transgress nation-states that are founded most often under the conditions of post-coloniality.

SUB-ALTERN PERSPECTIVES ON THE CHINESE GEO-BODY

As Thongchai Winichakul (1994: 15) has eloquently argued in his path-breaking work, Siam Mapped, modern nations become established through the imposition of borders, boundaries, and categories of configuration upon previously borderless, unbounded, or uncategorized regions, peoples, and spaces. The invention and "imagined community" of the geo-body of Thailand, Winichakul argues, is effected through the state-sponsored definition of boundaries, peoples, centers, and peripheries. It is clear that parts of China considered to belong to its "geo-body", such as Hong Kong, Taiwan, Tibet, and Xinjiang will never be considered released from Chinese authority. To do so, most Chinese believe, would be to er one's limb. Recovery of Hong Kong and Taiwan is merely reconstructive surgery.

Taking inspiration from subaltern studies in South Asian scholarship and studies in cultural criticism, this chapter seeks to understand the implications of China's increasing internal colonialism and notions of the Chinese geo-body for its subaltern subjects. Perhaps it is the recognition of and tolerance for heterogeneity that has led to the influential impact of subaltern scholars in India, producing almost no similar movement in China. The sub-altern studies movement has drawn together a diverse group of South Asian scholars, including Giyatry Chakrovorty Spivak, Ranajit Guha, Dipesh Chakrabarty, Partha Chatterjee, Homi Bhabha, Gyanandra Pand Shaid Amin, and Akhil Gupta, to name just a few, who share a common commitment to writing post-colonialist studies of Indian society.

As Edward Said notes in his introduction to the now classic 1988 Guha and Spivak collection, under the editorship of Rjit Guha, the first volume of Subaltern Studies: Writings on South Asian History and Society appeared in 1982, with the claim that "hitherto Indian history had been written from a colonialist and elitist point of view, whereas a large part of Indian history had been made by the subaltern classes, and hence the need for a new historiography". In China, a full-fledged "subaltern scholarship" has yet to emerge. While there is a growing dissident and women's literature, particularly from Chinese intellectuals living abroad, clearly there is very little written from the perspective of minorities or other disadvantaged and dispossessed groups. Women's studies and the study of women in Chinese society have begun to give voice to a wide range of opinion heretofore rarely heard.

These studies have begun to look at Chinese society through a multitude of voices, many of which have been suppressed or ignored. The Gilmartin, Hershatter, Rofel and White 94 collection, Engendering China, has sought to open up a wide variety of perspectives on Chinese society, demonstrating that the internal colonialism in China of constructions of gender influence not only how engendered subjects act in that society, but also how we see them. Yet there have been few studies giving voice to those subalterns who have independent histories and cultural memories that cry out for understanding on their own terms, rather than placed in a peripheral, sub-regional, or "sub-ethnic" position.

This is why at the end of this century the plight of China's sub-alterns becomes increasingly important, both for understanding China's increasing nationalism but also the nature of modern internal colonialism. For this chapter, "subaltern subjects" are the very groups, individuals, and subjectivities that continue to be regarded as somehow less authentic, more peripheral, and farther removed from a core Chinese tradition.

CHINESE NATIONALISM AND ITS SUB-ALTERN IMPLICATIONS

In a Far Eastern Economic Review (November 1995) interview, Liu Binyan, the former Xinhua journalist and now dissident Chinese writer living in exile in Princeton, clearly indicated that attention to China's ethnic "sub-alterns" is critical to our understanding of contemporary Chinese nationalism. "Nationalism and Han chauvinism are now the only effective instruments in the ideological arsenal of the CCP", Liu declared. "Any disruption in the relationship with foreign countries or among ethnic minorities can be used stir `patriotic' sentiments of the people to support the communist authorities". The recent outpouring of reports over the last few months in the official Chinese media regarding separatist incidents in Xinjiang and elsewhere suggests that Liu Binyan was perhaps correct.

After denying them for decades and stressing instead China's "national unity", official reports have recently detailed

Tibetan and Muslim conflicts activities in the border regions of Tibet, Yunnan, Xinjiang, Ningxia, and Inner Mongolia. With the March 7'1997 bus bombings in Beijing, widely attributed (though never verified) to Uyghur separatists, coupled with the Urumqi bus bombings on the day of Deng Xiaoping's memorial on February 25 (killing 9 people), Beijing can no longer keep them secret. The Yining uprising on February 7'1997 that left at least 9 dead and 100s injured, with 7 Uyghur suspects now arrested and most probably slated for execution, has been heavily covered by the world's media.

This distinguishes the last few events from on-going problems in the region in the mid-1980s that have previously met with little media coverage. In the northwestern Uyghur Autonomous Region of Xinjiang, the Xinjiang Daily reported five serious incidents since February 1996, with a crackdown that rounded up 2,773 terrorist suspects, 6,000 pounds of explosives, and 31,000 rounds of ammunition. Overseas Uyghur groups have claimed that over 10,000 have been arrested in the round-up, with over 1,000 killed. On March 2 the pro-government mullah of Kashgar's Idgah mosque and his son were stabbed by knife-wielding Uyghur militants, on May 27 there was aner attack on a senior government official, and September 1996 six Uyghur government officials were killed by other Uyghurs in Yecheng.

The government has responded with a host of random arrests and new policy announcements. On June 12 1996, the Xinjiang Daily reported "rampant activities by splittists inside and outside China", that contributed to the closure of 10 "unauthorized" places of worship, the punishment of mullahs who had preached illegally outside their mosques, and the execution of 13 people on 29th in Aksu county (an area that is 99 percent Uyghur) supposedly for murder, robbery, rape, and other violent crimes.

Troop movements to the area have reportedly been the largest since the suppression of the Baren township insurrection in April 1990, perhaps related to the nationwide "Strike Hard" campaign. This campaign, launched in Beijing last April was originally intended to clamp down on crime and corruption, but has now been turned against "splittests" in Xinjiang, calling for the building of "great wall of steel" against them.

The Xinjiang Daily on December 16 1996 contained the following declaration by Wang Lequan, the Region's First Party Secretary: "We must oppose separatism and illegal religious activities in a clear and comprehensive manner striking hard and effectively against our enemies". Intra-Muslim conflicts and anti-government protests among the Hui have occurred since 1992 in Xi'an, Yunnan, and Ningxia, China's only Autonomous Region for its largest Muslim minority. In Southern Ningxia, an intra-Sufi Muslim factional struggle in Xi in the Winter and Spring of 1992-93 led to the deaths of 49 Hui Muslims and the arrests of 4 local and provincial-level leaders, with 2 of them receiving life-sentences.

Though reported only in November 1996 in the New York Times, the government's harsh response to this and other local disputes have angered Muslims throughout China. Madrassahs, or mosque-related schools, have been closed and a moratorium on mosque-building imposed. This Spring (1997), the National Peoples Congress passed a New Criminal Law that redefined "counter-revolutionary" crimes to be "crimes against the State", liable to severe prison terms and even execution. included in "crimes against the state" were any actions considered to involve "ethnic discrimination" or "stirring up anti-ethnic sentiment".

Many human rights activists have argued that this is a thinly veiled attempt to criminalize "political" actions and to make them appear as illegal as traffic violations, supporting China's claims that it holds "no political prisoners". Since any minority activity could be regarded as stirring "anti-ethnic feeling", many ethnic activists are concerned that the New Criminal Law will be easily turned against them. Remarkably early summer 1996 a new directive requiring all Party Secretaries down to the village level to be Han Chinese in Xinjiang indicates the lengths the government is willing to go to re-establish firm control over the region. There are few Han Chinese at thillage level in Southern Xinjiang.

While much is reported about the policy shifts and re-imposed hardline in Tibet, including the prohibition of all public displays of the Dalai Lama's picture and the political re-education of monks, less is known about the extent of the unrest and cracowns in Xinjiang. Unlike Tibet, intra-Muslim factionalism and religio-political killings make the situation in Muslim areas much more complex and volatile. Without a Dalai Lama to sort out disputes and impose a restraining hand, China's Muslims who are riven by political, religious, and local factionalisms, are more susceptible to local and widespread violence. Muslims in China are distinguished from each other not only by linguistic, locality, and nationality distinctions, but also by a history of Islamic factionalism.

Though predominantly Sunni, Muslims in China have divided, sometimes violently, over Sufind reform movements often attempting to make Islam less "Chinese" and more true to their updated versions of its Middle Eastern roots. Since the Ming dynasty, overly harsh government responses to these intra-Muslim conflicts have often led to a unification of formerly factionalized Muslims against the intervening State. PRC officials have increasingly tried to nip intra-Muslim conflicts in the bud or mediate local conflicts, with varying success. It is clear that domestic disputes may have international implications.

The People's Republic of China, as one of five permanent voting members of the U.N. Security Council, and as a significant exporter of military hardware to the Middle East, has become a recognized player in Middle Eastern affairs. With the decline in trade with most Western nations after the Tiananmen massacre in the early 1990s, the importance of China's Middle Eastern trading partners (all of them Muslim, since China did not have relations with Israel until recently), rose considerably.

This may account for the fact that China established diplomatic relations with Saudi Arabia in August 1990, with the first direct Sino-Saudi exchanges taking place since 1949 (Saudi Arabia canceled its long-standing diplomatic relationship with Taiwan and withdrew its ambassador, despite a lucrative trade history).

In the face of a long-term friendship with Iraq, China went along with most of the UN resolutions in the war against Iraq. Although it abstained from Resolution 678 on supporting the ground-war, making it unlikely that Chinese workers will be welcomed back into Kuwait, China enjoys a fairly "Teflon" reputation in the Middle East as an untarnished source of low-grade weaponry and cheap reliable labor. Recent press accounts have noted an increase in China's exportation of military hardware to the Middle East since the Gulf War, perhaps due to a need to balance its growing imports of gulf oil required to fuel its overheated economy. Unlike Tibet, China can thus ill afford to ignore its Muslim problem.

Yet Chinese authorities are correct that increasing international attention to the plight of indigenous border peoples have put pressure on the regions, with even the German government calling for more human rights in Tibet following a June 15-17 1996 visit of the Dalai Lama. In Amsterdam, on June 2nd, Amnesty International supporters passed out fliers in Damme Square calling for the release of Kajikhumar Shabdan, a 72-year-old ethnic Kazakh, poet, writer, and radio broadcaster, who has been held in prison since July 1987. The fliers were printed on cards in Ensh and Dutch with places for signatures to be mailed to Abdulahat Abdurixit, People's Government Chairman of Xinjiang in Ürümchi. In Munich, on November 11, a "Days of Uygur Youth" conference attracted 100 delegates from Europe, Central Asia, and the Middle East interested in what was termed the "plight" of the Uyghurs.

Notably, the former chairman of the Unrepresented Nations and People's Organization (UNPO) based in Geneva is the Uygur, Erkin Alptekin, son of the Uygur Nationalist leader, Isa Yusuf Alptekin who died in Istanbul in December 1996 where there is now a park dedicated to his memory. There are at least five international organizations working for the independence of Xinjiang, known as Eastern Turkistan, and based in Amsterdam, Munich, Istanbul, Melbourne, and New York. Clearly, with Xinjiang representing the last Muslim region under communism, Chinese authorities have more to be concerned about than just international support for Tibetan independence.

The real question is, why call attention to these Tibetan and Muslim activities and external organizations now? The Istanbul-based groups have existed since the 1950s, and the Dalai Lama has been active since his exile in 1959. Separatist actions have taken place on a small but regular basis se the expansion of market and trade policies in China, and with the opening of six overland gateways to Xinjiang in addition to the trans-Eurasian railway since 1991, there seems to be no chance of closing up shop.

In his 1994 visit to the newly independent nations of Central Asia, Li Peng called for the opening of a "new Silk Road". This was a clear attempt to calm fears in the newly established Central Asian States over Chinese expansionism, as was the April 1996 Shanghai communique that solidified existing Sino-Central Asian Borders. This was perhaps the most recent and clearest example of Chinese government efforts to finally keep hold and fully map its "geo-body".

SUB-ALTERN SEPARATISM AND CHINESE RESPONSE

China's geo-body is not threatened by internal dismemberment. Such as they are, China's separatists are small in number, poorly equipped, loosely linked, and vastly outgunned by the People's Liberation Army and People's Police. Local support for separatist activities, particularly in Xinjiang, is ambivalent and ambiguous at best, given the economic disparity between these regions and their foreign neighbors, which are generally much poorer and in some cases such as Tadjikistan, riven by civil war. Memories in the region are strong of mass starvation and widespread destruction during the Sino-Japanese and civil war in the first half of this century, not to mention the chaotic horrors of the Cultural Revolution.

International support for Tibetan causes has done little to shake Beijing's gron the region. Many local activists are calling not for complete separatism or real independence, but more often issues express concerns over environmental degradation, anti-nuclear testing, religious freedom, over-taxation, and recently imposed limits on child-bearing. Many ethnic leaders are simply calling for "real" autonomy according to Chinese law for the five Autonomous Regions that are each led by First Party Secretaries who are all Han Chinese controlled by Beijing. Extending the "Strike Hard" campaign to Xinjiang, Wang Lequan, the Party Secretary for Xinjiang, recently declared: "there will be no compromise between us and the separatists".

Beijing's official publicization of the separatist issue may have more to do with domestic politics than any real internal or external threat. Recent moves suggest efforts to promote Chinese nationalism as a "unifying ideology" that will prove more attractive than communism and more manageable than capitalism.

By highlighting separatist threats and externintervention, China can divert attention away from its own domestic instabilities of rising inflation, increased income disparity, displaced "floating populations", Hong Kong reunification, and the post-Deng succession. Perhaps nationalism will be thely "unifying ideology" left to a Chinese nation that has begun to distance itself from Communism, as it has Confucianism, Buddhism, and Daoism in the past. As Bruce Kapferer has noted, nationalism "makes the political religious".

This is perhaps why regiously-based nationalisms, like Islamic Fundamentalism and Tibetan Buddhism, are targeted by Beijing. At the same time, a firm lid on Muslim activism in China will send a message to forn Muslim militant organizations to stay out of China's internal affairs. In a July 1994 interview with Iran's former ambassador to China in Tehran, I was told that Iran would never intervene in a Muslim crackdown in China, despite its support for the tring of Kubrawiyyah Sufi Imams from Gansu and close foreign relations with China. Any event, domestic and international, can be used as an excuse to promote nationalist goals, the building of a new unifying ideology.

As Shen Guofan from the Ministry of Foreign Trade and Economic Cooperation revealed in his statement concerning the most recent Sino-U.S. trade dispute : "If the U.S. goes so far as to implement its trade retaliation, China will, according to its foreign trade law, take countermeasures to safeguard its sovereignty and national esteem." Trade and separatism become obstacles not to economic and political development, but to preserving national esteem. Any action deemed by Beijing to be "unpatriotic" is quickly interpreted as an attempt to split the country, which runs counter to Chinese efforts at reunification of its entire geo-body. Hong Kong becomes the first example of the attainment of China's historic destiny, with islands such as the Spratleys and Diaoyutai, to say nothing of Taiwan, arded as impediments to national development and physical reunion.

CHINA'S EXPANDING INTERNAL COLONIALISM

In his recent visit to the U.S., Defense Minister Chi Haotian, declared: "We hope to see a peaceful settlement [regarding Taiwan] yet refuse to renounce the use of force.... The entire Chinese history shows that whoever splits the motherland will end up condemned by history". This follows the new Chinese History Project launched by Song Jian, Minister of Science and Technology, aimet writing a new chronology of China. In a Science and Technology Daily editorial, published May 17 1996, Song Jian stated that the project's goal was to demonstrates its 6,000 year "unbroken, unilineal" development. "Unlike those in Egypt, Babylon and India", Song declared, "the Chinese civilization has lasted for 5,000 years without a break".

The project, to be completed by October 1, 1999, clearly will take a dim view of anyone accused of separatism. As long as Muslim activism is regarded as "separatism", it will be regarded not only as going against China's national destiny, but against history itself. It is through the writing and re-writing of history that colonial and sub-altern status most often becomes internalized, both among the minorities and among the majority. This "internalized colonialism" lead to self and other-perception as "minority", and subject only to definition by state categories and policies. It also displaces indigenous prior claims to land and voice in the administration of local affairs.

Future prospects for the Uyghur in the 21st century may be low considering the proclivity of Chinese historiographers to write histories from the perspective of their "idealized" view. The Uyghur are in danger of being written out! This scenario was already pre-figured by the science fiction novelist David Wingrove in his eight volume futuristic novel, Chung Kuo (The Middle Kingdom). Once the Chinese have taken over the globe in the later 21st century, they re-write history, dating back to the first Chinese "conquest" of Central Asia in the Han dynasty.

"Pan Chao! It sometimes seemed as if half the films ever made had been about Pan Chao! He was the great hero of Chung Kuo-the soldier turned diplomat turned conqueror. In A.D. 73 he had been sent, with thirty-six followers, as ambassador to the king of Shen Shen in Turkestan... bringing Shen Shen under Han control... Over the next twenty-four years, by bluff and cunning and sheer force of personality, Pan Chao had brought the whole of Asia under Han domination. In A.D.97 he has stood on the shore of the Caspian Sea, an army of seventy thousand vassals gathered behind him, facing the great Ta Ts'in,the Roman Empire. The rest was history, known to every schoolboy.

Rome had fallen. And not as Kim had portrayed it, to Alaric and the Goths in the fifth century, but to the Han in the first. There had been no break in order, no decline into darkness. No Dark Ages and no Christianity - of, and what lovely idea that was : organized religion! The thought of it. In his version of events, Han science had stagnated by the fourth century A.D. and Chung Kuo had grown insular, until, in the nineteen century, the Europeans - and what a strange ring that phrase had; not Hung Mao, but "Europeans"- had kicked the rotten door of China in. Ah, and that too. Not Chung Kuo.

Kim called it China. As if had been named after the First Emperor's people, the Ch'in. Ridiculous!

He strugged. "I suppose you might call it an alternative history of Chung Kuo. Chung Kuo as it might have been had the Ta Ts'in legions won the Battle of Kazatin". The nationalist re-writing of history, Prasenjit Duara (1995) reminds us, is not unique to China, but accompanies nationalist projects around the globe. The threat of this re-writing is not to China's neighbors, for they do not belong to a nationalist history of China's past or future geo-body. Rather, the rise in nationalist rhetoric in China may have the greatest implications for its internal colonial others, it sub-altern subjects. And, one should not forget the ominous words contained in the Chinese national anthem: "The Chinese race is at a most crucial moment, we should stand up and build up a new Great Wall with our blood and flesh".

As Franke and Twitchett note in the introduction to their sweeping Alien Regimes and Border States:

"Traditional histories of China depict the Khitan, Jurchen, and Mongols as "outsiders", inrupting into "Chinese" territory. But this is a misleading oversimplification that needs to be laid to rest forever. In spite of what is shown in modern historical atlases, the T'ang, like its predecessors, never had any clearly defined and demarcated northern frontier... There was never a continuous defensive line or a defined frontier. There was a line of fortified border prefectures and counties, a few fortresses in strategic places, and a scattering of military colonies, military stud farms, beacon signal towers, and military picket-outposts. It was a defense in depth..." (Franke and Twitchett 1994 : 7).

The real question is, what will happen to those Chinese citizens on its borders, should a nationalist movement rise up that sees them as more of a threat than as part of a China that is multi-national and multi-ethnic. If nationalist sentiments prevail during this time of transition, what will happen to those sub-altern subjects currently living in China, but beyond the Great Wall? Europe made modernity both universal and uniquely European. Kenneth Pomeranz and R. Bin Wong tackle one part of that invention, the idea that Europe contained a unique, indigenous capacity to industrialize that made it a universal model for economic development. In the light of this idea, economic disparities among rich and poor countries seem to emerge because nations succeed variously in developing their own style of Western capitalism, as North America did most successfully.

Europe's modernity seems to be the secret of global success: the more integrated into the world economy any country is, the richer it becomes, as economies around the world converge along a trend of increasing productivity and material well-being in a historical process that is now called globalization. This entire scenario is in question, and these authors reconsider its original validity.

Pomeranz and Wong accept the idea that industrialization launches modern economic development and ask why it happened first in Europe and not China, specifically, in Britain but not the Yangzi Delta. Scholars have answered this question in the past by saying that no matter how rich China had once been, it was not ready for industrialization in 1800. Pomeranz and Wong conclude, however, that parts of China were indeed ready, which reopens the question, "Why Europe?" They argue that Europe's modern productivity did not arise from uniquely European modes of economic organization or from uniquely European levels or patterns of economic growth in early modern centuries. British industrialism depended on British natural resources and British assets in the wider world. It occurred during a particular conjuncture in world history and could have happened elsewhere.

This work sheds new critical light on modernity by detaching its origins from Europe and by arguing that early modernity was not modernity's logical precursor or inchoate immanence. Transitions followed unpredictable pathways. Contingency and conjuncture shunted China and Europe into discontinuous trends that Pomeranz calls "the great divergence." As Wong indicates, exogenous factors affecting

China and Europe moved inside networks of mobility that carried people, ideas, armies, commodities, technology, and finance all over the early modern world. These networks had a broad impact on regional histories in Europe, Africa, America, and Asia. Networks that connected regions of early modern China, each with their own individual histories, also ran into Central Asia and overseas. Europe had separate but connected regional histories that spilled outside Europe.

Activities in and across the Atlantic Basin, Indian Ocean, and Pacific Rim participate in both European and Chinese history. Early modern spaces did not enclose historical territories in the manner of modern national boundaries. In the course of "the great divergence," modernity disciplined the historical imagination inside national state territories, so that pre-modern histories appeared to operate inside the same national confinement. Pomeranz and Wong weave histories of China and Europe together in innovative and challenging ways. Changing times are changing historical thinking about modernity.

Here we have two historians of China, teaching in North America, writing for an American journal, doubly transgressing boundaries of European history, first by comparing Europe to China, and then by saying that Europe's take-off to modern economic growth was contingent, conjunctural, and partly exogenous. These ideas seem to be apt for the history of an age before modern boundaries arrived, and for scholars in a day when modern boundaries are dissolving, but transgressing national histories presents empirical, conceptual, and diplomatic problems for a profession built on national sensibilities. My comments here focus, therefore, on the importance of "the great divergence" as part of a larger historical process of modern inequality that runs across all national histories and into the intimate nooks and crannies of everyday localities on all the continents.

Pomeranz and Wong describe an early modern baseline from which to measure economic inequality between Europe and China. They see Europe and China as having similar potentials for economic development in the eighteenth century.

They argue that the great economic divergence of the nineteenth century defies explanation without taking into account exogenous assets that sustained Britain's original industrialization. These assets were exogenous in two senses: some lay outside Britain's national borders and others came from outside the market economy. Britain acquired coal, cotton, and profitable trade opportunities around the world by means other than "Smithian" market exchange.

These assets gave Britain economic advantages China did not have. Britain used these advantages to fuel a modern industrial development that spread across Europe and North America, as Western countries enriched one another with industry (and, we might add, with many assets acquired by non-Smithian means, including all the natural resources in the Americas). Early modern baseline similarities with Britain also characterized regions in South Asia, where merchants and manufacturers communicated and competed in networks of mobility that walked, ran, sailed, and then steamed from one end of Eurasia to the other.

As Wong points out, similarities among regions across Eurasia continued after divergence began. Industry actually spread faster in parts of Asia than in much of Europe and America. The first Indian cotton mill appeared in Bombay in 1853, and in 1881, the British government imposed the first Factory Act to counteract India's competitive advantage from low-cost labor and raw materials. In 1914, India had the world's fourth largest cotton textile industry. Textiles, coal, iron, steel, jute, and other industrial manufactures comprised 20 percent of Indian exports, valued at 10 percent of national income.

The American consul at Bombay then called India "one of the few large countries of the world where there is an 'open door' for the trade of all countries." In the next twenty-five years, Indian industrialization increased 58 percent, compared to slower, more uneven growth in Europe. Nevertheless, India's work force became increasingly agricultural and its population more subject to chronic hunger, in an open economy constructed on European lines, where most new farm investment benefited commercial crops destined for export. In 1943–1944, famine in Bengal-provoked by world war and spread by ubiquitous market forces-killed three million people in one year. Economic divergence thus involved more than rates of industrialization, and indeed, more than economics.

There were no statistics to measure diverging national incomes before 1870, but already by 1820, intellectuals in London and Calcutta claimed that Britain led the way to modernity. This claim did not arise from economic analysis as much as from the cultural impact of British military victories over Napoleon, Gurkhas (in Nepal), and Marathas (in western India). By 1870, divergence was a global cultural phenomenon. Official statistics became its instrument and indication. Like Malthusian ideas-which were used to explain famine and indentured labor migration in India long before census data could measure population pressure on the land -Europe's superior productivity compared to Asia was taken for granted before it became a fact, sometime after 1850.

Even then, belief in Western superiority did not need much empirical support, and its explanation still less, because the new idea of divergence simply translated old ideas about cultural difference into the market lexicon of industrial imperialism. By 1870, the supremacy of white Western men had assumed its modern industrial form. Modern theorists explained economic inequalities by reference to essential differences among people who ranked high and low on the economic scale. Difference explained inequality. Poverty marked inferiority and earned subordination. These basic principles of divergence applied equally to race, class, gender, and civilization.

Modern knowledge substantiated inequality and made it sensible. Like the making of the English working class, modern inequality began before large-scale industrialization. As British armies fought the French and Dutch in Europe and overseas, British authors like James Mill opened a cultural space for British supremacy. Across the later decades of divergence, Orientalism provided a flexible tool for explaining Asian backwardness that Karl Marx and Max Weber wrote into the foundations of social science. Social Darwinism evolved inside High Imperialism and implicated the poor in all societies.

Already by 1845, however, English urban poverty and Irish famine mortality had made economic divergence a political issue in the United Kingdom. Debates about the causes of the Irish famine mirror those about Indian famines: one side blamed native tradition, the other British imperialism. Such flatly two-sided debates became standard dramas of modern culture among educated middle classes, who learned to appreciate and normalize poverty as a feature of the modern world.

Among middle-class reformers and incipient development experts, it became common knowledge that ignorance, iniquity, and inequity thrived among poor people. These components of poverty became targets for reform. Missionary zeal arrived in India during wars with Napoleon, but British abolitionism launched the age of modern reformism, when free labor became the hallmark of progress just at the time when industry demanded armies of workers. After 1833, identical missionary and social reform efforts spread across the American South, Africa, and Asia. Reformers addressed a standard set of issues.

The natives' abuse of women became a favorite theme. Development discourse emerged on frontiers of poverty produced by modern inequality, as reformers attacked rigid native hierarchy, despotic native rulers, local corruption, irrational superstition, primitive technology, clannish and tribal closed-mindedness, and blind adherence to archaic ways. At the same time, however, native tradition-invented, rediscovered, romanticized, valorized, and enforced by law-became national culture. In 1880, Weber argued that each nation's unique identity made the national state the rational basis for modern political organization and economic policy-making. Weber spent the rest of his life sorting out cultural traits that constituted (universal) modernity and (national) tradition. By 1920, modernity and tradition evoked codified collections of cultural practices that respectively promoted and restrained economic progress.

National leaders promoted development with modern institutions and rallied the nation with tradition. In South Asia, linkages between modernity and tradition lay deep in "village society," where traditional order met rural development. Combining (Western) modernity and (Asian) tradition became the mantra of national governments as the subordination of tradition to modernity materialized in economic disparities between elites and subalterns. Tradition and modernity became political allies and adversaries as they attached variously to social conflicts fostered by modern inequality.

The great divergence is therefore neither a singular process nor a simple empirical fact, and it pervades modern history as it combines and connects differently constructed inequalities in and across national borders. In efforts to historicize modern inequality, two approaches are most prominent. One considers territories such as national states to be separate entities. Comparing and aggregating data from separate territories produces larger empirical patterns. The U.S. Census Bureau, United Nations, and all international development agencies use this approach. Its historical and political implication is that each geographical container for data is responsible for conditions inside its borders.

Another approach considers territories contextually inside wider networks of interaction, connectivity, and causation. This approach is more common in studies of poor countries subject to foreign intervention and external influence. Dependency theory and world-systems theory are two formal methods of contextual analysis that came out of research on Latin America and Africa, respectively. Studies of colonialism are always at least implicitly comparative. Comparative history is a different exercise in light of each approach: independent comparisons consider territories separately, and contextual comparisons consider systems of regional interrelations.

Pomeranz and Wong invite us to explore the overlapping of these two approaches and to follow evidence in historical sources back and forth between them. It is notable that economic historians of China who write in English typically adopt a national perspective on pre-modern China. This in part reflects the actual closure and self-containment of the huge Chinese economy in pre-modern times; it also reflects imperial and national ideas in Chinese policy, ideology, and statistical data. Historians of Japan also often stress Japan's uniqueness and closure in early modern times. In Japan and China, however, official ideologies and foreign accounts appear to have exaggerated the extent to which their economies excluded the outside world.

As Wong indicates, they both seem to have been very much part of an Asian trading world in early modern times. Pomeranz uses an array of data in cross-regional comparisons that lead him out of a strictly national perspective into wider early modern contexts of economic development. Economic history in South Asia has had a strong contextual impulse from the 1870s, when Dadabhai Naoroji argued that the British economy was enriching itself at India's expense. Naoroji wrote in England. He became a leader of the Indian National Congress. He invented economic nationalism "from below" in the midst of the great divergence, in a country supremely open to world markets under British control.

It is intriguing to imagine what impact Irish debates might have had on his thinking. The idea spread quickly that the world economy includes exploitative powers that benefit rich countries and deprive poor countries of assets they need to develop. In 1930, Jawaharlal Nehru expressed a homegrown underdevelopment theory by saying, "the great poverty and misery of the Indian People are due, not only to foreign exploitation in India but also to the economic structure of society, which the alien rulers support so that their exploitation may continue."

In this light, he clarified the project of nationalism by saying, "In order to remove this poverty and misery and to ameliorate the condition of the masses, it is essential to make revolutionary changes in the present economic and social structure of society and to remove the gross inequalities." Contextual dynamics of inequality inside South Asia have remained prominent since Nehru's day. Current academic efforts to track the local impact of globalization have a rich pedigree. New connections between the world economy and South Asian localities emerge every day. As I write, globalization seems to have increased violence against women over claims to dowry payments in India.

In the eighteenth century, multicultural enclaves of commercial capitalism in India seem to have sustained British trades and military adventures throughout Asia. Recapturing early modern history in its own context became more difficult as divergence progressed. British imperialists tossed aside Indian partners, and racial divisions hardened in India as British industrial supremacy expanded worldwide. Once set in motion, global divergence and modern inequality changed their composition, organization, and conceptualization during four broad periods: 1820–1880, 1880–1920, 1920–1980, and post-1980. Scholars in each period recomposed early modern history accordingly.

It now appears that early modern authors themselves did not live in a world of divergence. Even when they wrote about economic development, they did not describe diverging economies or domestic trends in inequality. Before 1800, inequality appears to be a static fact; and among places, it appears to comprise different amounts and types of wealth in different environments. In 1793, for example, Robert Bruce surveyed British activity in Asia without saying Britain was more productive or prosperous. He rather stressed that Britain and France sought to secure economic benefits in Asia with military victories, and that Britain had used its military "to revive its arts, diffuse its manufactured productions, restore its revenue, and once more, to give splendour to its empire."

Thomas Munro spent thirty years in India working for the East India Company, in its peak years of military expansion, and he concluded that Indians were as much a nation of shopkeepers as the British. In 1818, James Mill published his triumphal history of British India without claiming British economic supremacy. Three decades later, however, Marx took that supremacy for granted. Beguiled by the factory, Marx and his peers lost sight of early modern facts depicted simply and unabashedly by Bruce and Munro: the British military secured East India Company profits in India. A British alliance between the military and merchant capital had set the new empire in motion.

Bruce and Munro did not know how much of that merchant capital was Indian and could never have known how important the India empire would be for British industry. The surge in English factory production that beguiled Marx apparently began after Waterloo. British war expenditure supplemented private industrial investments, and Indian revenues supported British war finance. After the war, industry took center stage. British trade policies to support English industry impoverished weavers in Ireland and India at the same time as the great divergence began.

After 1880, High Imperialism reorganized global disparities on a larger scale than ever before and began to institutionalize economic development at the same time. In the 1920s, nationalist movements in Asia and Africa shifted debates about modern inequality into a national framework of analysis under the umbrella of the League of Nations and the British Commonwealth. After 1950, High Nationalism covered the world of conflict over socialist and capitalist development strategies.

Two international meetings represent the official reorganization of modern inequality under High Imperialism and High Nationalism. In the 1880s, treaties in Berlin partitioned Africa and wrote the collective power of rich countries into international law. In 1954, leaders of non-aligned nations met in Bandung, where they defined the First, Second, and Third World, thus formalizing a division of the world into rich and poor, and socialist and capitalist, countries. After 1980, modern inequality lost its Cold War guise, High Nationalism declined, the Second World disappeared, and socialist development options gave way to globalization. Moishe Postone describes the new context as characterized by "the weakening and partial dissolution of. . . national state bureaucracies, industrial labour unions, and physically centralized, state dependent capitalist firms."

He explains, "Those institutions have been undermined in two directions: by the emergence of a new plurality of social groupings, organizations, movements, parties, regions, and subcultures on the one hand and by a process of globalization and concentration of capital on a new, very abstract level that is far removed from immediate experience and is apparently outside the effective control of the state machinery on the other."

In this new environment, religiously inspired cultural nationalism expressed a new vision of modern inequality in and across national borders. Fundamentalism and majoritarianism flourished in rich and poor countries alike amidst invisible mysteries of the market, and in the United States, the great divergence exchanged its Cold War costume to become "clash of civilizations" and "global anarchy" infested with threats of global terrorism.

Freed from fears of revolution after 1990, experts have focused new attention on economic inequality untainted by class analysis. The results are stunning. In an essay written for the World Bank and aptly entitled, "Divergence, Big Time," Lant Pritchett calculated that ratios of per-capita income between rich and poor countries increased more than six-fold between 1870 and 1985, as income levels dispersed over an ever-widening range of variation and rich and poor economies clustered on either end of a broader spectrum. Today, inequality is increasing. The gap between the richest and poorest countries is growing.

The poorest of the poor are an ever-larger proportion of the world population. Absolute poverty increased in the 1990s most dramatically in Africa, where an average household now consumes 20 percent less than twenty-five years ago. These trends implicate history in various ways. Historians who write about high-income countries study a shrinking global elite minority. The population of the rich OECD countries shrank as a proportion of the world population from 20 percent in 1960 to 15 percent in 1993, and may be 10 percent by 2025.

Already, a mere 10 percent of the world's people live in twelve countries with over $20,000 per-capita GDP, mostly in the United States (45 percent), Japan (21 percent), Germany (14 percent), and France (10 percent). Rich islands of national history are getting richer and smaller at the same time, which encourages scholars in rich countries to expand their global reach through area studies, world history, cultural studies, and global studies. The best facilities for studying the world sit in rich countries. The United States has a dozen libraries with more books from South Asia than any library in South Asia. Most funding to study the world is in rich countries, where the most prestigious, well-funded academic paradigms emerge for economic and policy analysis as well as for history.

Meanwhile, 80 percent of the world's people live and work in thirty-six African and nineteen Asian countries with under $1,000 per-capita GDP, large proportions in China (34 percent), India (26 percent), Indonesia (5 percent), Pakistan (4 percent), Bangladesh (3 percent), Nigeria (3 percent), Vietnam (2 percent), and the Philippines (3 percent). Research and library budgets decline faster than national income as we move down the scale of national wealth. Even getting basic books and journals containing fundamental research on one's own country is impossible for most history teachers and scholars in poor countries. All this material is in New York, Amsterdam, Paris, and London.

Rich people are increasing their share of the wealth. In the thirty years after 1962, the richest 20 percent of the world population increased its share from 70 percent to 85 percent. Between 1977 and 1999, the richest 20 percent of U.S. households increased their share of national income from 44 percent to 50 percent, and the highest 1 percent increased their share six times more, from 7 to 13 percent. Economic disparities globally, nationally, and locally-in India, China, Europe, and North America-appear to be increasing in comparable, connected ways. In this context, Ken Pomeranz and Bin Wong invite historians to reconsider the rise of modern inequality in light of new perspectives on early modernity fostered by contemporary globalization.

From a historian's perspective, decolonization was one of the most important political developments of the twentieth century because it turned the world into the stage of history. Until World War I, historical writing had been the work of the European conquerors that, in the words of Oswald Spengler, had made the world appear to 'revolve around the pole of this little part-world' that is Europe.

With few exceptions, the regions outside Europe were seen to be inhabited by people without the kind of history capable of shaping the world. The process of decolonizaton, which began towards the end of World War I, was accompanied by the appearance of national historical consciousness in these regions, that is, the history, not of dynasties or the work of God/gods, but of a people as a whole.

To be sure, historical writing continues to be filtered through national preoccupations, but the rapid spread of modern historical writing to most of the world also enabled us to see how happenings in one region - no matter how peripheral or advanced - were often linked to processes and events in other parts. It became possible to grasp, as did the leaders of decolonization, the entire globe as an interconnected entity for understanding and action. There are remarkably few historical studies of decolonization as a whole, despite the importance of the subject. This is not entirely surprising because it is neither a coherent event such as the Russian Revolution, nor a well defined phenomenon like fascism. The timing and patterns of decolonization were extremely varied, and the goals of the movement in different countries were not always consistent with each other.

Indeed, we have had to exclude from our consideration the pre-twentieth century independence movements in the Americas from European powers, as well as the later decolonization of the Pacific islands from powers such as New Zealand, Australia, Britain and the Netherlands starting in the 1960s. In both cases, the circumstances of decolonization were very different from the core period and region of our consideration: Asia and Africa from the early years of the twentieth century until the 1960s. Within this approximate time and region, decolonization refers to the process whereby colonial powers transferred institutional and legal control over their territories and dependencies to indigenously based, formally sovereign, nation-states.

The political search for independence often began during the inter-war years and fructified within fifteen years of the end of World War II in 1945. It should be noted that there were many formally independent countries, such as Iran and China, whose leaders considered themselves to have been informally and quasi-legally subordinated to colonial powers, and who viewed their efforts for autonomy as part of the anti-imperialist movement. Therefore decolonization represented not only the transference of legal sovereignty, but a movement for moral justice and political solidarity against imperialism. It thus refers both to the anti-imperialist political movement and to an emancipatory ideology which sought or claimed to liberate the nation and humanity itself.

Even within these specifications, decolonization varied sufficiently from country to country, and often within the same country, to make generalizations quite risky. Take for instance, the case of China. Here was a vigorous anti-imperialist movement directed against the Western powers and Japan, based largely on an ethic of socialist emancipation. Yet there was no felt need to critique the West culturally – to ideologically decolonize in the manner of a Frantz Fanon or Mahatma Gandhi – since it had been only partially and informally colonized, and was occupied by an Asian power, Japan. Additionally, the meaning of decolonization as a process has itself been differently evaluated over time.

Our historiographical understanding of decolonization during the period when political independence from imperialist powers was taking place was shaped considerably by the writings of nationalist statesmen and historians, as well as a generation of Western historians who were optimistic or sympathetic to the process. More recently, the debates around post-colonialism have questioned the extent or thoroughness of 'decolonization' when independence from colonial powers meant the establishment of nation-states closely modelled upon the very states that undertook imperialism. Here again, the post-colonial critique has found more or less sympathy in different places according to the historical experiences of the people there. The volume will try to represent this variation without losing sight of the core historical character of the process.

If we can pinpoint a particular event to symbolize the beginnings of this movement, it would be the victory of Japan over Czarist Russia in the war of 1905, which was widely hailed as the first victory of the dominated peoples against an imperial power. Sun Yat-sen, the father of Chinese nationalism, reminisced about this event in a speech he made in Japan in 1925. He was on a ship crossing the Suez Canal soon after news of the Japanese victory became known. When the ship was docked in the canal, a group of Arabs mistook him for a Japanese and enthusiastically flocked around him. Even upon discovering their mistake, they continued to celebrate their solidarity with him against the imperialist powers. In the speech, Sun developed the theme of a racial or colour war against the white race for whom 'blood is thicker than water' and urged the oppressed Asians of common colour and culture to unify and resist imperialism.

Similarly, the event symbolizing the culmination of this movement was the Bandung Conference, a meeting of the representatives of twentynine new nations of Asia and Africa, held in Bandung, Indonesia in 1955, fifty years after the Russo-Japanese war. The conference aimed to express solidarity against imperialism and racism and promote economic and cultural cooperation among these nations. China, India and Indonesia were key players in the meeting. The conference finally led to the non-aligned movement in 1961, a wider Third World force in which participants avowed their distance from the two superpowers - aligning themselves neither with the United States or Soviet Union - during the Cold War. However, conflicts developed among these non-aligned nations - for instance between India and China in 1962 - which eroded the solidarity of the Bandung spirit.

With the dissolution of the socialist bloc and the end of the Cold War in 1989, the non-aligned movement - this in reality had included both truly neutral countries and those that were aligned with one or the other superpower - became irrelevant. The imperialism we are concerned with in this volume was the imperialism of Western nation-states and later Japan that spread from roughly the mid-eighteenth century to Asia, Africa, and the Caribbean and Pacific islands. The brutal and dehumanizing conditions it imposed upon these places have been well documented, most graphically by the independence movements themselves. At the same time, as Karl Marx noted, this imperialism represented an incorporation of these regions into the modern capitalist system.

As we shall see in the historiographical survey of imperialism conducted by Patrick Wolfe, debates continue about the purposes and nature of this incorporation, but we may make a few general comments about it. First, the colonial projects of capitalist nation-states such as Britain, France, the Netherlands, and later Germany, Italy, the US and Japan, among others, were an integral part of the competition for control of global resources and markets. The ideology accompanying the intensification of competition in the late nineteenth and early twentieth century was Social Darwinism.

This was an evolutionary view of the world that applied Darwin's theory of 'the survival of the fittest' to races and nations, and justified imperialist domination in terms of an understanding that a race or nation that did not dominate would instead be dominated. Imperialist competition for a greater share of world resources, particularly on the part of late-comer nation-states such as Germany and Japan, was an important factor behind the two world wars of the twentieth century. Ironically, however, both wars accelerated decolonization considerably. Second, from the perspective of the colonized, this incorporation inevitably involved the erosion of existing communities as they experienced the deepening impact of capitalism and alien cultural values.

The extent to which these communities were able to adapt to the new circumstances depended upon the historical resources they were able to muster, as well as their position and role in the imperialist incorporation process. Thus it was not uncommon to find a dualistic type of society in the colonies: on the one hand, an adaptive and relatively modern, coastal, urban sector, integrated under however unequal terms, with metropolitan society. On the other hand, a vast hinterland where historical forms of social life, economic organization and exploitation continued to exist, but hardly as pristine 'tradition'. This is the phenomenon known in dependency theory as 'the articulation of modes of production', whereby modern capitalism utilizes non-capitalist modes of production and exploitation for the production of capitalist value.

Whether responding to global prices or a plantation economy, these regions also serviced the modern capitalist sector of the metropolitan economy, but, typically, they received few of its benefits. In other words, the gap ought not to be seen merely as the difference between a traditional and a modern sector, but as different kinds of incorporation into the capitalist system. The gap between these two sectors and ways of life would often shape and bedevil the decolonization process. Anti-imperialist nationalism emerged historically from the urban, coastal sector where modern, capitalist forms of knowledge, technology, capital and organization had spread more widely.

Although there had been several major expressions of resistance to colonial powers organized around older, indigenous political patterns - such as the mid-nineteenth century Taiping Rebellion or the late-nineteenth century Boxer Uprising in China, the 1857 Rebellion in India, and the Senussi Uprising in Tunisia - as discussed by Geoffrey Barraclough in Part II, the successful movements of decolonization were almost invariably led by Westernized leaders from the modernized sectors of society. These were the would-be administrators and entrepreneurs who felt a very concrete ceiling over their heads, and educated Chinese who bristled at the signs declaring 'Dogs and Chinese not allowed' posted in public places in the foreign settlements in Shanghai and elsewhere.

These were people who experienced constant denial and humiliation because of their colour or origins, but they were also people who, like Mahatma Gandhi, clearly recognized the contradictions these actions presented to the Western doctrines of humanism and rationality. Finally, they were the people who understood the modern world well enough to know how to mobilize the resources to topple colonial domination. How did these modern nationalists and reformers mobilize the hinterlands and the lower classes of their society which were negatively affected by the modern incorporation and barely touched by modern ideas?

For many in these communities, loyalty to the nation-state was an abstraction quite removed from their everyday consciousness, and modern programmes of secular society, national education or the nuclear family were quite inimical to their conceptions of a good society – which involved regional, linguistic, religious, caste, tribal and lineage solidarity – and religious life. On the other side, for the modernizing elites, the peasants and the 'people' lived in a world that was increasingly alien and distasteful to them, and the new language of modernity, historical progress, citizenship and the like increased the gap between the two still further. To be sure, the process of transforming the hinterlands of Western nation-states in the nineteenth century was no less a forceful project of state- and nation-building. In the case of France, Eugen Weber has dubbed the process as the conversion of 'peasants into Frenchmen'.

But there were also significant differences between the two areas. The process in Europe grew out of historical conditions within those regions, and was not so sharp and wrenching as the process in the colonies. Second, colonies were disadvantaged by the unfavourable circumstances of imperialist domination absent in the European case; and finally, the prior development of capitalism in Western societies led to accelerated rates of growth and development that made it harder and harder for the disadvantaged societies to catch up and extend growth to the hinterlands. The great challenge faced by the decolonizers was not simply to bridge the gap between these rapidly diverging worlds, but to re-make hinterland society in their own image. This image derived both from their conception of humanistic reform as well as the need to create a sleek national body capable of surviving and succeeding in a world of competitive capitalism.

The decolonization movement was thus always faced with two tasks which were often in tension with each other: to fulfil the promise of its humanistic ideals and modern citizenship and to create the conditions for international competitiveness. To the extent that these conditions required the production of a homogenized people, there was also often a violent transformation of the lives and world-views of people who were forced to adapt to a world in which the benefits to them were not always clear. The various nationalist movements combined different strategies or methods of force and violence with education and peaceful mobilization to achieve their goals. Thus leaders like Nkrumah and Gandhi were able to achieve rural mass mobilization relatively peacefully, but in the absence of significant land reform or economic integration, the gap persisted. Revolutionary nationalists like Mao Zedong or Ho Chi Minh succeeded in restructuring the inequities of rural society, but often at the cost of massive violence. Other nationalist movements, like that led by Sukarno in Indonesia, were prevented by the structure of Dutch colonial control from achieving any significant rural mobilization.

Nationalists in the colonies - as in earlier nationalisms of the West - often justified the process of mobilization and transformation of the people by narratives of national belonging, or belonging to what Benedict Anderson has called the 'imagined community of the nation'. The imagined community refers to the sense that people who are differentiated by distance, language, class and culture are enabled by modern means of communication (from print to screen) to imagine themselves as part of a single community or family. These nationalists posited an ancient, even primordial unity of the nation that had gone into a long era of forgetfulness or slumber during the middle period between the ancient and the modern. The alleged ancient unity of the nation granted nationalists and the nation-state the right to make these transformations, and they described the nationalism they were seeking to foster as a national 'awakening'.

To be sure, this is not to say that there are no indigenous foundations of modernity. Nationalist historians and others have discovered the 'sprouts of capitalism' and 'alternative modernities' not only in China, but in India, Southeast Asia and elsewhere. Research on the Indian Ocean and East Asia from various different perspectives – Japan, India, China, Southeast Asia, Africa, the Arabian peninsula – reveals a dynamic and cosmopolitan world of commerce and cultural flows that long preceded the Western arrival.

However, the problem with the nationalist understanding is not that the research findings are wrong, but that these findings are located within an evolutionary paradigm containing the implicit (and sometimes explicit) argument that these developments would have ultimately led to modern capitalism and nationalism. This is an instance of how nationalists adopted the basic assumptions of the evolutionism of their colonial masters. One of the challenges of thinking historically about the problem of decolonization is to evaluate the importance of these historical developments without subscribing to the misguided evolutionary framework.

These long-term, often no longer extant, conditions must be separated from the more immediate conditions and circumstances which permitted decolonization or situated a society to quickly build a modern nationstate. Different societies were differently advantaged and disadvantaged with regard to this latter problem. Thus Japan's ability to rapidly build a modern nation-state in the Meiji Restoration (1868) had much to do with the presence of strong political and merchant elites. But it was also lucky in being relatively neglected by the imperialist powers; to be the last country to suffer the unequal treaties, and to be threatened by America, an emergent power with a rather different imperialist vision of the world. Indeed, after World War I, the circumstances for decolonization were generated as much from the international situation as any other.

First, the Soviet Union and the United States of America emerged as new powers with little stake in the old international order based upon the European balance of power, and were indeed, opposed to formal imperialism. Then there was the intensification of imperialist rivalries occasioned by the nose-thumbing, new imperialism of Germany and Japan, which often caused the colonizers to grant concessions in their colonies or promote opposition in others. These circumstances did much to undermine the facade of unity so critical to colonial control and superiority.

World War II made conditions still more unfavourable for colonialism. The spectacle of the old colonial powers being overrun by the Axis forces in North Africa and particularly by Japan in Southeast Asia (and threatening British India), the establishment of formally independent states in Southeast Asia under the rhetoric of pan-Asianism, the prominence of leaders like Sukarno and the Burmese leader U Nu who would lead nationalist movements against the returning colonial powers in the Japanese-dominated wartime governments, and the further rise of the United States and Soviet Union, made eventual decolonization a matter of time in most parts of the world.

The leadership of the modernizing nationalists implied as well that independence would not involve a return to the pre-modern ideals of the dynastic, imperial, religious, feudal or tribal systems. To be sure, as Frederick Cooper suggests, national independence was not always the goal of the decolonizing movement. In the Japanese and French empires, there were efforts on the part of both colonizers and colonized to create ideals of 'imperial citizenship' where equality would prevail in a multinational community (of the ex-empire), but ingrained colonial attitudes and escalating demands for autonomy (and defeat in the Japanese case) nullified these political experiments. Thus it turned out that the decolonizing movements sought to fashion themselves in certain basic ways as modern nation-states in the manner of their imperialist oppressors.

To what extent this would involve taking on some characteristics of the imperialist states themselves - acquiring neighbouring territories, exploiting the resources of peripheral regions within the nation - especially as they joined the competitive system of global capitalism, was yet to become clear. But what was clear to the nationalists is that they denounced imperialism and were determined to launch a new era of justice and equality both within their nations and in the world. As we shall see, the ideals of decolonization and the anti-imperialist movement were built upon two pillars: socialism and the discourse of alternative civilizations, or what I call the new discourse of civilization.

These two aspects were much more closely and deeply intertwined in the twentieth century than we have customarily believed. By socialism, I refer specifically to the Leninist programme of anti-imperialism and socialist equality, as well as state and party command over society. Some societies like China, Vietnam, North Korea and Tanzania adopted the socialist programme more completely, but most other decolonizing societies also reflected more or less the socialist ideals of equality, market restrictions and state re-distribution programmes as the alternative to the imperialist capitalism under which they had suffered.

Here we encounter these ideas among non-communists such as Sun Yat-sen and his successors in Republican China (1911–49), Jawaharlal Nehru in India, Kwame Nkrumah of Ghana, and Jalal Al-i Ahmad, an influential intellectual in Iran under the Shah.

One of the more important debates in the Third Communist International or Comintern, convened after the Russian Revolution, concerned the possibilities of developing socialist revolutions in the colonized world. In other words, they debated whether it was possible for decolonization to be accompanied by the birth not of a capitalist nationstate, but rather of an egalitarian socialist society.

This debate became more serious as the tide of revolution began to ebb in Europe, and in a reversal of the Marxist doctrine, European communists and the Russian revolutionary leaders in particular, began to consider the possibility that the road to revolution would not emerge from Paris and London, the centres of capitalism, but rather from Shanghai and Calcutta at the peripheries of the world capitalist system.

After all, even the Russian Revolution had taken place in one of the weakest countries of the capitalist world. Nonetheless, the communists recognized that the industrial working class or the proletariat in these countries often represented a tiny minority of the population, and the debate turned upon the extent to which communists ought to support the nationalist movements of 'progressive bourgeois nationalism' represented by leaders like Sun and Nehru. Ronald Suny has captured the essence of this debate, and we need not elaborate it here except to note that while rhetorically, the Soviet Union and the Comintern backed the decolonization movement, practically, the interests of the Soviet state under Stalin often determined which anti-imperialist movements it would support.

The impact of socialist ideas and the support of the Soviet Union – even if it was only moral support sometimes – upon the independence movements in the different colonies and informal colonies was, of course, widely welcomed by a range of leaders including Ho Chi Minh, Nehru and Sun. At the same time, however, socialist ideas and support also produced serious tensions within the nationalist movements. In his essay on African working-class movements, Frederic Cooper analyses how this movement became subordinated to the nationalist forces and was steered away from purely socialist agendas. But decolonizing leaders continued to inject at least a modicum of socialist egalitarianism into the nationalist ideology and programme.

This was also the case in many other countries, such as India, which under the leadership of Jawaharlal Nehru in the 1950s and 1960s, experimented with a 'mixed economy', combining state ownership of many economic enterprises with regulated private property.

Even the KMT regime in Taiwan, which came firmly under US hegemony after it lost the mainland to the communists in 1949, retained the strong state control over the economy and society that it had developed from Nazi and Soviet models in the 1930s, until as late as the 1960s. Conversely, in societies where socialist forces became dominant in the movement against imperialism, the leaders of the movement who based their organizational strength upon some combination of working-class movements and the land hunger of an impoverished peasantry, frequently had to appeal to a broader national coalition that included several elite and intermediate classes who were usually outside the scope of a purely socialist movement.

The best example of this kind of 'united front' thinking was to be found in the Chinese communist movement, which increased its power relative to the Nationalist Kuomintang party of Sun Yat-sen and his successor Chiang Kai-shek, during the anti-Japanese war in the 1930s and 1940s. Indeed, the Chinese communists were successful in riding to power on a massive revolution significantly because they combined their organizational techniques and reform projects with a call for national salvation, not merely class war. In 1940, Mao Zedong wrote On New Democracy, in which he declared 'The Chinese democratic republic which we now desire to establish can only be a democratic republic under the joint dictatorship of all the anti-imper ialist and anti-feudal people', and included in this common front, the proletariat, the peasantry, the intellectuals, the petty bourgeoisie and even sections of the capitalist bourgeoisie opposed to imperialism.

Not long after achieving power in 1949, however, Mao became increasingly intolerant of anyone who did not abide by his particular vision of communism. In the Cultural Revolution of the 1960s, he demoralized an entire generation by destroying the very party that had been painstakingly built since the 1920s. Just as socialism and workers' issues became inseparable from nationalism, so too did women's issues and women's rights movements. The relationship between the women's movement and the national movement is a complex and recently much debated topic that we can only introduce here. Together the pieces convey many of the problems associated with the role of women and gender in the nationalist movements of decolonization.

Fanon is widely regarded as among the most intellectually penetrating critic of colonialism, but he has also been taken to task for his understanding of women's roles, particularly in Islamic societies dominated by colonialism. The rights of native women were frequently championed by colonial powers and colonial reformers. Fanon grasps the ways in which colonial power seeks to invade the domestic realm of the colonized society by advocating the liberation of women and seeking to enlist their support for the colonial state, thus dividing the men and women of the nation. At the same time, feminists believe that this kind of critique of imperialism, which is by no means confined to Islamic society, but applies to nationalist movements in most other colonial societies in Africa, India, and East and Southeast Asia, tends at the same time to keep women within the structures of patriarchal domination.

To be sure, decolonizing nationalism did not envision a mere return to traditional patriarchy. The new woman was to be educated so that she could contribute to making the nation strong by rearing healthy children. Many women were also expected to be involved in the freedom struggle. But ideally, they were to be mothers of the nation, protecting and cherishing its inner values especially within the home, and not centrally involved in the public sphere.

As such, women's questions, particularly relating to changes in gender relationships or to their desire to undertake roles equal or similar to men's, were subordinated to the overall needs of the nation as perceived by men. The new patriarchy, as Partha Chatterjee has observed for India, was not a traditional patriarchy, but a nationalist patriarchy. Of course, we can scarcely expect to find the same conceptions of gender in every anti-imperialist movement, and we also need to recognize that for many women the enhanced role of motherhood may have been deeply satisfying.

Nonetheless, the idea that women's status and issues became the object of contestation between imperialists and male nationalists can be found across the territory of our inquiry, from Algeria to Korea. The priority given to the nation - or should we say, to the dominant conception of the nation - over the agenda of workers, feminists, ethnic groups or others was of course achieved, in part, by the appeal to present a unified resistance to imperialism. Still more important was the assumption that the nation was founded upon historically deep traditions or an ancient civilization whose timeless values could not be easily challenged or changed. Resistance to any radical transformation of gender conceptions, in particular, was often grounded in such claims. The new discourse of civilization appeared and spread around the world at the end of World War I.

The war threw European imperialism into an ideological crisis because its scale and brutality seemed, in the eyes of the colonized and many Western intellectuals, to expose European claims of civilizational superiority and 'the civilizing mission' as utterly hollow. As Michael Adas shows, this sense of the failure of the West led to a psychological liberation for many intellectuals in the colonized world, and John Voll reveals a similar pattern for intellectuals in Islamic societies during a later period. At the heart of the critique of civilization launched by Western and non-Western intellectuals after the Great War, was the universalizing promise of the 'civilizing mission' – a mission which exemplified the desire not (simply) to conquer the Other, but to be desired by the Other. In this critique, Western civilization had forfeited the right to represent the highest goals or ultimate values of humanity, and was no longer worthy of being desired, or even recognized, by the Other.

In some ways, the idea that there were other civilizations had been around in the West for a long time. Yet by the nineteenth century, European civilization based on Enlightenment ideas of progress came to displace the idea that other civilizations mattered. Indeed, the absence of such an idea of civilization in a society was sufficient reason to justify colonization. The war, the changed balance of power in the world, and the critique of European civilization restored the idea that other civilizations were just as (or nearly as) legitimate, and decolonizing thinkers associated civilization with claims to sovereignty, thus reversing the terms of the European assertion that denied sovereignty because of the lack of civilization.

The new discourse of civilization was a truly global intellectual product. Oswald Spengler's The Decline of the West, written just before World War I, and the postwar writings of Arnold Toynbee, converged with those of many Asian, and later, African, thinkers and writers. Among them were Okakura Tenshin and Okawa Shumei from Japan, Gu Hongming, Liang Qichao and Liang Shuming in the Chinese speaking world, Rabindranath Tagore and Mahatma Gandhi in India, and Léopold Senghor, Aimé Césaire and others of the Négritude movement. The view that emerged from this discourse was the world could be saved from materialist greed and technological destructiveness by combining the spiritual and moral qualities of other – such as Islamic, Hindu, African, Buddhist or Confucian – civilizations.

The validity of these civilizations was often established through three, sometimes combined, approaches. One was to find elements similar to European civilization within these societies: Confucian rationality, Buddhist humanism, Hindu logic, etc. Another found the opposite of the West in alternative civilizations which are 'peaceful' as opposed to 'warlike', 'spiritual' as opposed to 'material', 'ethical' as opposed to 'decadent', 'natural' as opposed to 'rational', 'timeless' as opposed to 'temporal', communal as opposed to competitive, and so on. Finally, these new nations would synthesize or harmonize these binaries and Western materialism would be balanced by Eastern spirituality and modernity redeemed.

In such ways, the discourse of multiple and alternative civilizations gave considerable authority and confidence to the critique of the Social Darwinist ideology that had fuelled imperialism and the imperialist idea of the civilizing mission.

The mobilizational value of this rhetoric of civilization made it an empowering and enabling force in the battle against imperialism. By the same token, however, it also subordinated other claims for justice and equality to the nation as the representative of a civilization. The ideals of egalitarianism, humanitarianism (or universalism) and the moral and spiritual values represented by the twin pillars of socialism and civilization discourse were frequently in tension with the programme of nation-making that decolonizing societies had to inevitably undertake. We have already alluded to several problems faced by modernizing nationalists, namely those connected with a hinterland society suspicious of modernizing projects, and with groups such as workers and women seeking greater rights. Added to these was a range of territorial and ethnic conflicts produced by the need to create a unified nation-state. Territorial maximization and the homogenization of the population were seen as necessary conditions for a strong nation-state capable of mobilizing its natural resources and population for the tasks of global competition.

These goals would have been largely foreign to pre-colonial historical empires or other polities in these regions. With respect to ethnicity, several historical empires, such as the Ottoman, the Chinese or the Mughal, had fashioned strategies for the co-existence of different ethnic communities, although local conflicts and violence were scarcely absent. Moreover, the frontier and peripheral zones of these empires and polities were typically regarded as no-man's lands: dark, forbidding wildernesses inhabited by barbarian peoples. Political control over these areas was at best informal and frequently multiple and changing: different neighbouring polities might make claims to them if and when they could or cared to. Many communities in these regions remained largely untouched by state power.

During the period of colonial empires, several developments took place that were to leave a different heritage for decolonizing nations. First, as a modern state, the colonial state was built upon the imperative that all global resources be controlled by territorially sovereign polities, whether nations or empires. This logic transformed the fuzzy frontier zones of the historical empires into the militarized boundaries of the modern state. The rulers of modern empires, such as the British, the French or the Japanese, were often obsessed by the need to maximize their territories and militarize their boundaries, often in remote, unprofitable regions.

Their actions provided the impetus for emergent nation-states like China, India, Nigeria, Iraq or Indonesia to maximize and militarize their own territories. Modern states have tended to incorporate contiguous, alien territories and peoples wherever possible, thereby blurring the practical distinction between imperialism and nationalism in these areas. This drive led not only to border conflicts among the new states, but also often meant the rapid deterioration of the environment - especially forests - and the elimination of the means of livelihood and cultures of indigenous peoples. In other places it often led to the alienation of larger populations, such as Kashmiri Muslims, the Tibetans, the Kurds or the East Timorese.

Second, the problem of ethnicity was frequently created and certainly compounded during the colonial period. Colonial states often created new categories of people - and even reified such categories as caste or tribe - for purposes of governance and to establish their power through a policy of divide and rule. In Africa, European colonialists reified a certain image of the tribe in order to co-opt chieftains whose power they had recently enlarged.

The British in India favoured certain 'martial classes' from the north, such as Sikhs or Gurkhas, in opposition to the 'effeminate' and politically restive Bengali intellectuals. More consequential for the South Asian subcontinent was the division of electoral constituencies in the twentieth century along religious lines, which had the effect of exacerbating and deepening tensions between majority Hindus and Muslim elites who felt they would be dominated in a new Indian nation.

Colonial policies encouraged and facilitated large-scale immigration from China, India and elsewhere to work on plantations and mines in Southeast Asia, the Caribbean and Africa. Colonial powers frequently used these immigrant communities as 'docile labour' or as junior partners of imperial rule - as merchants, intermediaries and functionaries - thus fomenting much ethnic strife between the local and diasporic communities, a strife that continues to the present. Just as important as the policies of colonial states was the broader discourse of national rights that emanated from the Americas and the French Revolution, intensified in nineteenth-century Europe, and was circulating globally by the early twentieth century. This discourse held that a people or nationality which could be shown to have had a long history (and civilization) had a right to a territory and a state of its own.

This is a discourse that we have, of course, assumed all along to have lain at the base of the decolonization movement. But while the discourse certainly enabled decolonization, it also divided the movement as it exacerbated ethnic tensions and led ethnic groups to demand nationality rights and a territorial nation-state for themselves.

The long drawn-out and violent decolonization of the French colony of Indochina was, as Stein Tønnesson has shown below, due not only to the tenacity of the French colonial rulers, the subsequent American support of the French, and collaboration by large groups of the colonized, it was also a consequence of the rivalry between different nationalists both within Vietnam and between the Vietnamese and the Cambodians and Laotians. In general, partitions of empire through the twentieth century in the Middle East, East Europe, Africa, South and Southeast Asia were a result as much of colonial desire to divide up spheres of influence (which continued under the Cold War empires) or to extricate the colonizers from increasingly sticky situations, as they were of ethno-national aspirations.

As Radha Kumar shows, rapidly devised colonial departure strategies of 'divide and quit' exacerbated many of the world's ethnic conflicts, and today represent a major legacy of the colonial period. In the end, the principal tension between the ideals of the new nations and their practical projects arose from the demands made by the very system which they sought to join. This was the Westphalian/Vatellian system of states which had once been a club of exclusive – and imperialist – nations, but which after World War I was in the process of transforming itself into a 'family of nations', originally through the League of Nations, and after World War II, the United

Nations. The United Nations crystallizes many of the ideals of the decolonizing era – a vision of global civilization, championing the rights of the oppressed, as well as the right of national self-determination.

The United Nations also represented a means to address the conflicts and problems among nation-states. That such conflict persists between and within nation-states is perhaps testimony to the driving power of competitiveness that is the underlying reason for the very existence of the system. It was, after all, the competition between nations for a greater share of the world's resources that had led to the world wars of the twentieth century. A good deal of the resource-maximizing and mobilization strategies of new nations derived from this imperative as well. Within the tensions of this larger context, how are we to interpret the decolonization movement of the twentieth century? In this volume itself we are able to trace several interpretive threads which should help us think our way. Geoffrey Barraclough's essay from the 1960s represents a sympathetic account of the movement. He recognizes the problems within the movements, but he is sensitive to the injustices and psychological injuries of colonialism.

In a way, we might say, his piece is morally – if not always intellectually – continuous with the writings of the nationalist leaders themselves. Like many of them, for him, decolonization represents a new beginning of development and fulfilment of the individual and citizen. For Louis and Robinson, European – especially British – imperialism hardly disappeared after World War II. It transmuted into a neo-imperialism led by the United States of America with Britain as junior partner.

They dominated the Cold War world by effectively controlling many formally sovereign nation-states through new forms of military and financial dependency. Kelly and Kaplan spell out the wider implications of this view, in which most of the decolonizing nations have become part of the 'Third World', formally sovereign in the nation-state system, but trapped by debt, alien institutions and cultural dependency in a world where many argue that the conditions for the great mass of people are not significantly better than in colonial times. They argue that decolonization mostly represented entry into a new world order dominated by the US, 'already tooled for purposes at best different than the aims of the anti-colonial movements, and at times, clearly obstructive of them'.

There is yet another interpretive thread. The East Asian countries have done notably better in developmental terms than the rest of the Southern World. We might say that they have been able to utilize certain institutional and historical advantages to mobilize the nation and prise themselves out of a peripheral and dominated status to become competitive players in the system, much as Japan had been able to do more than a century ago. In his comparative essay on Japanese colonialism, Bruce Cumings reveals that in contrast to European colonies in the same region, such as Vietnam, the Japanese colonial state built a strong institutional and developmental infrastructure in Korea and Taiwan in the 1930s and 1940s. Of course, the recent growth of China, which did not see the same kind of development under Japanese occupation, suggests that Japanese colonialism was at best just one factor, and others, especially the dynamics of regional economic integration, have been just as important.

It may also be argued that East Asian development represented a new or emergent moment in imperialist ideology when, in response to rising nationalism and intensifying economic competition, the relationship with the colony was re-thought. The colony was to be viewed less as an object of exploitation than as a partner - a dependent partner for sure - that could be economically strengthened through investments and infrastructure-building and mobilized in the global competition for wealth and power. Certainly Hong Kong, the last - and fabulously successful - British colony decolonized in 1997, represents this transformation, as Britain came to see it less as a symbol of empire than a critical piece of its strategy to remain a global power after World War II.

The economic development of the Japanese colonial empire also took place principally from the 1930s, after the establishment of the Japanese puppet state of Manchukuo in northeast China signalled an economic strategy of alliance and investment in these dependent states so that they could be more useful to the Japanese military's pursuit of world power. While we may think of the East Asian case as a sign of possibilities and hope, it is also important to remember that these nations participate in a system that is becoming increasingly volatile, both economically and politically. The late-1990s economic crisis in Asia and the longer-term decline of Japan is a sharp reminder that capitalist competition produces risks and uncertainties that may be even less controllable now than they were in the twentieth century, when several global empires were brought to the ground.

For decolonized nations, we have seen that the Cold War often meant new forms of dependence upon either the dominant capitalist powers or the Soviet Union. Non-alignment in any absolute sense was a chimera. Still, many new nations were able to play off the competition between the two superpowers to some advantage. The relatively restricted power of multinational capital allowed the nation-state to regulate relationships between national society and global society, although this varied from nation to nation.

Moreover, domestically, the nation-state form as an unprecedentedly strong interventionist and mobilizational agency was often able to achieve a measure of social justice and development. The higher ideals of justice, morality and equality that emerged in the course of the anti-imperialist movement still played an important role as regulatory or directive goals.

The end of the Cold War and the collapse of the socialist bloc and socialist ideology as a counter-weight to capitalism have produced a different scenario for these nations. They are confronted by a world dominated much more powerfully by multinational corporations, and they complain that these corporations and unfair trading practices in the mature capitalist economies continue to disadvantage their growth and competitiveness. Politically, they are more dependent on the US as hegemon and protector of the nation-state system which shows a dangerous tendency to exempt itself from the authority of the system. While it is arguable that some kind of equilibrium has developed between interdependence and hegemony within the nation-state system, discontent with the system is increasingly expressing itself from the interstices and the spaces between territorially bounded national units. Such movements of discontent, we have seen, are expressed in transnational ideologies with allegiance to the civilizational narratives and goals that were fostered in the encounter of imperialism and nationalism.

The era of decolonization may be over, but the pains of that transition have found their way into the new era of globalization. These represent a mixture of well known and relatively obscure pieces which discuss the ideals of the movement, the critique of colonial ideology, and the difficulties encountered in practical mobilization of the people. The 'Imperialism and nationalism', by contemporary scholars, discuss the role of imperialism and nationalism in the decolonization movement as global phenomena. The authors ask questions about the emergence of the movement in the changing role and understanding of imperialism and its ideology, such as the 'civilizing mission', about the role of peasant mobilization, ethno-nationalisms, and partitions, and finally, about the new nation-states and neo-imperialism or the imperialism of the 'new world order'.

'Regions and themes', also contains pieces by contemporary scholars which are thematically related to the rest of the book; but they address these problems from the viewpoint of a particular region. The relationship between decolonization and socialism is viewed from its point of emergence in the Soviet Union; the changing status of the West in the Middle East the tensions between the working-class movement and decolonization in Africa; the gender question in Korea; a comparison of the colonial experiences of East Asia and Vietnam; and the extended nature of decolonization in Vietnam, or the history of the Vietnam war are all discussed.

7

Women in Contemporary Asia

In traditional Korean society, women's roles were confined to the home. From a young age, women were taught the virtues of subordination and endurance to prepare for their future roles as wife and mother. Women, in general, could not participate in society as men did, and their role was limited to household matters. The situation began to change with the opening of the country to the outside world during the late 19th century. During this period modern schools were introduced, mostly by Western Christian missionaries. Some of these schools were founded with the specific goal of educating women. These educated women began to engage in the arts, teaching, religious work, and enlightening other women. Women also took part in the independence movement against the Japanese occupation, and displayed no less vigor, determination, and courage than the men.

With the establishment of the Republic of Korea in 1948, women achieved constitutional rights for equal opportunities to pursue education, work, and public life. There is no doubt that the female labor force contributed significantly to the rapid economic growth that Korea achieved during the past three decades. An increasing number of women work in professional fields. As economic development proceeded and the living conditions of Koreans improved, the educational attainment level of women also increased. In 1966, among those graduating from elementary school, only 33 percent of girls continued their education in middle school. The comparable figures for high school and university were 20 percent and 4 percent, respectively, during the same period.

However, by 1998, the comparable ratios reached 99.5 percent and 61.6 percent for high school and university. The economic participation rate of women also has increased steadily since industrialization from 34.4 percent in 1965 to 48.1 percent in 1999. In terms of characteristics of the female labor force, in 1975, only 2 percent of the female labor force worked in professional or managerial occupations, while 4 percent worked in clerical positions. However, by 1998, 12.6 percent of female employees were serving in professional or managerial positions, and another 16 percent were working in clerical occupations.

With an increasing number of women entering professional jobs, the government passed the "Equal Employment Act" in 1987 to prevent discriminatory practices against female workers in regard to hiring and promotion opportunities. Korean women today are actively engaged in a wide variety of fields, including education, medicine, engineering, scholarship, the arts, law, literature, and sports. Women are thus making significant contributions to society. With the launch of the new Administration in 1998, the Presidential Commission on Women's Affairs was established to handle issues specifically involving women.

The commission was elevated and expanded to become the Ministry of Gender Equality in January 2001. The new ministry set up 20 specific tasks to be achieved in six basic areas. These areas are: to revise and establish laws and rules that involve discrimination in any sector and to increase the representation of women, to facilitate women's employment and provide support for female workers, to increase educational opportunities for women to be competitive in the labor market, to provide social welfare policies for women, to promote women's involvement in various social activities including volunteer work and women's organization activities, and to strengthen the cooperation of Korean women's organizations with international women's organizations.

The women's movement, clearly the most influential social movement of the last century, has empowered women in most countries around the globe. By joining together, women at all levels of society are enhancing their capabilities, exerting their influence, and making their own decisions within their households and their communities. Utilizing this base of growing power and knowledge, many women are increasingly seeking seats in formal political institutions. However, the way women are wielding this growing power to build new societies varies widely and produces different patterns around the world. Such diversity arises from the cultural and religious characteristics of the societies in which they are embedded, as well as from the colonial and post-colonial economic and political systems of the countries in which they live.

Asia today illustrates the commonalities and diversity of women's paths to power. Given the broad and often contradictory trends among the countries and the ambivalent attitudes toward gender equality by women and men alike, any broad assessment of the region is impossible. Instead, to illustrate both the various approaches utilized by women's organizations and their achievements and problems, identified four distinct patterns that exist: in China, South Asia, Southeast Asia, and South Korea.

In each area the underlying culture with its overlay of religion, colonialism, and governmental system limit the choices available to women. A template exists to assess empowerment by noting how women use their power: enhanced services -from water to health to education- for their communities and families; greater opportunities for providing livelihood for themselves and their children; increased gender equality in household, community, and national decision-making; freedom from violence. How women seek to achieve such goals varies, but increasingly they utilize women's organizations directly or indirectly to reach accomplish their objectives.

National organizations often focus on legislation that would expand women's rights: to work, to divorce, to own land, to receive inheritance, and to give recourse to violence against them. But laws only indicate the direction of change which must come about through efforts of women themselves, uniting together. Their goals may be welfarist, but their methods require agency. 1 In early days of organizing, perhaps, agency was exhibited primarily by the elite leadership; but increasingly women at community levels are startling observers with their actions. An analysis of these paths provides explanations of the different ways women use power and suggests directions of their future empowerment.

FOUR ASIAN PATTERNS

The context within which women's organizations function explains their diversity. Hinduism, Buddhism, and Confucianism originated in region; Islam and Christianity arrived before Columbus sailed to the New World. All have adapted to local cultures as they spread. The migration of peoples throughout Asia is complex and contested, but patterns persevere. Societies in Asia have traditionally been stratified and, despite their constitutions which grant equality to all women and men, class and caste distinctions persist along with patriarchal dominance. India and China historically embodied a patriarchy that did not value women.

Separating these civilizations were mountains filled with migrant tribes whose subsistence activities promoted greater equality. From Ladakh through Nepal, Bhutan, and Burma these groups provide a different gender pattern which has spilled over into much of Southeast Asia. This pattern is characterized by greater gender equity in land ownership and in commercial activities. Asia was also influenced, if not actually controlled, by a spectrum of colonial powers that imposed different values and governing systems. While the British were the dominant force in the region, France, the Netherlands, Japan, and the United States instituted their own colonial versions of society and commerce.

Generally, the prevalent attitudes of the male expatriates reinforced existing patriarchal strictures. Colonial powers and missionaries also introduced western education for girls as well as boys, and so produced a cadre of elite women who became leaders in their countries' national movements. Most of these national movements were socially conservative; women involved in independence struggles did not make demands for change in women's social status. Even where education was made compulsory, by the US in both the Philippines and South Korea and by the communist Party in China and Vietnam, women's activism was conditioned by culture and religion. Post World War II Asia was a devastated region.

Fighting continued in Indochina and Indonesia as nationalist battled the returning colonial powers; Britain and the United States set dates for independence of their former colonies. Famines plagued India that had been pushed further into turmoil by the Partition which created Pakistan. In China the communists defeated the nationalists, then spread their influence to neighboring countries. First in Korea, then in Vietnam and Laos, foreign troops joined the fray. Poverty was pervasive; governments addressed the issues of food and of security in different ways.

Most created Five Year Plans; in none of them was women's economic contribution recognized. Present government systems in the various countries reflect both the colonial past and the education of the leaders. Thus Fabian socialists in India have promoted greater gender equality through politics and planning. In contrast, the socialist leader in Indonesia, Dr. Sjahrir, brought back from Holland the emphasis on women as mothers, a view that continues to constrict women in Indonesia. With the exception of communist countries, post-independence Asian countries preserved many elements of customary and family law which limited women's rights; yet even though new constitutions in the communist countries proclaimed women and men as equal, the gap between ideology and reality remained immense, especially in China.

Efforts by contemporary women's organizations throughout the region are addressing these inequities in many imaginative ways that go beyond legal changes. In contrast, in China, Laos, and Vietnam, women are organizing to maintain their legal rights in the face of patriarchal resurgence as their economies open to market forces. A majority of women leaders are drawn from the educated elite who, in stratified societies, rank above men of lower caste or class. In many Asian countries elite women have had a history of organizing and even protest, though such activity was often part of broader social or political movements.

What is new about women's empowerment today is its penetration to the community level in both rural and urban areas. Such change is a direct result of governmental efforts to modernize their economies. Hesitantly most government planning offices, pressured and funded by international assistance agencies, began to include women into the development process. Local and international nongovernmental organizations - often led by women- were instrumental in reaching poor women. Whatever the program goals, women were formed into groups. In many Asian societies the mobility of rural women has traditionally been extremely limited; and Asia was predominantly rural fifty years ago.

Allowing, even requiring, these women to leave their household compounds for reasons other than work in the fields, and to meet together had an extraordinary impact of these isolated women. Women's agency came slowly, impelled by consciousness raising; the male decision makers seldom noticed. Once again outside influences affect national policies as international and bilateral development agencies with their packages of projects designed to achieve economic development. Too often such programs fail to differentiate among recipient countries or to adapt to local circumstances.

Such is usually the case when the goals relate to women because their status within each society is embedded, as we have stressed, in the religious and cultural practices and in the history of women's activism and education. Further, the priorities given by different countries among the palette of development programs - health, education, family planning, agriculture, industry, informal sector, credit, community development - produced distinct patterns of modernization. The method of implementation and the strength or weakness of civil society contributed to these very different patterns.

As women have been incorporated into development planning at the community level, elite women became involved both in these efforts and in the burgeoning global women's movement that was facilitated and sustained by the United Nations world conferences on women beginning in Mexico City in 1975. Rapid economic transformation dislocates societies; changing women's roles have often produced a backlash from male leadership as women's traditional subservience vanishes. Male leaders in many countries have conflated nationalism with a return to tradition that privileges male dominance.

Vina Mazumdar finds that such anti-modern efforts are based on "a romanticized view of that traditional culture that is often quite divorced from historical reality. When played off against the negative consequences of Western-style development, however, such romantic images have power appeal". Many Asian women themselves are challenging modernization paradigms and the values that support them.

These leaders are utilizing the concepts of women's equal rights while also inventing new institutions for economic fairness and promoting new approaches to family and community that they believe are more appropriate to their cultures and values. Korea: family planning and universal education When Japan surrendered to the US in 1945, the Japanese occupation of Korea was at an end. But after communism triumphed in China, communist adherents in the northern part of Korea took over the government and invaded the south. United Nations troops joined the US government in fighting the invasion and secured peace in a divided peninsula.

The Japanese had reinforced the existing Confucian patriarchal system, impressed Korean men as workers in Japan, and seized many unmarried women for service as comfort women. The nationalist movement that arose was therefore not directed against European nations or the US. The cessation of hostilities in South Korea found a small country ravaged by the war, houses were destroyed in both rural and urban areas, the land was nearly devoid of tress, and farming was still largely subsistence. For many years the Korean military governed the country with the complicity of the US. Authoritarian political rule was reinforcing by Confucian tradition that made women subservient to men and men to rulers.

To promote rapid economic transformation, the government determined to reduce population growth and create an educated workforce. Both policies altered the traditional lives of women in Korea. To carry out efforts at birth control, adult women were formed into Mother's Clubs which met monthly to receive their allocation of birth control pills. All women of the village were required to attend. Dispensing the pills were educated urban women who imparted much more than pills as they taught the women about health and sanitation, and spoke about current events. These clubs responded to the government pleas for tree nurseries in order to reforest the hillsides. Some clubs not only sold the seedlings but planted trees as well.

Profits were used by the members as a group. Imagine the liberating emotions of a compound-restricted woman who suddenly has the opportunity to go on a pilgrimage to a Buddhist shrine on a train! The emphasis on reduced family size was a success: the fertility rate fell from 6 children per woman in 1960 to 1.6 in 1990. But pills are not widely used because those available in the 1960s produced many side effects because of their hormonal strength. Female sterilization is the primary method used; abortion is also high. Recently, ability to predict the sex of a fetus has resulted in a higher ratio of boys to girls born; this male preference is more pronounced after families already have daughters. Thus perversely, the ability of women to control their fertility has reinforced patriarchy, at least temporarily. But the organizing of women opened worlds for women to explore, particularly as the country rapidly urbanized: 28% of the population was urban in 1960, 75% in 1990. Government efforts to create an educated workforce began with the 1948 constitution which introduced universal education. Girls had to attend school and so were no longer available to help their mothers with the onerous chores of rural subsistence living - a trend that encouraged urbanization. This literate work force of young women became the foundation of later industrial development despite lower pay than men and deplorable working conditions in many factories. In the 1980s spontaneous rebellions began to break out in free export zones where unions were prohibited.

Despite government support for industrialization, reality in the factories was chilly because women were called by derogatory terms by men; once married most were required, and usually anxious, to leave and become a dependent housewife. By the late 1980s, active lobbying by Korean women's groups led to Equal Employment Act; but the intent of this progressive law was subverted by tradition.

Similarly, access to education for women has had mixed benefits. In-ho Lee complains that without women in educational administration and curriculum development, education has stressed conformity so that an inverse relationship exists between the level of education and workforce participation (1993). For university graduates, few opportunities are available, especially after the 1998 economic crisis. Many families still see higher education for women as a means to attract a higher status husband.

Women's activism Korea's constitution, drafted under American tutelage, granted women equality - as did most constitutions of newly independent countries, without any significant demand for this privilege. Previous women's activism was related to nationalist struggles or to rights for practicing Christianity which challenged the Confucian order. The contemporary women's movement in Korea came, according to In-ho Lee, "from imported academic feminism and the political context of grass roots demands to secure basic human rights.." (1993:98).

During the 1970s the focus of women's movement was on improving the situation of women in factories. As more women's groups appeared, the government set up Special

Commission on Women under the prime minister and created a Women's Development Institute.

Judged ineffectual by women activists, the Institute did offer employment to university educated women who wanted to work; studies that emerged fueled the emerging advocacy groups. To gain greater visibility, these groups, in 1989, formed the Korean Women's Associations United and helped ensure the passage of the Family Law Act in Dec 1989. The law finally brings family law under the constitutional provision of equality by granting women equal inheritance rights and provides for courts to decide custody rights of the parents.

Efforts to mitigate the oppressive nature of customary practice took over three decades, a effort spearheaded by Lee Tai Young, a lawyer and founder of the Legal Aid Center for Family Rights soon after independence. Women's power in Korea is still constrained by Confucian beliefs and traditional practices. The rapid economic transformation of the country from subsistence agriculture to an industrial urban nation did not purposefully liberate women. Cracks in patriarchal control began slowly with the Mother's Clubs but it was the plight of industrial workers that brought international activists to Korea to work on their behalf.

Educated women, activated by international contacts and women's studies curriculum, organized rights groups that addressed Korean specific inequities. Their role in formal political institutions remains minimal although since the election of President Kim Dae Jung two women were appointed ministers in the government and In-ho Lee became the first female ambassador, to Russia. Hampden concludes: "The greatest influence women have on the political decision-making process derives from the activities of pressure groups that have effectively mobilised public opinion on women's issues" (2000: 182).

DIVERGENT PATHS TO ORGANIZING LOCAL WOMEN

South Asia as a region was conditioned by nearly two centuries of British colonialism. Its society is still highly stratified as a result of the influence of the Hindu caste system which has also permeated both Islam and Buddhism as locally practiced. Many elite women and men were educated in English schools and adopted some of the values of the west, particularly regarding law and governance. While the British granted independence to the sub-continent following World War II, only Sri Lanka escaped riots and killing as India was partitioned into two countries. The remote Himalayan kingdoms of Nepal, Bhutan, and Sikkim had been under different forms of British control which India assumed.

Only Sikkim has been integrated into the India state. Women in contemporary India are active in a panoply of organizations that encompass dam building, land and forest rights, pavement dwellers, home-based workers, wife-burning, and much more. Their skills have been honed by nearly two centuries of involvement, first in efforts to reform Hinduism and then in the nationalist movement that demanded independence from Britain. Early women leaders represented the growing middle class whose members were drawn from the three upper castes; they sought western education as well as reforms of cultural practices such as sati, child marriage, and a ban of widow remarriage.

Some "modernist" Muslims supported education for Muslim women despite the prevalence of purdah, or the seclusion of women. Schools for girls in Sri Lanka were first started under the Dutch, then renewed by the British, in both vernacular and English languages. In all these countries, education of women was stressed, not to create a equal citizens but to help women fulfill their roles of wife and mother in a household headed by western educated men. Thus schooling for girls emphasized domestic skills and generally stopped at puberty.

By the end of the nineteenth century, South Asian men were enrolling in British universities; soon women followed. Study in England exposed women to the wide range of civil society organizations; on their return some started their own associations with both political and social goals. In 1926, the All India Women's Conference (AIWC) was formed to provide a nation- wide platform for women. By 1930, groups demanding improved working conditions for women workers in textiles factories and mines convinced the AIWC to hold a special session on labor practices.

But generally, these elite women emphasized religious reform, education, and suffrage that were of most concern to their own classes. Commenting on this history of women's participation, Jayawardene writes that "The most revealing aspect has been the essential conservatism of what on the surface seemed like radical change...women were kept within the structural confines of family and society" (1986:107).

Critical in changing these prevailing attitudes of organized women in South Asia was the influence of Mahatma Gandhi. He questioned many of the values of industrialization, and did so by wearing khadi, or homespun cloth; he lived in villages and among the untouchables and Muslims, countering caste and religious taboos; and he reached out to the entire country with his non-violent protests against the British. Muslim and Hindu women and men, many from abroad, joined Gandhi in his ashram.

In the spring of 1930, Mahatma Gandhi launched a salt satyagraha to protest a government tax on salt: women and men walked to the Gujerat coast and began illegally to make salt. The photographs of Indian women being arrested in this and subsequent protests helped create sympathy in Britain for Indian independence. Throughout the 1930s, as demands for self-government escalated, many Indian women withdrew from leading women's groups and focused on non-violent protests.

Experiences in jail converted many of these women into strong political figures who took leadership roles in independent India. Equally important, Gandhi's legacy gave moral legitimacy to women and men for working with the poor. As possibilities for the end of British rule grew, so did communal tensions between Hindus and Muslims. In the AIWC, Muslim women formed their own groups and by 1944 had withdrawn entirely from its membership.

Although both India and Pakistan declared themselves secular and passed bills to improve women's rights, because the reason for Pakistan's existence was Islam, religious conservatives grew in power in Pakistan and by 1977 the Islamization of the country had begun. Prior to that time, citizens in East Pakistan had began protesting repressive military actions and their treatment as a colony of West Pakistan. In 1971, the province fought for their own country; the new constitution of Bangladesh granted women equal rights in the public sphere.

INDEPENDENCE AND ECONOMIC DEVELOPMENT

In independent India, women formed new types of organizations to support women's equality as enshrined in the constitution. The country was suffering from destruction both from World War II and the Partition that created Pakistan out of British India; famines seemed endemic. International agencies poured economic development funds into the country, promoting a paradigm that rendered most women's work invisible.

In response, women founded both research centers and activist groups to address the often detrimental impact of development programs on poor rural women. Women's work in subsistence agriculture and household production was documented; the appropriate technology movement designed small machines such as grinding mills to alleviate drudgery and promoted new cookstoves; to introduce such innovations, women had to be persuaded.

Like the community development policies which were designed to increase agricultural production and improve health status in the villages, changes from traditional practices did not work without the inclusion of women. Caste and patriarchal dominance in these villages required the setting up of separate women's groups if women were to participate in the development projects. Once organized, such groups took on issues of local concern from setting up income producing activities to growing their own fodder for cattle on land they fenced off from cattle of better off villagers.

The emergence of the Chipko movement, women in the Himalayan foothills who hugged trees to prevent their harvesting, documented the negative consequences of rapid economic growth not only on the poor, but also on the environment. Recognizing the indigenous knowledge of such women about the sustainable uses of field and forest, women have organized to support traditional agricultural practices in Ladakh, and elsewhere, against high dams that would deprive many peasants of their land, and against "biopiracy" of golden rice or the neem tree. In Bihar, local women organized to obtain land in their own names.

Increased radio and television coverage of such events spread the word, and soon spontaneous groups of village women arose protesting local inequities. Women in hill tribes in Maharashtra shamed husbands who beat their wives by banging kitchen pots outside the offending man's house. Dalit (formerly called untouchable) women joined with devadasis (temple dancers) to protest the dedication of girls to serve in temples as "brides" of the gods – a sort of sanctioned prostitution. In central India local women challenged government sanctioned toddy shops because cheap liquor was increasing domestic violence while encouraging their husbands to spend their paychecks on the liquor; the shops were closed.

In cities, women earning livelihoods as vendors or home-based workers were organized into the Self Employed Women's Association (SEWA) in Ahmedabad (Jhabvala 1994) and in Madras (Chennai) in the Working Women's Forum. These large organizations, which support urban and rural poor women, were started and led by charismatic women. In contrast, similar groups in Bangladesh, Grameen Bank and BRAC, were started by and continue to be run primarily by men.

In Sri Lanka the major early community development organization, Sarvodaya, was also headed by a man. While the empowering effect of forming women into groups is similar, the lack of women in provincial and central positions illustrates the different trajectories taken in South Asia outside India and may be traced to the influence of the Gandhian movement that encouraged elite women to work with the poor.

Men trained in the Gandhian tradition worked with rural poor in both Pakistan and Sri Lanka; but their organizations, like that of Gandhi's, remained largely patriarchal. Increasingly, however, women's organizations in Bangladesh and Sri Lanka are forming women-only organizations themselves to work with the urban and rural poor. In India, women activists, legitimized by the Gandhian tradition to work with the poor, were emboldened by the women in development movement to work toward women's empowerment under female leadership.

PARALLEL EFFORTS FOR WOMEN'S RIGHTS

In all the countries of South Asia, elite women continued their efforts to reform religious limitations on women's equality that had been guaranteed by their constitutions when secular leadership was dominant In India, violence against women was the roots of campaigns directed against alcohol, the rape of lower caste and tribal women by landlords and police, and wife burning. These abominations occurred among all groups in the society and women of all religions and castes joined efforts to eliminate them.

Over time, however, more conservative elements, both Muslim and Hindu, began to influence politics. This trend was evident when, in the mid-1980s, a Muslim woman sued for support payments under civil law and the courts gave precedence to Muslim family law, effectively removing Muslim women from many protections in the constitution. The rights of Hindu women were challenged by the sati, widow immolation, in Rajasthan which appeared to be more like a murder than self-sacrifice.

During the 1990s and continuing today, increased communal violence has underscored the range of political and social views held by women as well as men. Identity politics led scholars to deconstruct the categorization of an Indian woman as an urban middle-class Brahmin. "The deep class and caste divisions in Indian society have inhibited the emergence of a unified feminist movement". But women are making their voices heard throughout the social, political, and religious spectrum; diverse groups took these issues to the Fourth UN Conference on Women held in Beijing in 1995.

In Pakistan, nationalism has led to a resurgent Islam that continues to contend with the modernist educated classes; most active women are both modernist and upper-class creating a chasm between their lives and those of the largely illiterate poor whom the educational system does not serve. The women's movement was energized and radicalized by the Hudood Ordinances put in place by the military regime of General Zia ul-Haq in 1979 to placate religious extremists. These ordinances superceded laws inherited from the British and enforced traditional Islamic punishments for adultery, rape, prostitution, etc.

Bari and Khattak record the difficulties of the largely middle class movement to challenge issues of family law, especially when they are seldom affected by extreme application. Rather, they argue, that the present women's movement in Pakistan "engages with the state to negotiate increased space and rights for women in the public and private arena through affirmative actions but not through direct political activism via party politics".

Instead of directly confronting family issues, many women leaders have set up or work with NGOs that are largely foreign funded to reach out to poor rural and urban women with programs about political empowerment, reproductive rights, and violence against women. Terming this flow of talent the "NGOization of the women's movement," Bari and Khattak conclude that these increased services must be weighed against the undermining of the movement's independence (2001: 238).

The ability of NGOs to provide services is questioned by Renken who noted that a majority of microfinance programs funded middle and upper class women, not the poor (2001). But Weiss argues that promoting microcredit in the walled city of Lahore has empowered women. The Bangladesh women's movement gained legitimacy on "visible and significant participation in the war for liberation in 1971 and the movement for democratization in 1980s".

Women's NGOs at first were research based; more recently some have begun social outreach programs that mirror those of BRAC and the Grameen Bank, and broadening their membership. Perhaps because men run those and other similar organizations and are working toward women's empowerment, the issue of western influence within the women's movement is seldom raised. Women do have to contend with the Jamaat party which promotes radical Islam and has encouraged attacks on NGO staff and beneficiaries.

Citing the growing strength and solidarity of the women's movement in Bangladesh, Jahan calls the prevailing mood as one of cautious optimism (1995). In Sri Lanka, feminists started a Center for Women's Research to focus on issues of concern to women. The Mahaweli irrigation scheme found that women were unable to benefit from loan programs if their husband's had defaulted on an agricultural loan.

These women lived in the same area where the government was encouraging export production village programs. In 1987 the Women's Chamber of Commerce started the Agromart Foundation to support such activities as exportation of ornamental tropical fish and cardamom. While these income activities did not alter gender relations, according to Samarasinghe, women in the program increased their self-confidence and had become more self-reliant (1993)

ELECTORAL POLITICS

The rising force of women organized at all levels of society throughout the world has given greater impetus to the 30% target for women in political positions originally promoted in 1995. Introducing quotas for electoral seats is considered an important strategy. The low representation of women in national assemblies contrasts with the number of prominent women political leaders in the region.

In Bangladesh the heads of the two major, and intensely competitive, parties are women. Both have served as the prime minister, neither espouse feminist causes, and both come from political dynasties: Khaleda Zia is a widow of an assassinated prime minister; Sheikh Hasena is the daughter of a nationalist leader. When Benazir Bhutto, daughter of another martyred prime minister, was in power in Pakistan, her ability to ameliorate the Hudood was circumscribed, but she supported women in their preparations for Beijing. Indira Gandhi, as India's prime minister, kept aloof from the feminist movement; after her assassination her son Rajvi became prime minister; after he was also killed, his wife Sonia -albeit an Italian by birth- was made head of the Congress Party and is being groomed for high office should the party win the elections.

Sri Lanka is unique in having had both mother and daughter as leaders: Sirimavo Bandaranaika, the widow of an assassinated prime minister, was the first woman prime minister in the world. Her daughter Chandrika Bandaranaika Kumaratunga is Sri Lanka's president but was also a prime minister; her husband was also assassinated. The dynastic succession is obvious. The reason these elite women could replace male relatives as their countries' leaders are due to class/caste identity and strong personalist politics in the region. Women's issues are certainly not privileged by such woman leaders; indeed, the strength of the women's movement is irrelevant.

With independence, the Indian constitutions recognized the intractability of the caste system by providing for representation of disadvantage peoples though a system that reserved specific constituencies for Scheduled Castes [untouchables or dalits] and Scheduled Tribes based on their population. Since many women prominent in the nationalist struggle were elected, no special provisions were deemed necessary at the time. Current women leaders, noting that the percentage of women members in Parliament has averaged 5 % since independence, have agitated for a quota without success.

While upper class women have had some representation in elective bodies, this was not the case in local elections for elective bodies at the village, county, and district levels of government when they were set up in the 1960s. This situation was changed by laws passed in 1993 requiring panchayats at all three levels to reserve one-third of their electoral constituencies for women. Furthermore, one third of all panchayats must elect a woman as chair. These quotas are achieved by rotation of constituencies and of electoral bodies. To date over one million women have been elected to local bodies. The southern state of Karnataka actually has 46.7 per cent women members, an indication that women ran for general as well as for reserved seats.

To assist these new legislators to understand their power and responsibilities many women's organizations have begun training courses for them. Activists at the local levels are generally impressed with the visible results of women in the panchayats, but skepticism is widespread among many feminists who question the ability of these women to understand the workings of the panchayats or to take positions independent of their husbands.

Srilatha Batliwala agrees with some skeptics who believe that quotas are "so much window-dressing and political gimmickry...in a narrow sense" but argues that such critics miss the potential that such participation has "to empower women and transform traditional gender relations" (1997:5). In sum, women's movements in the four South Asian countries discussed have at the very least been able to influence their governments for changes in women's rights. Their access to officials is facilitated by their membership in the modernist upper class.

Many women in these countries have begun to work with women of other classes though class, class, and religion seriously impede the emergence of a more unified movement. Gradually poor women in both India and Bangladesh are becoming empowered by development projects that reached to the village or community levels and organized them. This process in Sri Lanka was arrested by the years of ethnic conflict and in Pakistan by the increasing power of conservative Islam.

EGALITARIAN SOCIETY

The Hindu-Buddhist religions that expanded throughout the region left behind a status hierarchy that put the rulers, their armies, and the priests at the top. Commerce was less valued, and largely left to women or foreigners. More recent overlay of Islam and Christianity have not undercut this ranking although in Malaysia the Chinese filled the entrepreneurial niche as a conservative Islam was encouraging women to stay at home. Such displacement did not happen throughout Indonesia because Hindu-Bali beliefs have intertwined with Islam in much of Java.

But in contemporary times, women in Indonesia have not achieved the same level of prominence as entrepreneurs as have women in the Philippines and Thailand, perhaps because of the government sponsored campaign to keep women at home which has encouraged upper class women to participate in social uplift activities through government related women's organizations. Less well off women in Indonesia continue to work as do most women in both Thailand and the Philippines. Colonial policies in the region influenced women's educational opportunities.

In the Philippines, the UN introduced public schools throughout the country in the early 1900s which has resulted in a 95% adult literacy rate for both women and men in 1998, (UN 2000), with over one half of all students completing elementary school, a quarter finish high school. Torres argues that in terms of gender stereotypes, the new system did not "intrude on the value of male machismo" embedded in the culture by four centuries of Spanish rule, but rather reinforced it (1995:107).

Reflecting this emphasis on family, women who complete the university and graduate programs at higher rates than for men tend to dominate medical science (87%), food and nutrition (99%), and commerce (67%) - nurturing professions and trading. The abundance of women with college degrees and the lack of appropriate jobs, especially outside of Metro Manila, encourage women to join NGOs, if they can afford it, or to become self-employed. A study of street food vendors in

Ilo. Ilo found that 92% of the enterprises were headed by women; further 20% of these vendors had college degrees.

Women dominate the street food trade in Thailand as well, running 88% of the enterprises; women's adult literacy rate is 93%. In Indonesia, under the Dutch, education was limited and students were taught in Dutch above the elementary level. Only engineering and medicine were taught at university level in the country. After independence, the trading language Malay was adopted as the national language requiring new textbooks at all grades. Today women's adult literacy rate is 81%. The rapid expansion of the entire education system has allowed women and men to study, but shortages of teachers and books continue to be a problem.

Women continue to be prominent in the batik industry even under pressure from larger industry. In all three countries, women are expected to help support their families. In rural areas the lower income women work in agriculture, in cities they are engaged in small or micro enterprise. Young women often work in export industries that locate where women are educated. The income that women earn gives them status and relative independence, though women who sub-contract are frequently exploited.

In Thailand and in the Philippines, many women were drawn into the sex industry in response to large numbers of US troops and to the special package tours from Japan and Germany. Local women organized against US bases in the Philippines, and found international support that led to the down-sizing or closing of these installations.

ORGANIZING WOMEN

Three factors slowed the development of local women's local organizations in Philippines, Indonesia, and Thailand. First was the perception by most women of the region that there was gender equity: women accepted the division of labor within which they had considerable independence. Divorce is uncommon in the Philippines and Thailand, though concubinage/mistresses are widely acknowledged, perhaps giving wives more latitude. Most middle class women are involved in social service organizations that assist the poor; these groups are more likely to focus on societal issues such as housing, human rights, or the environment.

Until recently, few groups addressed more feminist issues relating to family law or violence. Only as exploitation of women in export factories and the abuse of Philippine and Thai women working in Japan, did specifically women's issues appear. Secondly, authoritarian governments in all three countries inhibited the growth of NGOs. In Indonesia, where women had been organized as part of the nationalist movement, women were "valorized" as mothers and wives. Under President Suharto, women's organizations were absorbed into the government under the control of the Ministry of Home Affairs.

Women's groups outside the officially sanctioned ones - known as GONGO or government organized NGOs- were viewed with suspicion. Activist women gravitated to environment and consumer organizations which were considered safe topics, and women headed several influential organizations. As the democratization movements grew in all three countries, women joined with men in more overtly oppositional activities.

In all three countries the oppositional NGOs were instrumental in the overthrow of regimes and the replacement with more democratic governments; spontaneous protests led by women over high prices of basic foodstuffs precipitated more general student strikes. Political participation Women in the Philippines have wielded power for many years indirectly through important men; Imelda Marcos was so powerful that she had her own ministry while the mistress of President Ramos had both visibility and influence.

Cory Aquino became president after her husband was assassinated; Gloria Macapagal, daughter of a revolutionary leader, became president in 2001 when the President Estrada was impeached. A 1986 law to limit terms has resulted in some wives replacing their husbands, but many wives have sought political office on their own. Roces concludes "Organized power is still very much the domain of men" (2001: 120). Indonesia has also seen the succession to president of a daughter of the first Indonesian president with Megawati Sukarnoputri.

Her election had earlier been blocked by conservative Muslims who objected to having a woman heading the government. The elevation of women relatives as symbols has no more to do with women's issues in Southeast Asia than in South Asia. The opening of political space for oppositional NGOs in the Philippines resulted in a rapid expansion of women's organizations during the 1980s, prior to that many groups focused on kinship politics even as they dispensed charity.

After the overthrown of Marcos, major women's groups, under the umbrella organization GABRIELA, became more feminist in nature. Roces argues, however, that except for nuns, women organizing outside the narrow construct of kinship politics are marginalized. Such groups are often sustained by networks with groups in other countries: ISIS publishes its Asian journal from the Manila and HomeNet, organizing home-based women workers, has enrolled 20,000 members in the country. The 1997 elections in Indonesia was the first time women's issues were discussed.

Middle-class women, both secular and Islamist, have started many overtly feminist organizations that have raised issues of domestic violence, marriage law, and the conditions of women workers. Since then, the tumultuous events revolving around the survival of democratic government have preempted focused action on revising the model of women promoted under Suha rto, but "The reform of gender relations is very much on the agenda of contemporary Indonesia"

Dismantling communist control in China, Laos, Vietnam When the socialist governments were set up in Vietnam, Laos and China, equal right were nominally granted to women, though scholars have pointed to discrepancies in gender treatment throughout the communist era in all the three countries due to persistent patriarchal values and attitudes

Edwards 2000; Unger 2000). Over the past decade, as leaders in all three countries have issued economic reforms designed to open their economies to the market economy, inevitable gender disparities that accompany rapid socio-economic change are eroding both achieved and theoretical equality.

For example, the countries decided to give land rights to the people though ownership remains with the state. Even though laws provide for land to be registered in the names of both women and men, women often see no reason for registering. Several international NGOs in Vietnam encouraged women to register in order to document their rights in case of divorce or death. In Laos the government sent teams to the countryside to talk to women about registering land especially among the lowland Lao who have matriarchal inheritance.

These women did not comprehend that they might not have their traditional rights to land. Under the new laws, equal rights are ineffective if women do not put their names on the documents. Registration for urban housing was a somewhat different issue. Housing had been predominantly provided through the work unit of the husband so that privatizing living quarters often deprived the wife of security of tenure in the case of divorce. In China, women were sometimes allowed to share the tiny housing space -diving the room with a blanket-for a year while they searched for alternative accommodation. Women researchers have publicized these problems, but the lack of locally led women's organizations means that appeals must be made to the government.

MASS ORGANIZATIONS

In communist Asia, workers, women, veterans, etc., each had a separate organization for representation and for control. Today, women continue to be elected to legislatures through women's mass organizations: Women's Union in Vietnam and Laos, Women's Federation in China. In interviews, women in these organizations are often dismissed as having less power than women in the regular party hierarchy. Historically such mass organizations usually functioned as a vehicle for the party to instruct the village women; Carol Ireson argues that in Laos, however, women's concerns were sometimes filtered upwards as well (1996).

Today, with the vast amount of development assistance flowing to poor women through both the Vietnam Women's Union and the Laos Women's Union and the subsequent training to the cadres in order to implement new programs, the status of union members has been considerably improved. Yet without a strong voice of women's organizations outside the government, women's concerns are those assigned by the party; but the mass women's organizations are beginning to challenge the narratives and policies in these countries. Communist regimes do not allow organizing outside party structures.

In communist Europe, women had not organized as women and often rejected the concept of a woman's movement as U.S. propaganda. Even today in Laos, Vietnam, and China, restrictions continue on types of organizations acceptable to the party. Professional groups are accepted, but organizations whose goals are to help others, not its own membership, are generally forbidden because social provisioning is the right and responsibility of the government. In Laos and Vietnam, where foreign assistance has focused on organizing poor women for microcredit schemes, international nongovernmental organizations are allowed to promote their programs but only through a official institution such as the Women's Union, universities, or research centers.

In Vietnam, in 1998, only two NGOs run by local citizens groups could be identified by the Ford Foundation as offering assistance to the poor. Both group s are registered under the 1992 decree 35 that allows scientists to set up groups outside the government for social purposes; and neither accepted foreign funding which might make them seem foreign agents in the minds of suspicious bureaucrats. In 1993, a retired female medical doctor whose speciality is gynecology had set up clinics in two villages with a population of 17,000. Her clinic emphasizes educating women about reproductive health and contraception.

Because the major problem in these villages is poverty, she uses locally grown medicinal herbs when possible, and collaborates with the Women's Union which she considers "still political." She subsidizes her village work through a private clinic in Hanoi. The second independent program was set up by a man long experienced in working with an international NGO. He earns money for the work by consulting with foreign NGOs, then invests those funds in programs whose design he believes will correct errors made by many of the naive foreign efforts. He trains young volunteers who, like Peace Corps volunteers, receive minimal pay.

These two organizations may predict the future of civil society organizations in Vietnam; today they are constrained by law and party to provide social service activities. However, even the officially organized microcredit groups I visited were receiving information as well as funding from the international NGO sponsors. Through research projects and international contacts with women's centers and local research organizations, the global discourse on women's rights is gradually filtering through to women working in government run universities, research centers, and the Women's Union; the internet is expensive but controls are sporadic. Vietnamese women travel abroad to attend international conferences and to study.

A growing network of women exists to influence and instruct policy on women. But as with women in the Philippines, most educated women in both Vietnam and Laos feel they have equity and are not yet engaged in feminist issues, while poor women are working hard to survive. But as rapid economic transformation erodes traditional family support mechanisms, women are beginning to realize the need for actions to maintain their status in the society.

In China, feminist issues that were slowly seeping in were given greater visibility by the UN World Conference for Women in Beijing in 1995 despite the government attempts as censorship. As the conference preparations were underway, a Journal Rural Women Knowing All was started to inform farm women of their rights as internal migration often left them to run the farms alone. Wu Qing, recent recipient of the Magsaysay award, helped start a hot line in Beijing; today over 200 such hot lines exist. While there is no network among them, the volunteers running them all know each other and refer problems back and forth.

Women's power in Asia today is growing from the community level to national and international women leaders in each country. Despite an historic disconnect between the village women and the educated elite, development projects and the global women's movement are providing an agenda that reaches all levels. To date, women's voices have seldom been heard in elected bodies even with quotas and reservations. Thus influence on legislation and policy is more likely to occur through media campaigns or lobbying than by standing for office. International networking, through the United Nations but also through development agencies including NGOs and the World Bank, adds to the pressure on decision makers to respond.

India has by far the most active women's movements at all levels of society, but feminist have not yet been able to achieve a cohesive national organization. Philippines has organizations of working women that exist outside the older women's organizations with their kinship/charity outlook. Throughout this part of Asia, educated women are articulate in global discussions and meetings about the need for recasting gender relationships. Their personal power in the family is often more egalitarian than the traditional stereotypes but legally they are often vulnerable. Women are walking on many paths to power, changing relationships within the family and community are palpable, but national power is elusive - but growing- in societies with strong patriarchal dominance of political institutions.

Bibliography

Avis, Paul D. *Eros and the Sacred.* London: SPCK, 1989.

Bennett, Anne M. From Woman Pain to WomanVision. Writings in Feminist Theology. *Mary E. Hunt, ed. Philadelphia: Fortress Press, 1989.*

Brock, Rita Nakashima. Journeys By Heart. A Christology of Erotic Power. *New York: Crossroad, 1989.*

Bruns, J. Edgar. *God As Woman. Woman As God.* New York: Paulist Press, 1973.

Cannon, Katie G. *Black Womanist Ethics.* Atlanta, GA: Scholar's Press, 1988.

Carmody, Denise Lardner. Seizing the Apple. A Feminist Spirituality of Personal Growth. *New York: Crossroad, 1984.*

Casey, Juliana M. Where Is God Now? Nuclear Terror, Feminism and the Search for God. *Kansas City, MO: Sheed & Ward, 1987.*

Chopp, Rebecca S. The Power to Speak. Feminism, Language, God. *New York: Crossroad, 1989.*

Christianity and the Goddesses. Systematic Criticism of a Feminist Theology. *London: SCM, 1988.*

Clanton, Jann Aldredge. *In Whose Image? God and Gender.* New York: Crossroad, 1990.

Cypser, Cora E. Taking Off the Patriarchal Glasses. *New York: Vantage, 1987.*

Daly, Mary. Beyond God the Father. Toward a Philosophy of Women's Liberation. *Boston: Beacon Press, 1974.*

Dematrakopoulos, Stephanie A. Listening to Our Bodies. The Rebirth of Feminine Wisdom. *Boston: Beacon Press, 1982.*

Dunne, Carrin. Behold Woman. A Jungian Approach to Feminist Theology. *Wilmette, IL: Chiron Publications, 1988.*

Engelsman, Joan Chamberlain. *The Feminine Dimension of the Divine.* Philadelphia, PA: Westminster, 1979.

Essays by Sivananda Radha, Dorothy Hale, Chandra Patel, Anne Lamb, Ochs, Carol. *Behind the Sex of God.* Boston: Beacon Press, 1977.

Fiorenza, Elisabeth Schüssler. *Bread Not Stone.* Boston: Beacon Press, 1983.

Garcia, Jo, and Sara Maitland, eds. *Walking on the Water.* London: Virago, 1985.

Giles, Mary E., ed. The Feminist Mystic and Other Essays on Women and Spirituality. *New York: Crossroad, 1982.*

Grey, Mary. Redeeming the Dream. Feminism, Redemption and Christian Tradition. *London: SPCK, 1989.*

Gross, Rita, ed. *Beyond Anthrocentrism.* Missoula, MT: Scholar's Press, 1976.

Gyn/Ecology: The Metaethics of Radical Feminism. *Boston: Beacon Press, 1978.*

Haddon, Genia Pauli. Body Metaphors. Releasing the God-Feminine in All of Us. *New York: Crossroad, 1988.*

Hammett, Jenny Yates. Woman's Transformations. A Psychological Theology. *New York: Edwin Mellen, 1982.*

Hampson, Daphne. *Theology and Feminism.* Oxford and Cambridge, MA: Basil Blackwell, 1990.

Iglehart, Hallie. Womanspirit. A Guide to Women's Wisdom. *San Francisco: Harper & Row, 1983.*

Kalven, Janet, and Mary Buckley, eds. *Women's Spirit Bonding.* New York: Pilgrim Press, 1984.

King, Ursula. Women and Spirituality. Voices of Protest and Promise. *Houndmills, England: Macmillan, 1989.*

Massey, Marilyn Chapin. Feminine Soul. The Fate of An Ideal. *Boston: Beacon Press, 1985.*

Mollenkott, Virginia Ramey. *The Naming of God.* Granit Falls, WA: Marvel, 1982.

O'Brien, Theresa K., ed. The Spiral Path. Essays and Interviews on Women's Spirituality. *St. Paul, MN: Yes International, 1988.*

Ruether, Rosemary Radford. Disputed Questions on Being a Christian. *Maryknoll, NY: Orbis Books, 1989.*

Russell, Letty M. *The Future of Partnership.* Philadelphia: Westminster Press, 1979.

Schmidt, Alvin J. Veiled and Silenced. How Culture Shaped Sexist Theology. *Macon, GA: Mercer University Press, 1989.*

Sexism and God Talk. Toward a Feminist Theology. *London: SCM, Boston: Beacon Press, 1983.*

Speaking of Christ. A Lesbian Feminist Voice. Ellen C. Davis, ed. New York: Pilgrim Press, 1989.

Spretnak, Charlene, ed. The Politics of Women's Spirituality. *New York: Doubleday Image, 1982.*

The elements within all great religious traditions that support the struggle for justice and liberation.

The Redemption of God: A Theology of Mutual Redemption. *Lanham, MD: University Press of America, 1982.*

Vorster, W. S., ed. *Sexism and Feminism in Theological Perspective.* Pretoria, SA: University of South Africa, 1984.

Winter, Miriam Therese. Woman Prayer. Woman Song. Resources for Ritual. *Oak Park, IL: Meyer Stone Books, 1987.*

Women's Spirituality. Resources for Christian Development. *New York: Paulist Press, 1986.*

Young, Pamela Dickey. Feminist Theology. Christian Theology. In Search of Method. *Minneapolis, MN: Fortress Press, 1990.*

Zola, Elemire. *The Androgyne.* New York: Crossroad, 1989.

Index

R

S

T

U

W

Z